SEASPRAY
AND
WHISKY

SEASPRAY
AND
WHISKY

Reminiscences of a Tramp Ship Voyage

Norman Freeman

A COMMON READER EDITION

THE AKADINE PRESS

Seaspray and Whisky

A COMMON READER EDITION published 1998
by The Akadine Press, Inc., by arrangement with the author.

Copyright © 1993 by Norman Freeman.
Afterword copyright © 1998 by Thomas Meagher.

A COMMON READER EDITION and fountain colophon are trademarks
of The Akadine Press, Inc.

ISBN 1-888173-38-6

10 9 8 7 6 5 4 3

To my mother, who waited
for all our homecomings

Introduction

The M.V. *Allenwell* was one of those ships most seafarers are careful to avoid. She was dirty and decrepit. The accommodation was dingy and the food unappetising. She was a tramp depending for gainful employment on securing charters from established shipping companies in need of temporary tonnage.

Such vessels tend to attract a motley collection of seafarers who might not easily find a berth on a well-run ship in the fleet of a reputable line. The captain could not be expected to be a paragon of propriety. Nor could the crew be expected to be the most orderly in the British merchant marine service.

The voyage on the *Allenwell* from Britain to the USA and back in 1961/62 was memorable largely because the ship itself was one of the eccentrics of the world of deep-sea shipping. A factor which dominated much of the voyage and which served to emphasise the rumbustious character of the ship was our consignment of Scottish whisky. When the last slingload of this precious commodity was deposited on the dockside in Houston, Texas, it was revealed that a substantial portion had disappeared. It could not be legitimately accounted for. The missing bottles most certainly accounted for a prolonged whisky-fest, which engendered riotous living afloat and ashore and which had some sad consequences as well.

In compiling this reminiscence of a very odd ship and an unusual voyage, I had some advantage in the form of notes, fortuitously scribbled down at the time. Yet, in recounting such a nautical experience, the selective memory tends to emphasise moments of piquancy and to underplay much of the monotony which attends seafaring. There is a suspicion that storms and fights acquire an exaggerated turbulence; that personalities appear larger than life; that outrageous behaviour is enlivened by a delight in recollection; that food is execrable rather than just poor. This may be so. The would-be raconteur must be accorded at least a little leeway in the interests of holding his audience.

Most likely the *Allenwell* has long since been dismembered in some breaker's yard, probably in the distinctive area of North-East England known as Geordieland, from which she and her rollicking captain originated. Many of the people recalled in this story are, I hope, still hale and hearty. Some may still be at sea. All will have some relatives living. Because some of the incidents related might prove embarrassing or hurtful, I have thought it wise to disguise the name of the ship itself and the names of some of those who sailed on our eventful voyage to the New World.

In writing this book I had the advantage of being an outsider – the curious if not inquisitive Irishman looking with some puzzlement as well as amusement at the antics of people of a familiar but different nationality in unusual circumstances.

I hope the book does justice to one of the great US cities, New Orleans, the scene of so much uproarious carousing and debauchery by the ship's rumbustious crew. It is seen from a sailor's perspective rather than the more cultured vision of the tourist.

1

'Dirty Old Tub, Isn't She?'

One cold and blustery night in December 1961 found me standing in a state of stunned dismay in a dingy cabin of a small cargo-ship berthed somewhere in the immense docklands of Liverpool. Outside, the wind howled about the deserted quays, the gaunt warehouses and the skeletal framework of the cranes. Inside, my despondency alternated with anger and resentment.

Despite the warmth from the gurgling pipes, I still wore my overcoat as if to emphasise to myself, if to nobody else, my extreme reluctance to accept this ship and this cabin as my abode for the next three months. My battered suitcase, with its precautionary leather strap still clamped about it, lay on the lumpy brown settee.

The cabin door was closed not just to keep in the heat. On entering shortly before, I had had to evict a sizeable rat, which was sitting on the centre of the floor with a proprietorial air. There seemed every chance that he might try to effect a re-entry.

On the bulkhead over the writing desk hung a badly printed calendar, bearing the greetings of one Mohandas Bannerjee of Cape Town, 'fabricator of high-excellency sandals, shoes and other footwear'. A row of dates on the month of November had been heavily crossed out, with a final date ringed in red pencil and an inscription beside it which read 'End of our voyage — thank Christ'.

It was not hard to understand the anxiety of the previous occupant of this cabin for the voyage to end or to imagine the speed with which he had scampered off the ship. I now found myself in his place, on board the scruffiest ship I had ever set foot on, because of a sly act of deception on the part of the staff clerk at the Marconi office that morning.

Up to this time I had had an extremely good run of ships: clean, well-run vessels, with excellent food and accommodation and companionable colleagues of my own age. Three years had been spent on the deck-passenger ships of the British India Company, a proud and aristocratic survivor of the days of the Raj. Goan servants solicitously attended all one's needs, laying out the spotless white uniforms one donned before going down to the festooned promenade deck. There might be a dance or a film show. One could sit in the comfortable bar, feeling glamorous, eyeing the exposed brown midriffs of the silk-sari-clad Indian ladies travelling first class.

During my time with the B.I., we would lean over the railings of the upper deck as the gleaming white ship went slow ahead towards the piers exclusively reserved for passenger vessels in Bombay or Karachi. We often looked down on battered cargo ships lying patiently at anchor in the roadways, waiting listlessly to discharge some unsavoury cargo when a berth became available. Men in dirty trousers and soiled singlets would be standing about, occasionally making suggestive gestures towards attractive girls lining the railings of our promenade deck.

These vessels, tramps and the down-at-heel carriers of the notoriously third-rate companies, were the ones most radio officers took pains to avoid. You might be away for anything up to two years, plodding between the more obscure ports of Asia, Africa and South America. Such ships came alongside in mosquito-infested creeks and river-ports, loading or unloading phosphates or molasses, carrying cashew nuts from Mozambique to the Malabar Coast, slinging bags of cement into rusty lighters miles offshore in the Persian Gulf. The food would be poor, the conditions on board uncomfortable, and the chances of savouring shore-life confined to shanty towns full of flies, offal and wandering pariah dogs.

The Marconi company always found it difficult to persuade men to serve on such ships. Many of the older radio officers, with years of sea service in their discharge books, refused to countenance them; their seniority entitled them to the passenger ships, the modern cargo vessels and the big ferries that ran between Britain and the Continent. Many of the younger men, who stayed at sea for an average of only five years, sought regular-run ships which returned home at short intervals; some were doing correspondence courses in electrical engineering and wanted to be on hand to take examinations or to grasp at the opportunities offered by the burgeoning electronics industry. Others simply had no wish to return home after two years, gaunt and haggard after an unrelieved diet of baked beans and hash. However, the Marconi company had contracts to lease radio and navigational equipment to a diversity of shipping concerns, together with the radio officer to operate and maintain it.

No doubt the staff clerk at the Liverpool depot, a sinister-looking individual with narrow eyes shifting about craftily behind horn-rimmed glasses, had been having some bother finding a man for the *Allenwell*. Then I, a newcomer to this office, presented myself at the counter. The staff clerk held your fate in his hands. The radio officer might want a good ship, but the staff clerk had to find men for every kind of ship — good and bad. This man eyed my anxious face carefully, holding a list of ships in his hand, in a way that made it impossible for me to view it.

'Well now, let's see what we have here,' he said with a cordiality that I later heard was entirely foreign to his nature. He ran his finger down the list.

'Ever been to the USA?'

'No.'

'Here's your chance. *Allenwell*. Sailing in six days' time. Only a three-month voyage. Now how about that?'

'What kind of ship is it?'

'Cargo. Not a Cunarder, but the next best thing to it — under charter to Cunard. Not bad, eh?'

Not bad at all. This had to be a reasonable vessel. And a

short voyage. I accepted immediately, gratefully, forgetting the old nautical adage about not taking a ship until you have had sight of her.

I emerged into the wet streets outside, buoyed up by the thought that my luck was holding out. After a warming meal, I began to browse about the bookshops, engaging in a pleasant preliminary survey of the books I might buy for the voyage ahead. When the dim day darkened in mid-afternoon, I sought the sanctuary of a cinema, feeling weary after the sleepless night on the squalid ferryboat from Dublin.

It was raining heavily when I came out. By the time I had managed to flag down a taxi, I was soaked. From the left-luggage department of Lime Street railway station I retrieved my bulky grey suitcase. All I wanted now was to be driven to a haven of rest and comfort, the radio officer's cabin on a ship chartered to Cunard. First thing would be to unpack, hang up my uniform, and dry out my shoes. Then, I might get a steaming mug of cocoa and a sandwich in the officers' pantry before turning in.

We drove along the wide road that skirts the miles of dockland. On one side was the high stone wall that encloses the port area. It still carried some of the dirt-encrusted iron structure of the defunct overhead railway. There was little traffic about. Work had ceased for the day in a port already going into a state of sad decline. On the other side of the road were shuttered warehouses, ships chandlers and many grim derelict buildings. A few pedestrians hurried along the pavements, huddled within themselves against the rain and wind.

At length we turned in at one of the huge gates. A port policeman, in a long black raincoat, glanced into the taxi and told the driver where the *Allenwell* was berthed. We cruised along under the high yellow arc lights, bumping over railway crossings and splashing through patches of rain-water, passed between the concrete end walls of two cargo sheds and emerged onto the dockside.

A long row of ships stretched down to the quayside. This is always a time when a flutter of apprehension courses

4

through the mind of the seafarer. One of these strange vessels is going to be his home, dominate his life for the months ahead. He wonders what kind of ship it will be, hopes it will be a happy one, that he will get along with his shipmates and those to whom he has to answer. Even with a very promising ship in the offing, it is a time of loneliness.

We drove slowly, peering up at the names of the ships on their bows or across their sterns. Several were modern cargo liners, with rows of gleaming portholes. Sometimes a ship under charter adopted the funnel colours of the chartering company; in my innocence, I was squinting down the line of ships, looking for the shiny red funnel which adorned such majestic liners as the *Queen Elizabeth*, as well as advertisements in society magazines. I wondered uneasily if Cunard standards of dress might be expected on the *Allenwell*; my sole blue uniform featured a decorative but eradicable mottling, the result of tropical mildew when it had hung, unworn, in wardrobes during my long period of Indian Ocean sailing with the British India Company.

'Here we are, lah. That's it there.'

'Where?'

'Right here. *Allenwell*.'

We were alongside a small tatty-looking cargo-ship. A few small cargo lights on the fore and after masts gave it a ghostly appearance. There did not seem to be a soul on board. One or two of the mean little portholes showed a dim light, but otherwise it looked as if she had been abandoned.

'There must be some mistake.' But there was no mistaking the white rust-blotched lettering under her bow.

'Dirty old tub, isn't she, lah? What do you want to do?'

There was nothing to do but get out, haul my suitcase after me and pay the taxi man. The thought occurred to me that, had I the money, I would have gone back with him to the city and looked for some hotel. The trouble was that I had accepted the ship, signed on the dotted line. If I was now going to refuse her, hold out for a better one, I would have to be able to say I had been on board, looked the ship over and found it intolerable.

As the red rear lights of the taxi grew smaller and then disappeared among the cargo sheds, I stood there uncertainly. Even in the shadowy light, one could see the pockmarks and weals on the black hull, where successive epidemics of rust had been treated by slapdash medication. Slimy brown streaks ran down from the discharge outlets on her side. The funnel was not the glowing red Cunard one, but a blemished buff-coloured affair.

My heart was as heavy as my suitcase as I climbed the gangway. There was no sign of the customary watchman on duty to check and identify boarders. It seemed as if this ship was destined for the breaker's yard, rather than New York and New Orleans. The iron deck was slippery with grime. Pieces of dunnage lay in wait for the unwary foot. As I made my way forward along the outer passage, I was relieved to hear the faint hum of a generator somewhere below in the engine room.

A door led into a badly lit foyer. It was bare of any furniture or decoration. No such thing as a framed picture of the company's founder or the British monarch on the bulkhead, and no brass plaque to commemorate her launching and indicate her age. Only a length of brown matting lay on the linoleum-covered deck. Obviously there was no need for a watchman on this ship. Any miscreant who slipped on board to steal something was bound to be disappointed.

For'ard of the foyer were the glass doors of a dark saloon. Across from it there was an open door into the galley. Its tiled floor was littered. On a big black range rested several huge cauldrons. A sour smell of old cooking hung about.

Peering down the starboard alleyway, I wondered if it would sound foolish to shout, 'Anyone on board?' Then a cabin door opened, and a figure came forward. It was small, with wide shoulders and short legs. It turned out to belong to a fellow in his early twenties, dressed in an anorak and dirty brown trousers.

'Excuse me — I'm looking for the duty officer.'

'You're looking at him,' he said with a lopsided grin, as if he found the title amusing. He stuck out his hand and we introduced ourselves. This was Pete Kendal, the third mate.

'You must have been caught screwing the Marconi manager's wife to get heaved onto this ship,' he laughed.

'Is it true she's chartered to Cunard for a three-month trip to the States?'

'Believe it or not. Cunard must be hard up.'

He had a wide reddish face, bumpy with the vestiges of adolescent pustules. His crew-cut showed off large protruding ears, giving him a somewhat comic appearance.

'When is the signing-on?'

'Not for three or four days. You still have time to back out.' He led the way to his cabin to give me the radio officer's bunch of keys.

'Lucky you caught me. Just on my way ashore for fish and chips.'

This was unusual. Duty officers were not meant to desert the ship and head ashore. In most reputable companies, such a dereliction of duty, if discovered, would have led to a severe reprimand, if not dismissal. But good ships usually had a well-stocked refrigerator at the disposal of those who had to remain on board in port.

'Where is everybody?'

'Captain and mate are away on leave. Second mate is ashore in the boozer. So are most of the crew. Oh, you'll hear them coming back, don't worry.'

Pete showed me my cabin, which was next to his and then sauntered off. My first task was to hunt out the rat. I remember the insolent manner in which he took his leave, nimbly hopping over the coaming. So here I was, fuming and fretting, sometimes standing, sometimes sitting.

I had decided to become a radio officer because it seemed an ideal way to see the world, free of charge, and to escape the claustrophobic environment of Ireland in the nineteen fifties. Only when I had been several months in the College of Science and Technology in Kevin Street in Dublin, did it occur to me that I had little aptitude for electricity, in theory or practice. I also found the Morse code exceedingly difficult to master. The concentration was lacking. My eye was apt to fasten on a seagull perched on the rooftop of the building opposite or covertly watch the instructor scratching himself.

Only after two attempts did I manage to get a second-class certificate. By the time the results were posted, much of what I had laboriously committed to memory had already evaporated. I tried hard. By the time I joined the *Allenwell*, I had attained some degree of competence and was able to get by. But I still had nightmares about sailing over a vast ocean, incommunicado, while I struggled haplessly for days on end with a seized-up transmitter. I was not the man to rush into battle with the staff clerk. He might call my bluff. I feared being sacked. I needed to hold my job because I was helping to support my mother and younger members of the family back home.

Perhaps it was this sense of my own weakness which made my predicament seem all the more galling. The *Allenwell* had to be the nadir of any radio officer's career. I wondered about those with whom I would have to live for the next three months, if I had no alternative but to sign on. Pete seemed all right. What about the captain? His character and personality would certainly set the tone on board. The captain of a tramp need not necessarily be an unpleasant bully or a martinet. Good or bad, he was unlikely to be an amateur watercolourist or a collector of antique books. I would be directly responsible to him.

Another thought occurred to me. If the *Allenwell* was likely to be manned by some odd characters, would one of them have been the previous radio officer? Would the radio gear be in good working order or as ramshackle as the ship itself appeared to be? It would be disastrous to discover that the labyrinthian innards of the radar or the main transmitter had recurrent intestinal trouble which required the ministrations of an accomplished physician.

The radar was likely to be the biggest source of worry. Before boarding, I had noticed the banana-shaped scanner on its sturdy mast just abaft the monkey island. If it was a fault-prone affair of vintage make, the radio officer would have much to keep him occupied.

Wearying of all this speculation, I took off my coat and looked about the small cabin. The wooden bunk lay fore and aft with two big drawers beneath. It was something of a pleasant surprise to find that the bed linen was newly laundered. The washbasin was spotless, smelling faintly of cleansing fluid. The old writing desk, against the for'ard bulkhead, was scored and scarred, but it had been well waxed and polished. Obviously the cabin steward took some pride in his work.

Feeling I needed a breath of fresh air before turning in, I went out on deck and stood at the railings outside the foyer. At least it had stopped raining. Just as I was about to go back inside, there came from afar an echoing chorus of voices raised in ragged song. From between the cargo sheds there emerged a swaying, stumbling group of men. Two of them, with uncontrollable rag doll legs, were being supported by their companions. The bawling, shambling cavalcade made towards the *Allenwell*. Coming abreast of the gangway, they wheeled in and began to clamber cumbersomely up. Several cradled big brown paper bags, heavy with clinking bottles. One celebrant collapsed in mid-ascent and had to be hauled and pushed to the top, like a sack of potatoes. The party disappeared below to the crew quarters. Their passing was marked by a single shoe lying at the foot of the gangway.

When I returned to my cabin, I would hear them directly below; the muffled sound of bellows and guffaws, hoarse singing and tuneless music-making. Presently there was a pause. Then through the iron deck came the tones of a mellifluous tenor voice, rising and falling easily, accompanied by a slow quivering cascade of notes played tremolo fashion on a mandolin. The indistinct notes, surging and fading, weaved a tantalisingly incomplete pattern. At length the voice soared to a high note, lingered there and ceased. An uproar of applause followed. (This voice turned out to belong to a small wiry Welshman, whose dark hair and black moustache gave him a villainous aspect.)

The revelry continued below. Other, less talented voices endeavoured to entertain. Soon there came shouts of 'Pipe

9

down' and 'Shut up'. Then came the rumble of chairs, the scrabbling of feet and what sounded like the thud of fists. I tip-toed up to the galley and stood at the top of the stairs leading below. The fight had spilled out into the lower alley-way. Above the thumping rumble a high-pitched voice cried out repeatedly 'I'll get you — you twat!'

A tangled mass of shoulders, arms and heads locked in ineffective combat, appeared at the bottom of the stairs. The narrow alleyway and the drunkenness of the participants made it difficult for anyone to land a telling blow; but it occurred to me that if the struggle moved into the galley there was a fearsome array of potential weaponry there in the form of cleavers, skillets, ladles, pots and pans. I scurried to my cabin and locked the door.

There was no sign of Pete returning. At any rate it might have been unwise of him to venture below to assert his authority and quell the disturbance.

Shortly afterwards the sounds of struggle died down and then ceased. The brawl did not augur well for the behaviour of the crew during the forthcoming voyage. Not long after, I was surprised to hear from below a chorus begin to sing the old sea-shanty 'Shenandoah'. It sounded like an anthem of peace and forgiveness, accompanied by the mandolin, which apparently had escaped destruction.

2

Day of Observation

Waking next morning was aided by the sound of Pete's radio next door. It seemed that his enjoyment of music was in direct proportion to the loudness of the sound. Experience was to prove this surmise correct.

For some time I lay contemplating the cream-painted steel deckhead over the bunk, with its rows of rounded rivet-heads. This was to be a day of observation and assessment. I would have to learn more about this ship, but more particularly, the people who sailed on her. The radio room and gear would have to be checked. If it seemed that life on board the *Allenwell* was likely to be intolerable, then I would have to screw up enough courage to confront the staff clerk the next day. Yet a night's sound sleep in the bunk had alleviated much of the gloom and anger of the previous night.

As an indication of my uncommitted status, I did not don my uniform with its zig-zag stripes of gold braid on the cuffs. Instead I put on my sole suit, a dark green check affair, shapeless after five years' use. I imagined this to be a subtle gesture of defiance. On my previous ships the wearing of civilian dress while the ship was in port was not encouraged. The uniform was a tangible indication that duties were being taken seriously, that discipline prevailed even in the relaxed atmosphere of a ship in port.

My supposed act of independence was a fortuitous one. To have appeared in uniform for breakfast in the saloon of the *Allenwell* would have caused amusement if not hilarity. I was to find out that the wearing of uniform, in port or at sea, was

11

looked upon as a pretentious eccentricity. The crew, leaning over the railings, were in the habit of hooting derisively at uniformed men from nearby ships passing along the quayside. 'Hey look! There's a sailor!'

The saloon was empty when I entered. There were two tables. Not knowing where the radio officer's place was, I hesitated and decided to stay about the foyer until Pete arrived. In the galley two figures were moving about in a fog of blue smoke and the smell of singed bacon. Both were dressed in baggy check trousers and soiled white jackets. One was a small ferret-faced man who hopped about energetically; the other one, an elderly man with a fan of thick grey hair and horn-rimmed glasses, lumbered awkwardly.

Pete appeared, brisk and grinning, in the same attire as the previous night.

'Where does the radio officer sit, Pete?'

'Anywhere you like.'

'Isn't there a designated place?'

'The Sparks is meant to sit at the starboard table, second seat down, starboard side.'

'I'd better sit where I'm supposed to.'

'Suit yourself', he said, going to the other table.

'Who else sits here?' I called across.

'Captain, mate, chief engineer. The second engineer too, but he always eats in their mess.'

This information was received with a mixture of satisfaction and unease. I had never sat at the senior officers' table before. On the other hand, I tended to be ill-at-ease in the presence of captains, not relishing any mealtime scrutiny.

Suddenly there came an angry yell from the galley: 'You clumsy fucker you,' shouted a sharp Liverppudlian voice.

'Don't shout at me, you bollocks,' came the reply in a hoarse London accent. This was followed by a deep gong-like sound of a frying pan being slammed on the cooker plates. Pete was smiling.

'Old Charlie and Little Alex are at it again!'

'Does this go on much?'

'It's time to start worrying when it doesn't.'

The row ended as suddenly as it had begun. A few moments later came a different but equally disturbing sound — a succession of gurgling, heaving, rasping coughs such as brings saliva to the mouths of hearers. The source of this exertion appeared in the doorway and made his way slowly to the table. It was an old man with a huge tiara of grizzled hair. He breathed laboriously as he shuffled, like a patient in a geriatric hospital ward. This man sat down opposite, observing me from cough-watered eyes.

This was Mr Albert Yardley, chief engineer and a native of Kingston-upon-Hull, Yorkshire.

'The last Sparks was Irish too,' he said reflectively. 'McCarthy. A good enough lad when he was sober. The trouble was, he was drunk as a fiddler's bitch most of the time.'

This unwelcome item of news about the previous custodian of the radio room seemed a little ironic coming from Mr Yardley. He bore all the signs of one who had devoted much of his life to heavy drinking. His face was blotchy; he had a big soft nose which was embellished with a mosaic of tiny red veins. His hand shook as he held the square of cardboard with handwritten inscriptions which served as a menu.

'What speciality has our chef in store for us this morning,' he said with a tight smile, investing the word 'chef' with malicious disdain. He spoke in a flat Yorkshire accent, but with a studied sense of refinement in his choice of words. While he was looking balefully at the menu, a lithe figure, clad in tight-fitting red trousers and impeccable sky-blue jacket, glided into the saloon. He stood attentively at Mr Yardley's shoulder.

'I think I'll have a fried egg and bacon this morning, steward,' said the chief engineer, as if there was a wide choice and he was in the habit of choosing something different each morning. I ordered the same, eyeing the steward with some curiosity. He seemed to be in his early forties, and had a fine-boned sallow face. More noticeable was the blurred make-up round his eyes and the pair of small ear-rings. His frizzy brown hair was carefully styled. He disappeared soundlessly.

'Oh yes, Sparks, we have all kinds on board this worthy vessel,' said Mr Yardley. 'A full cast of comedians, clowns and piss-artists — not least our distinguished captain.'

That the captain should be spoken about in this way by the chief engineer to a complete newcomer was unusual. I made no comment.

'He's now in the loving arms of his good wife. She's a member of a very distinguished family — the O'Flahertys of South Shields.' Mr Yardley chuckled. 'A very forthright lady indeed. Last time she was sitting at this table, she belched and said, "Better out than in." That kind of insouciance only comes with breeding.'

Uncomfortable at the turn the conversation was taking, I asked him if he had been aware of the fight down below.

'Don't let that kind of thing bother you, Sparks,' he said soothingly. 'That comes under the category of "Marine Entertainment."'

Seeking reassurance, I asked about the Cunard charter.

'Don't ask me how we got it. But it doesn't alter the fact that this ship is a tramp. You can dress a tramp up in white tie and tails and send him off to dine with the aristocracy — but he's still liable to get gloriously pissed on brandy and champagne, steal the silver, aim a kick at the peacock strutting about the garden, and end up trying to screw one of the lady guests. Or, if he doesn't succeed, trying his hand with one of the maidservants.'

Mr Yardley had the air and manner of an embittered provincial professor, caustic and erudite, who might have been dismissed from his post for some failing, probably insobriety. When the breakfast plate was put before him, he surveyed it bleakly.

'You know, Sparks, it takes a chef of considerable genius to spoil the simple English breakfast', he said, looking at the bacon which was burned black along the edges, and the eggs, fried solid into little wizened pancakes.

After breakfast Pete told me that the chief engineer's shattered condition was largely due to emphysema, a chronic distention of the lungs which leaves the sufferer constantly fighting for breath. 'It makes him cough and splutter every hour of the night and day.' I wondered how this afflicted man managed to make his way down into the engine room, descending the narrow iron steps of the steep companionways into the steamy, oily world where you had to shout at the top of your lungs to be heard above the trembling noise of the motors and the pistons, which kicked rhythmically like a chorus line.

'It's simple. He doesn't go down at all. Hasn't been for at least two years. He depends on the second engineer to keep things going. But he has an instinct for engines. He can tell if something is wrong, just sitting in his cabin listening to the sound.'

When I asked Pete how long he had had his second mate's certificate, he laughed. 'I sat for it about a dozen fucking times, but I haven't got it yet. Next time lucky.'

'But do you keep a seagoing watch?'

'Of course I do. I'm the third mate. Okay, the Old Man signs the log-book and all that, but I'm the fellow on watch. He pokes his nose in now and then, and makes a nuisance of himself, but mostly he leaves me alone and that's the way I like it.'

The ship ploughing along on a pitch dark night with an uncertificated officer in charge might not bother everybody, but the British Board of Trade would not approve. I asked about the second mate.

'That was him you saw in the galley a minute ago.'

On the way out of the saloon, I had caught a sight of a big flabby man with a brown balding head leaning against the galley table. His feet were splayed out behind him as if he were trying to push the table forward. He was eating from a plate with a spoon.

'That wasn't him, was it?'

'Frank Bradshaw — Brad for short.'

'Does he often eat in the galley?'

'Always — he never comes into the saloon.'

'Why not?'

'Search me. Why don't you ask him yourself?'

It was time to inspect the radio room and gear. The inner stairway led up from the foyer. On the deck above was a door with a small brass plate on which the word 'Captain' was indented. I peeped in the window and saw a fairly spacious cabin, well furnished. I did not linger long in the vicinity of the captain's quarters. Though I had been told he was not on board, I felt that the door might suddenly be flung open and a personage, bristling with authority, demand 'Who are you?'

When I climbed the stairs to the bridge deck, I was struck once again by the strange silence and lifelessness that envelops this hub of nautical activity when a ship is tied up in port. The small chart room seemed subdued by the still air. The wide chart table, with its rows of long drawers beneath, smelled of wax. It was bereft of charts, callipers, pencils and erasers. The squat clock above it ticked faintly.

It was not the brass-bound telegraph nor the big mahogany wheel that caught my attention when I went out to the bridge. There in the corner, solid in its grey metal casing, stood the viewing unit of the Marconi Mark IV radar, a sturdy and reliable set whose vital organs I knew something about. As I peered into the darkened vision tube, my fingers automatically moved to the familiar control switches. It could not be tested until the current had been switched on in the radar hut abaft the monkey island above.

When I unlocked the door of the radio room, Mr Yardley's remarks about the insobriety of my predecessor were somewhat dispelled. I found a large, airy and tidy office. Most importantly, it held an array of equipment with which I had a respectful familiarity. The main and emergency transmitters, the two big marine receivers side by side in front of the desk, the automatic alarm and the direction finder unit, all solidly bracketed to the bulkheads, were in a state of hushed suspension. They exuded the thin metallic beeswaxy smell of radio gear.

Only at sea did the radio room come into being. With the long aerials hoisted high, the receivers pulled in the twittering tin-whistle orchestra of the Morse-world wavebands.

16

Here thousands of jostling streams of dots and dashes sped over sea and land or bounced back and forward and onward between earth and ionosphere. The ship's radio room was a floating outstation of this universe of communication, whose language, the fluting sounds of Morse, whistled from loud-speakers and earphones.

It would be wrong to depict the radio room on a ship like the *Allenwell* as a busy hub of contact, with the transmitter constantly droning and the ping of incoming signals resounding during every watch period. The place essentially served a small floating community and most of the time resembled a sleepy village post office. On a three-month voyage there would not be much more than forty incoming and outgoing telegrams to handle. Sometimes, in the middle of a vast ocean, it might take time to raise one of the high-frequency stations and clear or receive a telegram, but all in all there was not much work of this kind to keep one occupied.

The equipment and R/O were on board primarily in the interests of safety of life at sea. I switched on and tested both transmitters. They were in good working order. On the bulkhead over the desk was a large age-browned card with the ship's four letter call sign. Automatically I found myself tapping it out and making slight adjustments to the Morse key's delicate springs. Every Morse-man has his own individual style and rhythm — 'fist' as it is called. Adjusting the tension and bounce of the gap between the contacts to suit his wrist is one of the first things a radio officer will do on taking over a station. Perhaps it was a first unconscious move towards accepting the *Allenwell.*

The automatic alarm and the echo sounder passed the routine test procedure. The Mark IV radar set gave a very well-defined picture of the Mersey estuary on its cathode ray tube. The drawers were well-stocked with telegram forms, receipt books, radio logs, account sheets and stationery. The dozens of boxes and containers in the spare parts lockers were neatly annotated and arranged; the checklists pinned to the inside of the doors bore little pencil ticks beside each item. All these valves, capacitors, resistors, commutator brushes, solder-spools and a hundred other items would have to be tallied if I decided to sign on. But my estimation of McCarthy was tending towards the benign. Last of all, I uncovered the bank of six-volt batteries in their locker outside; the hydrometer readings showed them to have been well cared for. Then I locked up and went below, feeling a little more buoyant.

This mood subsided somewhat when I looked into the officers' recreation room on the starboard side of the saloon. This area, intended to be the focal point of communal relaxation and social intercourse, can reveal a good deal about those who use it, the general atmosphere on board, and the company's concern for its employees. Its centrepiece was a decomposing dartboard hanging on the inner panelled bulkhead. So pitted and pockmarked was this vintage affair that it was difficult to discern the colours behind the scarred wire frame. Battered chairs were arranged in a semi-circle about it. There were a few small tables whose surfaces were covered with an intricate chain-mail design which seemed at first glance to have some artistic merit; on closer inspection, this proved to be the accumulated imprints of wet beer cans and bottles.

Someone had painted a makeshift white throwing line on the threadbare carpet. The panels on either side of the dartboard were covered in a wayward pattern of pit-marks, up to the deckhead and down to the wainscotting. Clearly it would be wise to stay well clear when games were in progress. But I was to discover that this was the scene of the most extraordinary games, with admirable skill displayed under the handicap of a ship rolling in the ocean, as well as the blurred vision and unsteady hands of some who were drunk.

My attention was caught by a faint sucking sound. It came at regular intervals. I glanced quickly about the floor, wondering if the rat expelled from my cabin had found a new abode. Then I noticed a man standing outside the door, gazing into space with a sad smile. He had the puffy profile of a nineteen thirties' film star or bandleader gone to seed, with jet black hair brushed flat on a well-shaped head. Every so often a corner of his mouth twitched. Later on I was to time this sucking habit and found it came almost exactly every ten seconds. No doubt it was one of those personal peccadilloes that begins innocently and grows until it becomes so firmly established that only a tremendous shock will cure it. I passed in front of this man and was ready to nod a greeting, but he seemed so absorbed in his own thoughts that he did not notice me. On a ship where wearing a uniform was regarded as a form of exhibitionism, it was impossible to guess who he might be. I described him to Pete.

'That's our chief steward, Ted Wrignall. Dreamy sort of fellow, isn't he? Lives very much in his own world. I was ages on this ship before I realised he was just pleasantly drunk all the time. I can't say I've ever seen him sober. A harmless sort of fellow.'

Harmless indeed, but it did not exactly fill one with great expectations about the standard of food and provisioning.

While chatting with Pete, I became aware of sounds from my cabin, which I had been careful to lock. I rushed around and found the effete steward who had served breakfast vigorously polishing the brass of the porthole. The bunk had been made up, the floor swept and the writing desk waxed.

'Hello, Sparks,' he said chirpily. 'I'm your steward. Tony is my name — spelt TONI — in case you ever send me a postcard.'

I engaged in a cautious conversation. He immediately volunteered the information that, before he came to sea, he had been a valet for several distinguished people in London.

'Last one was a retired general. Used to chase me around the house, did that man. Caught me a few times as well,' he said saucily. When in turn he asked me if I had ever 'Done anything like that', I gave a sullen, belligerent 'No!' No sooner had he departed with a cheery 'Bye bye!' than I hurried round to Pete.

'Don't worry, Sparks, he won't bother you. Seeks out his own kind. And a bloody good steward. Married too.'

'Married?'

19

'Well he was, at some stage. Two children too. She came on board a few days ago, demanding money. What a battle-axe! If I was married to her, I'd probably turn arse too.'

At lunch I sat alone until, preceded by the sound of a most excruciating succession of coughs, Mr Yardley made his way in slowly. His chest heaved as he lowered himself into his seat.

'I believe the captain and the mate won't be back till later this evening,' I opened.

The chief engineer vented a savage chortle. 'The mate will be even sourer than usual – if that's possible – seeing that he obviously failed to find another ship. One voyage under our Master Mariner was enough for him.'

'Is that so?'

'Some of our gallant crew got out of hand during the voyage. The mate tried to exercise his authority, but of course Thompson wouldn't back him up and he lost face. Our captain, you see, wants to be the star of the show, popular with everybody, boozing with every Tom, Dick and Harry. He'll be disappointed to see the mate back. We won't see much love lost between those two during the voyage,' he concluded with a smile of malevolent anticipation.

For lunch that day we were served stew. It was not too bad, and the prospect that meals would be garnished by the acerbic comments and anecdotes of Mr Yardley had a certain attraction.

I decided to defer checking the spares until the next day and to head ashore. Pete, who was on cargo duty, suggested that we meet later in the city and go for a meal together. Our meeting place was to be outside Lewis's department store, under the huge male nude statue over the main entrance.

'If it's raining, don't stand directly below,' he warned, 'the rain runs off his prick and showers down on the pavement.'

From the quayside in daylight the *Allenwell* did not look all that bad. She was tatty but compact. There was a certain grimy solidity about her. The buff-coloured funnel seemed too large, like a nose that appears to increase in size with age. Some of the previous night's revellers lined the railings, smoking and clutching mugs of tea, subdued. They breathed in the misty air like seals emerging from a long underwater swim. The winches of the derricks rattled gratingly as cargo was swung aboard.

The *Allenwell's* port of registration was Sunderland, in North-East England. Isolated by stretches of moorland to the north and south and bounded on the west by the Pennine range, facing the sea and Norway on the east, its people have a distinctive character. They are down-to-earth people, outspoken in accents that have a Scandinavian lilt. They frown on social pretention. The North-East has always had a strong nautical tradition.

Geordie ships had a reputation for being spartan. Hardy seafarers reared under the cold grey skies of the North Sea, they had little time for frills and niceties. The area's coalmining and shipbuilding industries had been hard hit by the Depression of the 1930s; hunger and hardship had been common. Deck officers from the more southerly parts of England were inclined to look down on the Geordies. 'The Geordie will put up with the worst kind of food, bad conditions on board, bad everything — he doesn't know any better,' they said.

After wandering about the department stores and bookshops for a few hours, I met Pete at Lewis's. We went to a Chinese restaurant.

'Captain's back. So's Misery.'

'Who's Misery?'

'The mate. Misery Muir. Just had another run-in with him. Didn't want me to go ashore. Oh, I told him to get fucked,' Pete laughed. He had a large loose mouth with no clear line between lips and red-skinned cheeks. 'He wanted to turn in for the night, straight after tea. Sleeping is his favourite form of recreation. Trouble is, the *Allenwell* isn't the ideal kind of ship for a man of his habits. A lot of boozing and shouting.'

'I heard some of it last night.'

'Yes. That's another thing bothering him. He knows all the regular piss-artists from the last voyage will be back with us again. A floating home for alcoholics, the *Allenwell*.'

21

'What's the captain's attitude to all this?'

'Turns a blind eye to it. A boozer himself. He runs an easy ship. Oh, he tries to throw his weight around the bridge now and again, but I don't take too much notice of him,' said the uncertified third mate. 'He's a bit of a showman. Wants to be the centre of attention.'

This sounded like a flippant judgment on the master of the *Allenwell*. But shortly afterwards, unexpectedly, I was to see this rollicking master at first hand. When we alighted from the bus at the dock gate, Pete suggested that we cross the road for a cup of coffee in the big public house. In the bitter December night, its tall windows glowed a welcoming orange. As we approached it, the sound of muffled music came from within. Over the door a big wooden sign, depicting a sailing ship, swung creaking in the wind.

'Watch how you go, Sparks — someone's spewed his ring up.'

We stepped around the asterisk of beer-smelling vomit and pushed our way through the heavy doors. The sudden impact of noise, heat and light was startling. This nautical drinking den was jam-packed. Sailors, stevedores, truckers and female companions sat cheek by jowl at marble-topped tables festooned with glasses and bottles that reflected the yellow glare of the high ceiling lights. The bar was hidden behind a shouldering wall of bodies as men clamoured for attention from the perspiring barmen. The air was full of the smell of beer, damp clothing and perfume. There was an eye-watering fog of blue tobacco smoke. Above the bellowing, the shouted conversations, shrieks of laughter, a three-piece band battled manfully to entertain in one corner. All you could hear was the dull thud of the drum, a drowned trickle from the piano and the odd disjointed blare of the saxophone.

'I think we can forget about the coffee, Pete.'

'Would you fancy any of the women?' he shouted in my ear. There were a few young vivacious women scattered about the tables, giggling and looking around. But there was a large contingent of blowsy, raddled women whose life-scarred faces were flushed with alcoholic cheer.

'If there's one place to catch a dose, it's here, Pete.'

Patrons in this establishment were encouraged to perform. It was the ideal place for the untalented to work off their fantasies; croaking out-of-tune voices were screened from serious scrutiny by the uproarious din. A fat woman, stuffed into a red costume, much the worse for drink, began to bawl into the microphone. A mass of peroxide blond hair fell over her face; one could just glimpse the heavily lipsticked mouth opening and shutting.

Pete grabbed me by the arm. 'Hey — there's the Old Man.'

'The captain? Here?'

'Over there — with Brad, Ted and the cooks.' As I squinted among the tables, I wondered if Pete was pulling my leg. No captain I had ever sailed under would be seen in a raucous boozer such as this. And most certainly not in the company of the cooks and chief steward. British captains tended to be conscious of their rank and dignity both ashore and afloat. The command structure on British ships usually reflected the country's class structure, with its overtones of selective breeding and snobbery. This helped to reinforce the distinction between the higher ranks and the less exalted. The captain of a Cunarder or a British India vessel would deign to socialise ashore only with his very senior officers. Even in the relaxed atmosphere of some club or restaurant, there would always be a veil of deference between the august personage and his companions. If wives were present, it was tacitly accepted that the captain's wife had a sort of seniority that put her slightly above the other ladies.

Pete pointed out the table and I craned my neck. The ferret-like face of Little Alex, the chief cook, became visible in the throng; Old Charlie was gesticulating energetically; Ted was sitting there, looking handsomely sad, and I could see the frieze of jet black hair which hovered over Brad's skull. All I could see of the man whom Pete said was the captain was a pair of round shoulders and a round brown head like a big weathered pumpkin, with wispy hair swept back. Just then the female performer gave up the effort and stumbled off the little stage. This man rose to his feet.

'The Old Man's going to sing,' yelled Pete gleefully. I saw a low-slung rotund man, with bushy eyebrows and a pouting lower lip, push his way between the tables. Just as he reached the stage, a rival entertainer appeared, a skinny young fellow who affected a jaunty air. But the fat one thrust out a stout arm, glared truculently and the youth sidled off.

'Give us a song, captain,' came several roars from tables, which Pete told me were occupied by crew members and female friends. The Old Man had a word with the musicians and then came forward and tapped the microphone with a stubby finger. A momentary silence fell. He cleared his throat with a rasping amplified sound and then in a quick emphatic Geordie accent said, 'I'm going to sing a song and if any bugger wants to join in he can, and if he doesn't, he can shut up his mouth and listen.'

The band played a few introductory notes. The captain cleared his throat again. The introduction was repeated. Then in a flat, harsh voice he launched into an inspirational song, beloved of the Victorian English, called 'If I can help somebody, my living will not be in vain.' He took liberties with the lyrics. When he came to the line 'If I can do my duty as a Christian ought,' he substituted 'If I can do my duty on the *Allenwell'*. This spontaneous inventiveness was lost on the audience. After the first few bars, a hum of conversation began and increased in volume, interspersed with a few derisory guffaws. This seemed to annoy the performer. He filled his paunchy figure with air and bellowed into the microphone. His voice had a curious resonance which I imagined came from the echo-chamber formed between his heavy jowls.

Catcalls were flung towards him; a few of the audience theatrically clamped their hands to their ears. Suddenly he stopped. The band stopped too. A puzzled hush descended. The Old Man puffed out his cheeks and frowned threateningly towards those tables where his crew and their women were carousing.

'Some buggers are laughing and not listening, but they

won't be laughing when I stop the allotments.'

This reference to the arrangement whereby absent sailors had monthly payments made to spouses, common law wives and shore-side strumpets brought a roar of laughter. Instinctively sensing that it was the right moment to act, the Old Man waved cheerily and, in a storm of applause, made his way back to the table. I wondered what the staff clerk at the Marconi office would have thought of the captain of 'the next best thing to a Cunarder' performing in the 'Windjammer'.

Pete shook his head. 'Alright — now that we've seen the star of the show, let's get back on board.'

The ship looked dim and deserted. As we passed along the outer passageway, Pete indicated the curtained porthole of the mate's cabin and made a sleeping gesture with cheek on palm. There was nothing to distract the mate's slumber until about two hours later. Then the wooden steps of the gangway began to clatter under misdirected footsteps. Curses and huzzahs resounded. I wondered if there would be a repeat performance of the 'marine entertainment' of the previous night, but there was nothing more than a few random shouts. Presently a growing rumble of voices, punctuated by outbursts of cheering, drifted down the alleyway. I put down my book and went out. A darts game was under way in the recreation room.

About a dozen men were hunched together in the small area, with two crates of communal beer cans on the floor. I edged inside without anyone taking notice. The captain was in the act of throwing. He came forward to the line, gave a preliminary burp, then thrust out his ample belly as if to intimidate the dartboard. He shifted and settled his heavy bandy legs, encased in floppy trousers. He blew out his cheeks like balloons, eyeing the target from beneath his bushy eyebrows. Then, with a deft flick of his thick hairy wrist, he let fly. Successive cheers went up as each dart embedded itself in the board. The Old Man grinned, looking about.

Little Alex was less successful. He flexed his shoulder and

pulled his arm back as if he was about to throw a javelin. Two darts plonked into the panelling and one hit the board but fell out. A roar of disparagement greeted his effort and someone shouted superfluously 'That man is drunk.' Ted sat in a chair, gazing at the dartboard like someone watching a scenic sunset.

The captain easily beat Little Alex and challenged Brad to a game. The flabby brown-faced man shambled to the line with a throaty laugh. He had delicate, expressive fingers and held the darts like a fastidious painter putting the final touches to a picture. But Captain Thompson got the better of him, hitting the finishing double first time, to a reverberating roar.

I drifted out and went down to my cabin. As I was about to go in, I saw the door of the mate's cabin wrenched open. A long bony head on a thin scrawny neck, with a prominent Adam's apple, was silhouetted against the light. It had a big beakish nose and a pointed chin which almost met one another, like the pincers of a crab. The sunken mouth opened and a flat plaintive voice called out 'Could we have a little quiet, please?' This plea was either ignored or unheard by the bibulous gathering. The uproar continued. 'Noisy cunts,' the voice spat, the head was withdrawn and the door banged shut. This was my first sight of Misery Muir, mate of the *Allenwell.*

The day of inspection had come to an end, I sat with feet propped on the writing desk, thinking it over. Those who shy away from confrontation usually try to justify their lack of spirit. If I aroused the vindictiveness of the staff clerk, I might end up on an oil tanker monotonously plying the oceans between one isolated oil terminal and another for nine months. Here was a chance to see New Orleans and the ports along the sunny Mexican Gulf. What had I come to sea for in the first place? To earn money, certainly, but also to see the world, to taste life, meet all manner of people. You could not expect to get good ships all the time. Someone had to take over the radio room on the *Allenwell,* and the gear was in good working order. After the three-month trip was over, I would always be able to say 'I've sailed on everything — from deck-passenger ships east of Suez to rusty old tramps.'

Besides, the bizarre character of this ship was already exercising an attraction, stimulating a curiosity. There would not be many ships afloat where the captain performed in dockside taverns, the chief engineer never entered the engine room, the second mate never entered the saloon, the chief steward was perpetually stewed, and the cooks made the galley a mealtime battleground. And a rough-neck crew of proven rowdiness.

There was another reason that helped me decide to sign on. I was easily unnerved by haughty, authoritative captains. Thompson was, I felt, a man who would give me little bother. I probably also sensed that here was a ship where the oddities of my own personality, rooted in painful shyness and uncertainty, would go unnoticed. The *Allenwell* was a ship where any seafarer could find a niche.

3

'The Flower of British Manhood'

Next morning I sat alone in the chill saloon, listening to the bickering of the cooks. Then the voice of Alasdair, the young Scottish steward, rang out: 'The chief's alive — I just heard him coughing'.

Mr Yardley came slowly in, dabbing watery eyes. His hands and arms were shaking after the convulsions of a cough-bout. He nodded bleakly in my direction. Presently a thin bony man of middle age entered with a sliding pigeon-toed gait and sat down next to me. He was neatly dressed in khaki pants and tweed jacket. The sandy hair at the top of his long narrow head was closely cropped. The prominence of the beak-nose and pointed chin of Misery Muir were diminished by the installation of a full set of small false teeth.

'Another Irish sparks', he said with a thin, turned-down smile of disapproval when we introduced ourselves. He scanned the menu sarcastically.

'I think I'll try a few cornflakes, steward,' he said in a slow reluctant voice.

Mr Yardley eyed him with faint amusement and pronounced: 'Eating is nothing more than a habit. I only eat myself because people would think me peculiar if I didn't.'

Such subtle mockery was completely lost on Misery. He began a dreary recitation of his activities since he had arisen. He had a strong Geordie accent, pronouncing his 'I's as 'Ah's. 'Ah got up at seven. The cup of tea ah got was cold. Then ah smoked a cigarette. Then ah had a pee. Then ah washed and shaved. Then ah went out on deck to see the cargo started working'.

Mr Yardley nodded sagely. 'The excitement of it all. No wonder you can't stop adventurous young fellows like Sparks here from haring off to sea.'

Misery's face was the texture and colour of fine sandpaper. He had light blue eyes, arched bitterly, and thin lips that he barely opened when talking, as if breath was a commodity he did not care to expend freely.

Mr Yardley said gloatingly, 'The captain was in good form last night by the sound of things.'

'A darts game going on until all hours, keeping every fucker awake,' said Misery sourly.

Just then the subject of the conversation appeared in the doorway, his belly hanging over the belt of his trousers. He grinned slyly as he took his seat at the head of the table and grunted a vague greeting, sharp eyebrow-shaded eyes darting round the table. Misery looked down at his plate.

'Married an Irishwoman myself,' the captain laughed when I introduced myself.

'I bet you didn't tell her everything about last trip,' said Mr Yardley.

Captain Thompson grinned roguishly. Then he belched and patted his stomach. 'Bugger won't stop rumbling. I ate a bad meat pie in the pub and I've been blowing from both ends the whole bloody night.'

'Yes indeed,' agreed Mr Yardley. 'Bad meat pies are always a danger. It's never the fourteen pints a man drinks that causes the trouble. Meat pies are the things you have to watch out for.'

'Any news of a new bosun?' asked Misery, not looking directly at the captain.

'Not yet. Hope he's better than the last bugger' chortled Captain Thompson, as if the memory of a man who was apparently disastrously incompetent as boss of the crew was a matter of amusement. Misery was silently resentful.

'I suppose we'll have the cream of British manhood on board again for the voyage. Our marine superintendent, Mr Hall, will see to that,' Mr Yardley's voice grated with disparagement. The captain grunted wryly. For all his supposed stomach trouble, the Old Man ate his breakfast with relish, round cheeks expanding and contracting, heavy jowls quivering as he chewed vigorously on the stringy bacon. He and the mate ignored one another.

The tangible air of strain at the table was broken when Misery rose abruptly. 'Ah better see how the cargo is coming on,' he said, with an air of a man who was attending to his duties while others were neglecting theirs. Captain Thompson was visibly relieved at his departure. He sat back and opened a packet of oval-shaped cigarettes called 'Passing Clouds'. These cigarettes, in their pink-coloured packet, seemed at variance with his robust character.

'Ever sailed the North Atlantic in winter before, Sparks?'

'Never sailed it at all, captain.'

'He has a treat in store for him, especially on this bloody ship,' said Mr Yardley.

'Never mind, Sparks. When we get down to New Orleans, the women will be waiting for you.' He smiled impishly. 'Caught a dose from a black lassie there before the war.'

'Doses are an occupational hazard,' said Mr Yardley thoughtfully. 'I've often wondered why the National Union of Seamen never used it as a bargaining counter in wage negotiations with the shipowners.'

Captain Thompson belched, said 'There's nowt more to eat,' got up and plodded off with a bow-legged nautical roll. Mr Yardley glanced over his shoulder, shook his head and said 'That man.' Into these two words he compressed an accumulation of scorn. He pressed his lips against his teeth to form a compact smile of derision.

When you begin the task of settling into a ship's cabin you invariably come across little mementoes of the previous occupant. It is like unpacking in a hotel room where your predecessor has been in residence for some months. You stir up a residual spirit of the other's personality. As I opened the drawers to stow away underwear, socks and shirts, arrange books on the little shelf, put notebooks and paper into the writing desk, I uncovered some of the little life-signs of McCarthy. An empty whisky bottle rolled forward when I pulled out the top drawer of the desk. In one of the pigeon holes was a packet of contraceptives bearing the reassuring inscription 'electronically tested'. In another drawer was an envelope addressed in an elegant female hand 'John McCarthy, c/o *Allenwell*, Cape Town.' It exuded a faint perfume. It was disappointing to find it empty. In the bottom of the wardrobe was a pair of warped, mildewed shoes, heels worn down from determined walking.

Just then a voice behind me said, in a tone of appraisal, 'So you're the new sparks, eh?' Leaning against the doorway was a tall man in an oil-stained boiler suit. A round pasty head sprouted from a long neck. He was bald except for a smudge at the top of his forehead.

'The last sparks was a rum bugger all right,' he said in a nostalgic, admiring way. 'Never stopped drinking and as soon as the ship docked he was away ashore after a bit of tail. Some fellow was McCarthy.'

The second engineer's big heavy nose seemed to pull his black eyes together and dominated his small energetic mouth.

'He had two women on board at the same time in Durban. One slept on the settee, the other on the bunk there — he had to doss down on the deck himself. I don't know how he managed it,' he said enviously.

'How long have you been on this ship?'

'Too bloody long. This is my last trip. I am jacking it in at the end of the voyage. Going ashore for good. Getting married,' he said in a vaguely dissatisfied way. Then he returned to the subject of McCarthy's amorous exploits and his drinking capacity.

It was not hard to get the impression that he thought that I was something of a dullard by comparison with my illustrious predecessor. I did not take to him very much. Because of his rodent-like facial features, I mentally christened him 'Rat' and now cannot remember his real name.

Whatever about McCarthy's drinking and womanising, he

had left the radio room in first-rate order. Even before I was halfway through the tiresome business of ticking off each item in the spare lockers, I was sure that the full regulatory quota was there.

Just as I had finished, I heard someone pulling out the creaking wooden drawers in the chart room next door and the heavy papery sound of a chart being unrolled. When I peered round the door there was Brad, feet splayed out behind him in the same posture as in the galley, gazing quietly at a big chart he had pinned on the board. With nimble fingers he was automatically rolling a cigarette.

His round light-brown face was full of warmth and ease. One of his parents obviously had originated east of Suez, possibly Burma or Malaya, but he had the build of a well-fed European and his accent was pure Geordie.

'That's the bugger we have to cross,' he said placidly, tapping the white expanse of charted ocean with a sensitive finger. I looked at the map with some concern. Only at the edges of his immense waste was land visible; the rocky sea-battered headlands of Brittany, Ireland and Britain to the east; away on the other side the grey indented coastlines of bleak wintery regions like Newfoundland and Nova Scotia; at the top was the barren shape of Iceland, with hard Nordic names on its stormy capes.

'How long is it going to take?'

'Fourteen days. It'll be heavy going. Rough weather.'

I had heard much about the North Atlantic, of the great storms that tumbled ceaselessly across the dim shelterless ocean in winter.

Brad looked at me with dark oriental eyes and said reassuringly, 'We'll be all right a few days out of New York, when we head south past Cape Hatteras. The Gulf of Mexico will be lovely sailing this time of the year.'

This placid man was somewhere in his mid-forties. You could see his shiny brown skull, but he was not completely bald, for a mist of black hair hovered over it like a magnetic field. The only disconcerting thing about Brad was that his dentures were loose; when he spoke, they moved a fraction of a second behind his jaws, slightly out of synchronisation.

'Let's see how the cargo is coming along,' he said and moved out to the wheelhouse. I had seen items of cargo being loaded in Number Three and Number Four holds, so nondescript that I cannot remember what they were. When we looked down at the scene on the Number Two hold, it was evident that something unusual was going on. There were port police standing on the dockside in attitudes of watchfulness. The fork-lift truck drivers and the stevedores seemed to be taking special care with the rectangular wooden crates being carried from the cargo shed and stacked ready for loading. At that moment a slingload of crates was gently hoisted up from the quay. For a few seconds it swung in mid-air before being lowered into the hold. It was possible to discern the stencilled inscription 'Vat 69 – Produce of Scotland'.

'Where is the whisky for, Brad?

'New Orleans and Houston. A fair amount,' he said with apparent indifference.

Apart from the fact that this precious commodity needed to be loaded carefully, it did not seem to me to have any other practical significance. I noticed, however, some of the crew members watching with intense solicitude.

When I locked the radio room and went below, I found the foyer full of the smell of burning. In the galley three cauldrons hissed and bubbled on the ranges. The heavy lids trembled and heaved, releasing clouds of steam and a thick liquid which ran down the sides and dissolved into brown vapour when it reached the hot plates. The cooks were nowhere to be seen. Why had they abandoned their posts at such a critical time in the culinary process?

The answer was provided when I looked into the recreation room. There were the two with faces pressed against the for'ard porthole. Ted stood behind them, craning his neck. All three heads moved in unison, like spectators watching the kick-out at a football match. They presented a picture of total absorption as they followed the journey of each slingload of whisky. The pointed face of Little Alex, raised skywards, reminded you of one of those minor figures you see on an enormous canvass depicting the ascension into heaven of some saint. The tousle-headed Old Charlie's spectacles were halfway down his nose, so that he had to tilt his head further back, giving the impression of a grandfatherly toad gazing at the full moon. From Ted the steady succession of sucking sounds seemed to have increased in pace, as if to denote a heightened awareness of life. Even then I did not realise the implications of this excessive interest in our cargo.

The most immediate result was seen when a dark brown viscous substance appeared on our plates at lunchtime.

'Irish stew, by God,' said Mr Yardley scathingly. 'If St Patrick could see this production, he'd turn in his grave.'

Misery prodded the mess with his fork, making a tense grimace with his lips. As if there was some connection between the stew and the crew we were to sign on next afternoon, he said, 'No doubt we'll have the dregs on board again for this voyage.'

'Why shouldn't they sign on?' reasoned Mr Yardley. 'They know that can get away with anything on this ship. You can't expect Mr Hall to weary himself selecting a proper crew.'

The contempt in which the marine superintendent was held and the way in which it was expressed almost openly to his face was one more abnormal aspect of the *Allenwell*. As the men who represented the owners, with overall responsibility for the management and profitability of a company's vessels, marine superintendents were usually personages of authority. They were shown considerable deference, especially by masters and senior officers, whom they had the power to hire and fire.

There were certain reasons why Mr Hall was regarded with something less than awe on the *Allenwell*. He came on board at ten o'clock each morning with the gait of a man intent on briskly performing onerous duties. He would spend some time with Captain Thompson, who thought it proper to offer him beer while they discussed business. Mr Hall would then go to the chief steward's cabin, presumably to deal with matters related to the provisioning of the ship. By lunchtime his step was unsteady rather than decisive, beads of perspiration decorated his red face, and his magisterial mien was replaced by a glazed look.

Just then the man himself stumbled in, clutching a sheaf of untidy documents. He lowered himself awkwardly into one of the seats.

'Everything all right, Bob?' asked the captain between mouthfuls.

'I've done the best I can. I think we have a bosun that'll keep the crew toeing the line.'

Mr Hall's speech was slurred. His head kept falling forward a few inches. Captain Thompson seemed unconcerned, but Mr Yardley and Misery eyed the marine superintendent scornfully.

The signing-on took place next afternoon at three. The table-cloth on the captain's table in the saloon was removed. A varied collection of men began to assemble in the foyer. Each one held a grimy seaman's discharge book in fingers calloused or oil-stained. Many were old hands, signing on for the umpteenth voyage. These men joked and bantered amongst themselves.

'You're here because you wouldn't be taken on board another ship.'

'Look who's talking!'

Those signing on for the first time were quieter, but most looked as rough-hewn as the old lags. The total assemblage represented men of all ages, conditions, shapes and sizes. Some were beer-bloated, others gaunt; a few pale-faced young fellows, some beefy men of middle age and quite a few grizzled sea-dogs. Almost all were badly dressed, as if their clothes had been bought in the musty second-hand clothes shops in the side-streets of the dockland area.

There was a momentary hush when the rotund figure of the captain waddled into view, accompanied by the perspiring Mr Hall and two seedy-looking clerks from the shipping office, who had an array of ballpoint pens in their breast pockets as symbols of office and literacy.

Captain Thompson smiled as he sat down at the head of the table, like Old King Cole enjoying his regal role. Mr Hall and the clerks sat on either side of him, with the crew list on the table before them. The men formed a straggling queue and began to shuffle forward towards this tribunal of inspection. Beneath the elbowing banter was a current of tension. The captain has the power to reject those whom he considers unsuitable, men with known records of misbehaviour, with 'Decline to Report' written in their books under the heading of 'Conduct'.

Misery stood to one side, watching the scene from hostile blue eyes. He was like a general at the final call-up during a prolonged, disastrous war when the war-machine, desperate to replace casualties, casts aside all standards, overlooking physical and mental disability, even criminal records.

'The flower of British manhood!' he said to me, shaking his head with disapproval. He was watching the trouble-makers, layabouts and heavy drinkers who had enlivened the previous voyage. If he had had his way, they would have been summarily sent packing.

Captain Thompson, however, had the air of a kindly and amiable magistrate. As each man presented his book, he flicked over the pages with short gingery-haired fingers. His sharp eyes, behind rolls of flesh and canopy eyebrows, briskly scrutinised each man's face and then gave a friendly nod. On a few occasions he hesitated theatrically, looked at the man's record a second time, gave the applicant a small look of warning and then, with a tolerant smile, nodded.

Some signed awkwardly, gripping the cheap ballpoint and signing heavily on the list. Toni signed delicately, with a cheeky pursing of his lips. Little Alex signed with a great flourish, like a dignitary putting his name to an international treaty of historic significance.

Misery's bitter disappointment shaped his thin mouth into a downward crescent. All very well for the captain to display monarchal magnanimity, but Misery was the one who was going to have to control the deck crew. His gaze kept returning to a burly, bear-like fellow, with shaven head and flat battered face. This tough-looking veteran was Ben Jennings, the bosun unearthed by Mr Hall to act as Misery's right-hand man. He certainly seemed very capable of keeping order amongst the crew, by force of fists if force of personality should fail. Misery regarded this man with some suspicion.

The officers signed on last. When my turn came, Captain Thompson turned the pages of my discharge book, noting the other ships on which I had served.

'Well, Sparks, this ship is a bit different to your British India boats — but we're lively enough in our own way.'

4

Rough Sailing

'Third mate — is that rag flying up there supposed to be the Blue Peter?' the Old Man called across the saloon to Pete at breakfast.

'It's the only one we have.'

'It's as tattered and torn as the old red flannel drawers that Maggie wore.'

Below the rag flapping from the foremast in a rising wind, the last slingloads of cargo were swung aboard. The ship made preparations to sail. The deck crew bustled about, under the command of the bullet-headed Ben Jennings. He in turn was being silently nagged by Misery, who picked his pigeon-toed way about the littered decks, his thin spiteful figure shadowing the bulky frame of the bosun.

The crew heaved and hauled at the heavy wooden hatch-boards and slid them into place over the holds. The canvas covers rasped as they were spread over the boards, pulled taut and fastened. The closing of the hatches for a deep-sea voyage is one of the rituals of sailing day. Before they are uncovered, surging sea-water may have swept over them, ice formed or snow fallen on them, tropical sun blazed down on the canvas. Their reopening in distant ports will be under skies of a different climate, with stevedores shouting in strange accents or languages.

'Make sure they're all battened down, bosun,' called Misery, looking at the clouds rolling in from the north-west.

'Aye, aye sir', Jennings said resolutely and shouted orders to his disparate band.

The bosun was less formidable at close quarters. After I had replaced several of the big brown china insulators at each end of the main aerial — the result of its careless lowering at the end of the previous voyage — I went to him to have it hoisted aloft. He was an agreeable man and helped me straighten out the kinks in the sea-greyed wire before directing some of the men to haul on the ropes at the foot of the foremast. Lumbering about on flat feet, with battered face and bristling skull, he seemed like a seedy convict; later, word got round the ship that he had in fact done time for some unspecified misdemeanour. As the aerial rose jerkily upwards, he turned to me and said, in a confidential tone, 'I'm worried about the crew, Sparks, I don't mind telling you. I reckon there's a lot of plonkies on this ship. I won't be surprised if there's trouble before the voyage is out.'

He spoke with a West Country accent, the words coiling slowly out of a grey sunken mouth that held a few isolated teeth. It never occurred to me at the time that he may have been hinting that the presence of whisky in Number Two hold might be a source of temptation to our men.

When I had given the radar a final run-through, I prepared to nip ashore to post a letter home. Captain Thompson was in the foyer. 'Stocking up with French letters for New Orleans, Sparks? Listen — while you're at it you can buy me a few sex yarns as well', he said, giving me some money. Several men pressed letters into my hand at the top of the gangway. For married men, especially those with young children, those with strong family ties, this was a day tinged with sadness, one of final phone calls and letters: 'I hope you will all have a very happy Christmas. I will be thinking of you all on Christmas Day.'

But sailing day evokes an excitement, even an ebullience, on board. For the true seafarer, a few weeks in one place, even in the warm bosom of his family, stirs up a restlessness deep in his soul. He may say his goodbyes with a lump in his throat, but he cannot help feeling a sense of relief to be heading back to the sea which is part of his very being. He may dismiss anything which smacks of adventurousness, be scornful of the notion of renewing any mystic relationship and adversity with the ocean; yet a certain light comes into his eyes when the Blue Peter flutters to the masthead and he smiles easily as he walks about. For young fellows like Pete and I there was a sense of excitement about heading out into the North Atlantic, as well as the prospect of eventually sailing under balmy blue skies towards Louisiana and Texas.

'We'll have some sport when we go up the Mississippi and come alongside in New Orleans,' Pete predicted happily.

Tattered grey clouds were streaming over a yellow western sky as the tugboats came alongside to take us out into the Mersey estuary. I had scribbled down the forecast; predictions were dire. A depression had rolled across the Atlantic like a huge roundabout, spinning storm-force winds from its centre. Brad, marking it on the chart, reckoned it would come thundering over the north-west coast of Ireland just as we emerged into the open ocean the following afternoon.

On the bridge Captain Thompson ambled about in a dirty duffle-coat, a big black beret clamped over his head. Brad trundled away to cast off aft, rolling a cigarette as he went. Only Misery wore a uniform cap as he stood at the prow, supervising the taking on board of the tow-rope and the hauling in of our last link with the land. The spruce Mersey pilot bounded onto the bridge. He looked about superciliously.

'Where's the captain?'

'I'm the captain' growled Thompson 'Let's shift our arse.'

'I'm ready when you are.'

Captain Thompson cupped his hands and roared like a foghorn to Misery, 'Let the bugger go.' Misery cast off.

Mr Hall stood on the quayside as we drew away. There was a look of achievement on his florid face. He waved at Captain Thompson and shouted, 'Have a good voyage then.' The Old Man returned the wave cursorily, said 'Bollocks' in a low tone and turned away.

The deck trembled slightly as the propeller began to churn the muddy water. When we emerged into the Mersey estuary, the grey panorama of Liverpool spread out on our starboard side: buildings and rooftops, chimneys and spires, with the twin bird-topped towers of the Liver building dominating this dull and misty vista.

As I peered into the radar viewer, Pete came up.

'By the way, I may as well warn you that the Old Man isn't too well up on radar.' Thompson came over and Pete moved off.

'Radar OK, Sparks?'

'Fine, captain. Take a look.'

'Don't let the third mate play around with this thing. He fucks it up every time he goes near it.'

The captain took over the controls and began to change ranges, back and forth, with alarming speed. I could imagine the whining trigatron valve up in the radar hut flickering as it changed tone, like a clarinet player trying to keep up with a manic conductor. I walked away in annoyance. A minute later Thompson called, 'Sparks – this bloody thing seems too have packed up.' I hurried over. He had succeeded in wiping the picture off the tube by misuse of the controls. I retuned it and the outline of the estuary reappeared.

'It's set in the correct position again, captain.'

'Good. Don't let the third mate get his fingers on those knobs.'

The Irish Sea was full of choppy bouncing waves as the pilot launch came alongside, gathered our pilot and swerved away shorewards. The deck was shifting and swaying as we headed into sea and wind. From now on the movement of the sea was going to dominate. You begin to balance yourself against the rise and fall and yaw. It becomes almost automatic after a while; you place your feet carefully, widen your stance for stability. You have to relearn the language of sea-movement, accommodate yourself quickly to its varying rhythms if you are to avoid bumps or injury.

In the radio room I called up Anglesey radio station. 'MV *Allenwell* leaving Liverpool bound New York and New Orleans.' It sounded like a final confirmation that we were on our way.

Out in the chart room Brad was leaning over the table,

laying off our course. We were to go west of the Isle of Man, up through the narrow strait between Ireland and Scotland and then out into the North Atlantic.

'It will be a bit rough out there,' he said quietly.

Once a ship sails, the treadmill of watchkeeping is imposed on most. The hands of the clock, the ship's bell, rule one's waking and sleeping hours. Through the twenty-four-hour day the watches change in the engine room and on the bridge. At the beginning of each radio watch, the short-wave traffic list has to be copied down, the weather forecast taken twice a day, the time signal given to the bridge. The sense of excitement that attends putting to sea subsides after the first few watches, especially on a murky December day in the Irish Sea.

Early next morning I went out to the port wing of the bridge to stare westward. There was nothing to be seen but low cloud being whipped along over the sea. Somewhere out there was the dark shadow of the Cooley Mountains and just north of them the sloping Mountains of Mourne. In between was the thumb-shaped inlet that the Vikings had named Carlingford. Not far from the rocky shore, dark with damp brown seaweed, was the cottage where my mother lived at Omeath. I wondered if some of the sharp-winged seagulls swooping round the masts might seek shelter there from the coming storm and look down on the little house where I longed to be.

By afternoon we had gone through the narrows and come abeam of the north tip of Donegal. Now there was no protection whatever from the huge black waves which had built up on their unimpeded way across the vast watery plain ahead. They advanced towards us like long mountain barriers, their crests topped with spray. Above the howling of the gale you could hear a deep thunderous rumble as the waves approached.

The prow of the *Allenwell* met each one with a shudder and an explosion of water. White cascades surged out on either side. Great plumes of spray rose into the air; the wind grasped them, bent them and flailed them into spray which came flying towards the superstructure. It crashed against the streaming windows of the wheelhouse and deluged the open wings of the bridge.

Those first few days of North Atlantic storm-sailing provided some unforgettable moments of exhilaration. I used to get into a set of crews' waterproofs and wellington boots and go out on the wing of the bridge to watch the spectacle. The deck rose steeper and steeper as the ship climbed up each massive wave; if you did not cling to the parapet, you were likely to slide back down the deck. Then the 'boom' as the prow broke through the crest; the ship plunged down, the deck falling away beneath your feet in a way that brought a ticklish sensation under the heart. Then the ship steadied and began another ascent.

Out there on the wing you had to crouch behind the parapet, ready to duck each time a cannonade of white water came roaring towards you. But there was no avoiding the pellets of rain and spray if you were to watch the turmoil of the storm. Your face glowed red, your eyes winced, your hair was tugged and tousled, your arms ached from holding, but you felt like a Viking chieftain.

Sometimes Pete and I stood there together, laughing and shouting obscenities at one another that were whipped out of our mouths by the wind and sent flying aft, barely heard above the tumult. A rolling grey mattress of cloud raced by overhead, seeming to touch the swaying foremast. Wave, wind and cloud swirled and melted, parted and joined in confusion as the ship rose and plunged like a bucking bronco in slow motion.

At first I was cautious about leaving the radio room to watch the storm when the captain was on the bridge. But he was ever jovial, liking to have someone to talk to; he had an easy-going attitude towards the rules, both as they might apply to himself and to those under his command.

Occasionally he emerged from the wheelhouse to the open wing, grinning exultantly as he gripped the parapet with stubby fingers. A sort of sea-bond grew between us in those moments.

Most of the time he was content to remain in the wheel-house, peering out through the whirling glass windscreen. He would curse the weather cheerfully, telling little anecdotes of North Atlantic sailing.

'Those are the biggest waves I've ever seen, captain.'

'Ah, this is bugger-all, Sparks,' he shouted above the roar of wind and wave. 'I sailed through the great storm of 1918. We nearly turned turtle off the west coast of Scotland. Bloody great waves smashed the wheelhouse, made match-wood of it. I was at the wheel. Couldn't hold the bugger. Got my bollocks tangled in the spinning spokes. Lost a ball I did,' he grinned, as if this was a hilarious event.

I mentioned this unfortunate accident to Mr Yardley later.

Oh yes — I heard about that — too many times. Well it certainly didn't put him off his stroke. Indeed, I imagine he used his anatomical deficiency to arouse the curiosity of women he was trying to seduce. If anything, the loss of a ball stimulated his sexual activities.'

It would be wrong to give the impression that those hours of losing oneself in the turmoil of the storm made the crossing an enjoyable one. Most of the time it was tiresome and miserable. Every moment of the day you had to struggle to keep your feet whenever you stood up or tried to move from one place to another. You had to cling to doorposts or railings to prevent yourself being tumbled onto the deck or flung headlong down stairways. Out on the bridge you could see what was happening, ready yourself for the rise and plunge; but floundering along the alleyway, legs and arms braced, stumbling from one safe foothold to the next, could be a stomach-churning experience.

In the radio room the chair on which I sat strained against the stout chain that shackled it to the floor, like a bear making ponderous attempts to free itself. Copying down traffic lists or weather forecasts or sending the very occasional message meant wrapping one leg about the desk-leg to try to keep steady. It took one hand to keep the message-pad or logbook on the desk; when the Morse hand was in use, the pencil had to be clamped between the teeth; if I inadvertently left it on the desk, it immediately rolled off and skittered away about the deck and I had to chase it on all fours, like a naturalist in pursuit of an elusive cricket. I had forgotten to lock two of the drawers and they had shot out with a tremendous bang, scattering their contents about the floor. It was a Herculean task to gather them up and slam the drawers into place again.

My off-duty hours were spent lying on the settee, feet jammed against the wardrobe, arms against the side of the writing desk, trying to get some rest. All the efforts to maintain balance, to get through the watch duties, exacted a toll on muscles and energies. After three or four days continuous storm-sailing, it wore down the spirits as well. All you wanted to do was to lie down and close your eyes. At night you had to brace yourself against the bunkboard to stop yourself being heaved out onto the threadbare carpet; a full night's sleep was impossible.

Even some of the most seasoned seafarers had to endure days of wretched sea-sickness. There were haggard faces everywhere as the ship was tossed about in the maelstrom. Though I did not suffer to the same degree, my stomach was in a constant state of queasiness. The wastepaper bin in the radio room had been emptied in case my innards decided they could stand no more. Smoking a cigarette was out of the question; a single cough might have brought on a spasm of violent retching on an almost empty stomach. By the time we reached New York, the smoking habit had disappeared, along with my initial enthusiasm for North Atlantic sailing.

I cannot think of that horrendous voyage without once again feeling the nauseous emptiness of a stomach ravenous for food but which recoiled at the very sight of it. At the best of times the food served up in the saloon was never appetising. In those dreadful conditions, the greasy brown stews and oily soups were sickening to behold. Mr Yardley, Misery and I sat at table chewing bread and butter, nibbling at the odd piece of potato speared from our plates. 'Reluctant participants at life's banquet' was how Mr Yardley balefully described us.

But not Captain Thompson. He would bowl into the saloon, beaming at the prospect of food, lower lip pouting in expectation. He scooped up his soup, head bent over the plate like a famished tom-cat. The stews he devoured with relish. When a lump of fatty meat, slithering about, eluded his fork, he would solve the problem by catching it between his thumb and forefinger and popping it into his mouth. He never left a scrap on his plate, scouring up the gravy with a crust. He often finished his meal with an explosive belch of approval. 'My father used to say "Gie us summat wi' a bit o' meat in it".'

Captain Thompson was one of those who had long ago accepted the rough realities of seafaring and had decided they could just as easily be enjoyed as merely endured. From casual remarks, anecdotes and snatches of reminiscence, it was possible to piece together an outline of his seagoing life. He had gone to sea as a boy, sailing as ordinary seaman with tough Geordie companies. By the early nineteen thirties he had acquired his master's certificate. In the great Depression of those years, when rows of idle ships lay rusting at anchor in the river Tyne and many seafarers spent years on the beach, Thompson had managed to stay afloat. By the time World War II had broken out, he was captain of a small deep-sea vessel. By the time it was over, he commanded a sizeable ship in a medium-scale cargo line, which had nine vessels in its fleet.

'That was the top of the ladder for him,' said Mr Yardley as we sat alone one morning after breakfast. 'From then on he slipped down from one rung to the next until he's fetched up here. You ask me why, Sparks? No man can run a ship the way he does and expect to escape trouble. He gets away with it for a while and then it catches up with him. And, of course, he won't allow himself to be reprimanded by any shipowner. He'll bluster and lie to get out of a corner.'

One lunchtime, when we had reached the halfway mark of our tempestuous crossing, the Old Man gave an amused chuckle as he finished his coffee. This was always the signal that he was about to launch into some yarn. Misery quickly absented himself while Mr Yardley winked at me from a watery eye.

'It was round here that I lost a bloody ship,' said Captain Thompson, as if this was a matter about which it was proper to boast. Mr Yardley set to contemplating the pattern of over-lapping brown stains which successive sloppings had imprinted on the tablecloth. Apparently this was an oft-tale that he found boring and bombastic.

'Lucky no bugger lost his life,' the captain continued in lighthearted vein. He related the story in short bursts, without any dramatisation, as if describing a minor cycling accident. His ship had loaded in St John, New Brunswick, on the east coast of Canada, and had set sail for Liverpool. It was mid-winter. The ship had been buffeted and battered by stormy weather as soon as it got out of the lee of the land. The cargo shifted in the holds somewhere in mid-ocean and the vessel began to list dangerously. They could do nothing to right it. They sent out an SOS. Several ships came to their aid and stood by. The list got worse. There was nothing for it but to abandon ship. They managed to launch the starboard lifeboat, but several men, including Captain Thompson, had to jump into churning seas and cling to life-crafts. It was pitch dark, but the searchlights of the rescuing vessels kept them in sight. They were all picked up after some hazardous moments. By that time the stricken vessel had gone down.

Captain Thompson warmed to the story when he came to the sequel. The Canadian shippers and the insurers main-tained that the cargo had been lost, not by an act of God, but because of the careless way in which it had been stowed. The court case was heard in the King's Inns in London. The plaintiffs engaged an eminent Queen's Counsel to represent them. Apparently a battle of wits developed between this legal luminary and the chief witness for the defence, Captain Harry Thompson.

'This bugger strutted around the courtroom in his gown and wig. "Captain Thompson" he said in his posh accent, "has any vessel under your command ever been overloaded?" "Yes" I says. At that he looks about the courtroom holding

47

out his hands. I took the smug look off his face when I butted in, "During the war under Board of Trade special regulations." Even the fucking judge smiled.'

Thompson said that it took the distinguished jurist some minutes to compose himself after this sally. Then he returned to the attack.

'"Captain Thompson – there seems to be a remarkable inconsistency in your capacity to remember things."

'"What are you talking about?"

'"You seem rather hazy about the way the cargo was stowed. And when you abandoned ship, you apparently forgot to take the ship's logbook, the cargo plan and other important documents with you. On the other hand, you did not forget a sea-bag containing certain personal belongings."

'"There wasn't time to think of everything."

'"Indeed. Your memory seems to have been rather selective. You have just given the court the most vivid description of the exact circumstances under which you quitted the vessel."

'"Listen here," says I, "if you had to jump over the side in the middle of the North Atlantic in mid-winter, in the middle of the night, and you couldn't swim, you'd remember it too".'

Thunderous applause, according to Thompson. The judge had to hammer the bench with his gavel to restore order.

The verdict went in favour of of the shipping company and Captain Thompson.

'Afterwards I bumped into this Q.C. fellow in the restaurant and he congratulated me. "I must say you comported yourself well during this difficult case, Captain Thompson," he says. "Well," I said, "I believe in telling the truth. Once you start telling lies, you're likely to get all mixed up and end up making a bollocks of it".'

Mr Yardley winked at me, made a little burst of laughter and quoted 'Oh, while you live, tell the truth and shame the devil.'

Then Thompson, to bring the story to a conclusion, laughed and said, 'Next day I got the fucking sack.'

Mr Yardley nodded his head slightly as if to acknowledge

that the story had come to an end, but also giving the impression that he considered Captain Thompson's dismissal well-deserved.

Whatever his misfortunes, there was no aura of failure about our jolly captain. He seemed in no way dissatisfied with his lot, carried no regrets for a man who had known better ships and better days. In fact, it was hard to imagine him as other than master of a ship like the one he now commanded.

What a contrast between this jovial fat man and the bony bitter-faced mate! During his watch hours Misery was a dank grey presence on the bridge. He bore the buffeting of wind and sea with bleak fortitude. In his oilskins he seemed like a forlorn scarecrow, with drops of rain and spray dropping from his frozen red beak. A peevishness hung about him like a sodden shroud. He was critical of everything on board in a snide, petty way. From the start he was at pains to let me know that he had once commanded a ship of his own. He began sentences of sour censure with the words, 'When I was master' . . . . '

'When I was master I wouldn't tolerate any cracked mugs on the bridge,' he said, sipping lukewarm tea from a mug that he held with demonstrative distaste. 'Them cooks would be put in their place, smart.'

He never made any direct criticism of the captain, partly because it would have been bad form and partly because he preferred to disparage with indirect remarks, silent scoffing and looks sharp with resentment. He told me he had been captain of one of the Tate and Lyle ships transporting raw sugar from the West Indies to the refinery in Liverpool. But he did not enlighten me as to how he came to be mate on the *Allenwell.*

'Pig-headed pride is the answer,' said Mr Yardley. 'Tate and Lyle decided to sell some of their older ships and use charters instead. Muir's ship was sold to some Greek outfit. He had to revert to being mate. He would have none of it; he wanted to be captain or nothing. I don't imagine that his rather dismal personality had endeared him to the company.

When he tendered his resignation, they snapped it out of his hand before he could change his mind. He looked about for another captaincy, but he had no luck. He just sat at home until his money ran out. In the end he had to take anything he could get — and so here he is, enlivening this ship with his gaiety and good humour.'

At breakfast Misery never failed to say, 'Ah think ah'll try a few cornflakes,' as if reluctant to affirm the life-sustaining properties of food. Occasionally he would pick up the milk-jug, peer at its contents and hand it to Toni with the words 'Could we have a little more milk in the water, if you don't mind.' Misery interpreted Mr Yardley's faint smile as acclaim for his witticism. As soon as the Old Man took his place, Misery would relapse into sullen silence. This only served to stimulate Thompson's ribald humour; he would tell coarse jokes and stories, beaming with delight at the punch line. Mr Yardley's eye-signals across the table, flickering with amused disdain for the captain and for Misery's prudish discomfiture, lent a pointed humour to these mealtime scenes.

Misery never said as much, but he clearly felt that Brad's habit of taking his meals in the galley, hob-nobbing with the cooks in his off-duty hours, undermined the structure of authority of the ship. It was just the kind of thing you could expect from a half-caste, someone who had not the same degree of propriety and intelligence as your fresh-faced Britisher.

Brad blithely ignored the mate's silent strictures. There was not an ounce of bad nature in this moon-faced man; he was always in a state of mild good humour that he never lost, even when bad times fell on the *Allenwell* during the latter part of our voyage. He rarely spoke about himself, his back-ground or his seafaring career. Whenever I heard him shuffling about the chart room on the afternoon watch, I would go out to join him. He would be contemplating the chart, delicately twirling a pencil over the estimated position.

'How many times have your sailed across the North Atlantic?'

'Too many times, Sparks.'

'What kinds of ships were they?'

'Oh — all kinds.'

'Ever been shipwrecked or anything like that?' Pete had told me that Brad held a master's ticket.

'Near enough'. He deflected all questioning with a slow smile. All I could glean from him was that he had been raised by a grandfather in South Shields, and had gone to sea at sixteen on the colliers of William Corey and Sons. I sometimes wondered if his mixed parentage had attracted cruel jibes when he was growing up and if his genial reticence was part of a defensive cocoon within which he had placed himself.

After the late-night watch finished, I often stayed on in the radio room to listen to the radio broadcast bands and would go out to exchange a few words with Brad when he came on watch at midnight. I began to get a smell of whisky from his breath, though he was never even marginally tipsy. I knew he was in the habit of going to Ted's cabin for half-an-hour before he came up to the bridge. I assumed at the time that Ted and the cooks had a private supply of whisky to supplement the daily beer-ration. Not just in the evenings but at odd times of the day, there seemed to be an unusual amount of coming and going from the chief steward's cabin. Brad, Rat, Old Charlie and Little Alex had formed a sort of companionable clique whose meetings were held behind the closed door. By this time Mr Yardley, whose cabin was next to Ted's on the port alleyway, started to complain about the laughter and shouting that went on until the small hours.

'No wonder the grub-spoilers can do nothing right. You can't get on with your job if you're on the piss every night.'

On several occasions I had peered into the galley as the lunch or evening meal was in the course of preparation. The two cooks were to be seen floundering about, abusing one another in slurred voices, clanging pots and pans in demonstrations of bad-tempered truculence.

'That's one advantage of rough weather,' said Mr Yardley savagely. 'It acts as a camouflage. If one of the cooks falls flat on his face, or a pot of stew gets spilled all over the deck, you can blame the sea. But they don't fool me — I'm too long at this bloody game.'

These were the first signs that whisky drinking was being pursued with dedication by some on board. But neither Pete nor I, nor Mr Yardley nor Misery nor, perhaps, the captain had any inkling of the great bacchanalia that was enveloping the *Allenwell*.

The camouflage for those unsteady on their feet also deadened one's sense of awareness, brought on a great lassitude, and numbed one's interest in anything outside of the work one had to do. I copied down the weather forecasts wearily and with an increasing hatred of the North Atlantic. There was no let-up. One depression followed on the seething circle of its predecessor, while another formed, ready to roll, off the coast of Newfoundland. They were like the huge illuminated wheels that course endlessly across the massive neon signs over the nighttowns of Reno or Tokyo. The inevitability of it all was galling.

Gone were the times when I went out on the wing of the bridge to savour the power of nature. After clambering leadenly up to the radio room, I flopped into the chair and sat there, holding onto the desk, making tiresome entries in the log until the watch was over. As soon as I reached my cabin, I lay down and sank into a state of dispirited and comatose fatigue. It was a time when one was prompted to ask 'What am I doing here?'

5

'What Am I Doing Here?'

The notion of going to sea as a radio officer seemed like an ideal means of escape from the damp green land of Ireland in the early nineteen fifties. In those dismal days the country lay under a pall of economic depression. We school-leavers scrabbled about in a state of bewilderment, seeking the few jobs available, meeting to exchange scraps of information as we sat on creaking bicycles in the windswept square in Thurles.

The chances of getting any kind of job were poor. Tens of thousands of the country's most enterprising young packed suitcases, put on their best clothes and, with a meagre store of cash pinioned to inside pockets, set off for the ports. Many went to North America, to Australia and far-flung places about the globe. Others went to Britain, often ending up in industrial warrens that could not have been more different from the open countryside they had just left.

My elder brother Tom saw an advertisement for a radio school in Limerick: 'Sail the seven seas as a radio officer. Good pay and conditions. A Second Class Certificate in 18 months'. Off he went, staying in a frugal digs during the week, and cycling the 35 miles home at weekends. After I had spent many frustrating months trying to get a job on one of the local newspapers, the idea of going to sea became very appealing.

The Irish country boy's knowledge of seafaring in those days was hazy. It was gleaned from adventure stories in books borrowed from the town library and from Hollywood films. The sea meant palmy beaches and coral reefs, where tepid waters broke on white sand to the sound of Hawaiian guitar music. It was a place of crowded docksides where barefoot men in straw hats humped huge stalks of bananas up narrow gangplanks, apparently keeping time to the rhythm of the samba. It was a vision of watching equatorial sunsets, porpoises and flying fish from the bridge of some South Seas freighter. Dark, husky-voiced women, with hibiscus blossoms over one ear, sang sinuous songs in port side cantinas, casting loving looks toward the table where their clean-cut nautical heroes sat. There might be thundering adventures too, rapping out the SOS as the ship crunched onto the Great Barrier Reef on a remote coral island in the South Seas, while spear-wielding natives, noses decorated with finger bones, lurked behind the tropical foliage to await the survivors.

The first step on the road to adventure was leaving home in the quiet rural heartland and taking the train to the bustling capital city of Dublin, there to look for lodgings and to enrol in the radio school of Kevin Street College.

There seemed to be a foretaste of the sea-rover's unrestricted lifestyle in the contrast between the atmosphere in the massive red-bricked building that housed the College of Science and Technology and that which pervaded the chalk-smelling classrooms of the secondary school in Thurles. The Christian Brothers placed a strong emphasis on religious observance and dogma. The long days were punctuated by parroted prayers. To keep the minds of adolescent scholars on a spiritual plane, the corridors and classrooms were sombre with crucifixes, plaster statues of Italianate gaudiness and heavily framed pictures of religious significance. Vehement lectures on the evils of sexual licence, drunkenness and blasphemy were regularly delivered by the celibate ascetics of the order. Books, plays, films, painting and sculptures with the slightest real or imagined hint of lewdness were denounced, along with communism, socialism and what were referred to as 'pagan influences'. Smoking was strictly forbidden within the precincts of the school. Coarse language was regarded as a prelude to a life of lechery and brought down wrath on any student unlucky to be overheard using it.

The scene in Kevin Street was decidedly different. The corridors and wide stairways boomed with shouting and raillery. Spears of wit and banter, pointed by sharp nasal Dublin accents, were flung back and forth. Youths leaned against the radiators outside the classrooms, sucking minuscule cigarette butts held stoically between finger and thumb. There were rumbling stampedes as fellows raced towards the lecture theatres and instruction room at the very last minute, many exhaling the last lungful of cigarette smoke as they took their places.

Conversation amongst students in the radio classes was eloquently garnished with four-letter words.There was a feeling that facility in obscene language was a prerequisite for the nautical life we hoped to embrace, almost as important as the Morse code. The tall elderly Morse instructor, in his baggy pepper-and-salt suit, and the barrel-chested man who taught the practicalities of handling marine equipment were regarded with something akin to awe. Both these stalwarts had spent years at sea, and their language and attitude seemed to have an appealing marine flavour. Rumour had it that they had lived adventurous lives, been torpedoed or shipwrecked, swum through shark-infested waters and had recuperated from their ordeals in the loving care of scantily clad native girls, who had restored them to full health with yams, palm wine and physical caresses.

The Morse instructor was a picture of benign patience as he sat at the head of the class, his grey head adorned with the earphones that enabled him to listen to any one of the twenty Morse keys being hammered awkwardly by the students.

'Go easy, go easy, you fellows. You're all going hell for leather as if you were in the Grand National. Use your wrists — not your whole bloody arm. Like this.' He would hold up his big hand and wave it delicately, like a conductor taking the clarinet through an intricate passage.

He had an endearing air of world-weariness, a man who had been everywhere, done everything, lived life to the full during his long sea career and had achieved in the end a deep inner peace. Occasionally he would make a passing reference to the amount of money he had spent on drink and women. He did this with a wry humour, regretful but understanding of the excesses of his youth. This decent man evoked great affection and admiration amongst his students. We felt that we could arrive one day at this state of tranquillity and benevolence only if we too drank deeply from the cup of life, preferably in boisterous portside taverns and murky nightspots.

Even when he shouted at latecomers, 'You fuckers can't get out of your bunks in the morning,' this was taken as a kindly admonition and the scolded ones nodded and smiled.

The equipment instructor, a man in his early forties, had left the sea only six or seven years before. It seemed to us that he was having difficulty accommodating some of the bacchanalian habits he had acquired at sea with the curbs imposed by shore-side living and the administrative demands of the college. He went to great pains to project an image of stern dignity, striding along the corridors with out-thrust chest and an aloof frown on his face. The waves of thick black hair which slanted back from his wide forehead were carefully oiled and combed. What tended to spoil the impression of solidity were the little pieces of toilet paper that covered shaving cuts on his face and the aura of stale beer that surrounded his presence. Some of the smart fellows nodded and said approvingly, 'There's a man who likes his jar.'

One morning his bearing was even more grave than usual. The reason was clearly to be seen — an impressive black eye. A titter of amusement broke out amongst the top tiers of the lecture theatre. He rounded on the culprits.

'Some fellows up at the back there are breaking their arses laughing, but they won't be so cheerful the day of the examination.'

The smiles disappeared abruptly. A man who went about

with a black eye was deserving of respect.

On odd occasions the mask of dignity was cast aside. One afternoon the class was interrupted by one of the girls from the administrative office. She was blonde, bosomy and bottomy, her figure displayed in a light green dress of silken material. Pale pimply-faced students eyed her over the top of the tiered benches. Her plump, happy face was close to the instructor's as they examined some document that she was holding. He nodded in a serious concentrated manner; but when she was not looking, he cast theatrical glances of lecherous appraisal over her. When their discussion had ended, she walked towards the door. In a completely unexpected movement, our stern instructor tiptoed after her, an outstretched hand hovering within inches of her see-sawing buttocks, like the grab of an excavator. Just as suddenly he stopped short, quelled the grins of onlookers with a frown and continued the lesson as if nothing had happened. A far cry indeed from the ordered piety of the Christian Brothers!

The most immediate breath of the nautical life was provided by those ex-students who had been to sea with Second-Class Certificates and now returned to study for further qualifications. Though they were only slightly older than most of us, their sea sojourn placed them apart. They walked about confidently in polished patent leather shoes, treated the lecturers as equals, inviting them for a pint when the day had ended. They had wallets filled with notes. Their natty suits and blazers contrasted with the rumpled attire of the majority. Some had acquired a taste for aromatic Dutch tobacco or Burmese cheroots. They had also acquired regular drinking habits, along with a philosophic and worldly attitude towards the amount of money spent the night before. But any morning-after odours were lost in the pungent shaving lotions which they had taken to using.

These bronzed men of the world tended to club together. When they stood about exchanging stories, a crowd of raw students gathered round the periphery, listening intently to references to the Malabar Coast, the South China Sea and the Bight of Benin. What caused the circle of ears to bristle were the descriptions of the throbbing nightlife of places like Recife, Buenos Aires, Hong Kong and Saigon, sweltering bordellos and dives where naked female flesh gyrated on the dance floor to the sound of bongo drums, and tables glittered with bottles and glasses of incendiary spirits distilled from sugar cane, rice, dates and coconuts.

'Jaysus, I'm going to study and work like a whore from now on,' hungry students would say determinedly as the class bell rang.

Much of the more innocent romanticism was dispelled by the seafarers. There were tales of rough sailing, of ice-covered decks, of bodies decorated with insect bites and heat-rash, of explosive bouts of diarrhoea caused by exotic but contaminated dishes, of hours spent grappling with faulty equipment, of clashes with bullying captains, and of venereal disease. But even these events were related with a verve which lent them an adventurous sheen.

This sort of selective recollection was natural enough. The sea is a great university of the story-telling art, where the times of exhilaration and fear, delight and disaster are emphasised, made part of a narrative which diminishes the long days of tedium between the peaks. Nobody was likely to return to Kevin Street and announce, glumly, that sea-going was a sore trial, that he had been wretchedly sick for most of the voyage, been bored to tears on a trans-Pacific crossing and had no intention of ever setting foot on board a ship again.

The Marconi company, desperate for a continuous supply of radio officers at a boom time for shipping and when the burgeoning electronics industry was steadily attracting the sea-going staff, was not above painting a rosy picture of what lay in store for those who managed to acquire a certificate. The company had a close relationship with the College in Kevin Street, going back to the days when Marconi conducted his experiments in trans-Atlantic radio communication from the west coast of Ireland. All the equipment was supplied by the Marconi organisation; its personnel were always welcomed fulsomely. One day, not long before the examination, we had a visit from an eminent personage from the head office in Britain. He was a tall, dignified man whose mane of white hair emphasised his sun-browned face. He smiled benignly at us from a mouth full of large gleaming teeth.

'Now, chaps, as someone who has spent twenty-five years at sea, I can tell you that there is no better life. The Marconi company services ships that go to every corner of the world — Sydney, Vancouver, Bombay, Yokohama — everywhere. Drink is duty-free, of course. A tin of fifty cigarettes is just three shillings.' Here he performed an elaborate piece of mimicry, displaying fingers stained darkly with nicotine. Then this elder statesman raised an eyebrow roguishly and an expression of remembered delight suffused his face.

'You fellows will get a chance to meet women of every shape, size and colour — black and white, coffee and cream, yellow — anything you fancy.'

Nothing seemed further removed from such fantasies as being on a seedy trampship on grey dismal days in the North Atlantic when the gale howled ceaselessly outside and the ship clawed its way up the slopes of the huge dark waves and then plunged down the other side.

6

A Spirited Christmas

As the *Allenwell* gradually drew nearer to the North American continent, the turbulence of sea and wind began to subside. It was still heavy-going, but the straining and creaking of the woodwork ceased. Shrunken stomachs began to regard food with reviving interest. A bitterly cold wind, blowing steadily from the frozen land-mass to the west, swept away the low, tattered cloud cover. The weak wintry sun now peered down from behind immensely high plateaus of thin white cloud which seemed like ice-floes. At night the sky was full of coldly glittering stars. Rime glistened on the decks.

'This is the time to bring out the fur-lined French letters,' said Captain Thompson.

At night on the medium-wave broadcast bands the brash vigour of the American stations replaced the more sedate, disparate voices of Europe. Through the frosty night came the jingle of sleigh bells, the tinkle of tinsel and the ring of cash registers. Admixed with the endlessly revolving spectrum of the Nation's Top Fifty were new Christmassy songs, brassy and banal, composed and recorded with mercantile zeal the previous July while the sun baked the pavements outside the recording studios. As a gesture towards the spiritual dimension, almost suffocated beneath the weight of colourfully wrapped Yuletide bargains, the odd carol was played.

The commercial announcements were enunciated with such electric joy, in tones of frenzied preachers bringing the

Good News to the populace, that it was hard to detect any nuances of greed. The air vibrated with tantalising offers, magnanimous reductions, fantastic promotions.

'Hurry on down to the corner of Concord and sixty-fifth to get your life-size Christ doll at only five dollars ninety-five. They're going like hot cakes, folks. And — wait for it — absolutely free with each one — a special three dollar voucher for our gigantic after-Christmas sale.'

'Here's something for all you late, late shoppers. We stay open right through Christmas Day. Now how about that?'

An enthusiasm for pre-Christmas celebration began to manifest itself on the *Allenwell*. The sound of voices raised in song could be heard from the crew's quarters at night.

'The bosun hasn't put a foot on deck for the last two days,' complained Misery. 'Says he slipped on ice and hurt himself.'

'As good an excuse as any,' said Mr Yardley, who had had a run-in with Rat over two of the junior engineers indulging in a series of noisy post-midnight races up and down the port alleyway.

One night the quartermaster gripped the wheel as a means of support rather than steerage. He purred quietly to himself and, by the dim light of the compass, his lips could be seen pouting spasmodically, like a fish hauled from the ocean depths. In the chart room Pete murmured his suspicions.

'There's a smell of whisky all over this ship. Where it's coming from?'

At table Mr Yardley and Misery began to make veiled references to the possible source. They did so only when the captain was not present. Neither did they openly voice the opinion that the cargo had been broached. This was too serious a matter for casual speculation. It was a criminal offence. There was the possibility of one day finding themselves in court or at a police or company investigation, being asked when they first became aware of the barratry and what steps they had taken to counter it.

'It's the captain's responsibility; he knows what's going on,' said Mr Yardley. 'He should put his foot down. But he won't. He's turning a blind eye because all his boozing pals are in

61

on it, that's why.'

On the night before Christmas Eve there was an extraordinary scene on board which, amongst other things, seemed to reinforce Mr Yardley's strictures. When I came down after the late night watch, I was surprised to find the recreation room lit up. A darts game was in progress, but this was no ordinary game. The rough weather may have abated, but the deck still rose and fell, rocked and yawed. The dartboard itself swung like a battered pendulum.

Yet here was Captain Thompson, heavy legs set apart to counter the movement of the ship, big belly seeming to act as a kind of stabiliser, darts in hand. Grinning at the challenge, he waited until the board came level with his eye and then, at the precise split-second, flicked each dart theatrically. He achieved a very good score. His opponent, Little Alex, still wearing his filthy checkered pants, squinted at the moving target, his sharp nose following it like a gun sight. He was handicapped somewhat by being drunk. Spectators kept well away from the area of the board; the darts thunked into the wooden panelling anywhere up to six feet from it.

The real star of this unusual show was not the captain but an unobtrusive fellow who peered out at the world from behind a pair of big bottle-lensed spectacles which earned him the nickname 'Lambton Worm', derived from a children's ditty popular in Northumberland. This tousle-haired player was the third engineer, John Wright. He was uncannily accurate. He did not wait until the ship was momentarily level but flung the darts with amazing precision, whether the board was above head height or down at knee level. When he hit the treble twenty, as he did several times, a roar of approval went up.

Wright would have won hands down against any opponent. His task was made easier by the fact that he was drawn against Ted. The chief steward battled away sadly, sucking his teeth, wincing as he tried to focus bloodshot eyes. He rarely hit the board. Then, while facing up for another go, the ship rolled. Ted lost his footing and fell backward, hitting his brilliantined head against the corner of one of the

62

wooden coffee tables. He had to be lifted onto the settee and was declared disqualified from any further participation in the game.

There were two or three cases of beer lying about. The hiss of cans being opened lent a festive air to the occasion. In the foggy atmosphere, with the portholes tightly battened, a distinct smell of whisky was wafting about. Every now and then men excused themselves on the pretext of going for a pee. Little Alex, Old Charlie, Ted and Rat appeared to suffer from incontinent bladders. They returned with glistening lip and transitory sparkle of eye. Captain Thompson guzzled beer, yet his round fat figure absorbed it like a sponge; he was merry, but his sharp eyes missed little. It was hard to believe that he was unaware that whisky was being drunk copiously.

Just before I left, I happened to glance towards the door and saw the hunched figure of Mr Yardley. There was a look of anger and disapproval on his blotched face as he surveyed the scene; the waves of hair on his big head were ruffled combatively. I was sure he was going to burst in, but he disappeared. Next morning he had a flaming row with Rat. He was not at all pleased that engineers who were meant to take charge of the engine room at midnight or 4 am should be up drinking and playing darts into the night.

'What can you expect when the master is the boozer-in-chief? Leading by example, hah!' he said after breakfast when the captain had left.

There was another reason for Mr Yardley's dislike of the captain. The chief engineer was a self-educated man, a voracious reader with a wide span of interests. He was especially erudite on Greek and Roman culture, on economic and social history, particularly that of England. His mind was a bank of information about the development of construction and engineering, from prehistoric times up to the present. He had a remarkable memory which retained the vast store of knowledge which he had accumulated over the years. More than that, he had an exceptional capacity to arouse interest and curiosity in anyone who cared to listen to him. His dis-

sertations were peppered with satire and a caustic, perceptive wisdom. When he realised that in me he had an attentive
hearer, he began to discourse regularly in the saloon on his
favourite subjects. I shall always be grateful to that old
Yorkshireman for the way he helped broaden the scope of
my mind.

The problem was that it was difficult for Mr Yardley to
hold forth while the captain was present. Thompson had no
interest in the chief engineer's enthusiasms. His literary interests were largely confined to the lurid paperback novels that
I had bought for him in Liverpool; on several occasions I had
spied him curled up on his settee with one of these gripped
in his stout hand. Moreover, he liked to be the dominant
voice at table. He would become tetchy at Mr Yardley's lectures, like a star performer easily aroused to jealousy. His
strategy was to interrupt and to trivialise the scholarly and
erudite.

'Them ancient Greeks were arse-bandits, one and all.'

At lunch on Christmas Eve Mr Yardley started to give a fascinating account of the ingenuity and courage of the North
American railroad engineers. He described how they had
performed prodigious feats in laying tracks across deserts,
rivers, ravines and over and through the Rocky Mountains. In
the middle of this, the captain appeared and took his place at
the head of the table. He listened for a while, eyeing Mr
Yardley from beneath bushy eyebrows. Then he butted in:
'That reminds me of the story of the two blokes travelling on
one of those old-fashioned trains with no corridor. One
bloke is dying for a shit. "I don't know what I'll do" he says.
"Listen" says the other, "stick your arse out window". So he
sticks his arse out window. Train goes flying past a small station. Porter on the platform is watching it whiz by. Next
thing – wham! He gets a turd right in the eye.' Here Captain
Thompson cupped the fingers of his right hand and, with an
expressive gesture, wiped an imaginary turd from his eye
and flung it on the floor. 'Porter goes straight into station
master to complain. "Did you get a good look at the bugger?"
asks the station master, getting out the complaints book and

licking his pencil. "Yes," says the porter, "he had two fat cheeks, only one eye, a moustache and his tongue was hanging out."'

Thompson chortled with delight. Mr Yardley speared him with a look of utter distaste. When the captain had left, he said 'That man wants to bring every subject down to his own vulgar level.'

As it happened, the train story was one of the captain's favourites. He repeated it at table several times during the voyage, despite the fact that it evoked little amusement apart from his own. He was apt to regale gatherings afloat and ashore with it, no matter how unsuitable the occasion, often to hearers who did not appreciate or even understand its niceties.

During the first moments of Christmas Day occurred an indistinct yet telling incident. After the last watch on Christmas Eve, I remained on, listening to the outpouring of schmaltz, melody and patter from one of the powerful New York broadcast stations. It was well past midnight when I switched off the receiver. It occurred to me to wish Brad a happy Christmas and I went out to the wheelhouse.

'He's somewhere out on the wing,' said the quartermaster. It was freezing cold outside and so I stood before the window, letting my eyes adjust to the dark. Gradually the forepart of the ship took shape; it was not totally dark for there was a moon somewhere above a thin layer of frosty cloud. I happened to look down at the Number Two hatch and was surprised to see a cluster of dark figures gathered round one corner. They disappeared quickly. Then the door to the port wing opened and Brad came in. If he had proffered any explanation for the men's presence below, I would have accepted it without question.

'Everything OK, Brad?'

'Yeah. Any change in the weather forecast?'

'Pressure is rising.'

'Good. Well – three more days and we'll be in the Land of the Free.'

On my way down, I noticed the light off in the captain's

cabin. Its for'ard portholes looked down on the hatch. Just as well for those who may have been replenishing their supply of whisky, if that is what they were about. The captain could never have ignored a hatch being tampered with, no matter how tolerant he might be. I was never to know to what degree Brad was implicated in the pilferage. Such a dangerous subject could not be a topic of conversation. I might have learned more about it or even participated in it had I been a member of the drinking cell which met in Ted's cabin. But because of my father's alcoholism, which had darkened the years of youth and adolescence, I never drank liquor and shied away from the bibulous cliques which naturally formed on board every ship.

The stars still hung in the sky when I went up to the radio room at seven o'clock on Christmas morning. There were a few greetings telegrams to be taken from Portishead Radio, the British short wave station, including one for Captain Thompson from his wife. When I had dealt with these and contacted the New York marine station on medium wave to let them know we were now within earshot, I went out to the bridge. There was Misery, standing looking out at the sea like a famished barnacle goose.

'Happy Christmas, Mr Muir.'

'What's fuckin' happy about it?' he asked, the last three words rising into the high Geordie interrogative pitch.

You could not help wondering if his wife and daughters bore his absence from the Christmas table with some serenity; it was doubtful if he was capable of shedding his mantle of bile along with his overcoat when he entered his house. It was men from happy homes who were most assailed by loneliness and homesickness. I noted some remarks overheard that morning.

'My kids will be tearing open their presents just about now.'

'My missus will be putting on the turkey soon.'

'Never mind — I'll have my Christmas dinner when we get back. It's always cold and miserable this time of year in England anyway.'

66

There were those who were glad to be at sea. They were the estranged, the loners, the isolated. Christmas in their homeland served only to emphasise the lack of warm family ties. Yet the indifferent, along with the lonely and the cheerful, felt that the occasion called for some celebration. Tumblers clinked in gestures of camaraderie, draughts of good cheer helped anaesthetise feelings both of home longing and rootlessness. Christmas at sea was better endured with warm innards and flushed face. All ship owners and some masters were uneasy about Yuletide bonhomie while the ship was under way. The charts of the world's coastal regions are marked with those little lopsided triangles denoting shipwrecks; a suspiciously significant number of these occurred around Christmastime.

No cautionary mood prevailed on the *Allenwell*. The sound of singing and laughter could be heard in the alleyways of the crew's quarters from midday onwards. In the galley Little Alex and Old Charlie staggered about, shouting and yelling at one another. An ominous smell of burning suffused the foyer and drifted up the stairwell to the radio room. Just as we assembled at one o'clock for the Christmas meal, the scuffling of feet, grunts and thumpings came from the galley. It was concluded by the sound of a pot being banged on the range-top, like an enormous tuning-fork.

'Peace on earth to men of goodwill,' intoned Mr Yardley.

'If I don't get something to eat soon, I'll go in there and give the two of them a boot up the arse apiece,' Captain Thompson growled.

'Unfortunately they're too drunk to do any real harm to one another,' Mr Yardley said, eyeing the captain; he was not impressed by Thompson's facile threat to his erstwhile drinking companions.

'We really ought to preface the meal with a prayer or at least a carol,' suggested the agnostic Mr Yardley. 'Sparks here is the possessor of one of those Irish tenor voices feared and dreaded the world over.'

'There's been plenty of singing below already,' said Misery peevishly. 'I wanted to get the bosun to sweep down the decks, but he was flaked out on the floor of his cabin.'

'Shame on you to speak of our bosun in that manner,' chided Mr Yardley. 'Being pissed before noon is an essential part of the traditional British Christmas.'

'Got a telegram from the wife,' beamed the Old Man, tapping the envelope in the breast pocket of his jacket. 'She and the mother-in-law will be pissed as newts before this day is out.'

'They won't be the only ones,' added Mr Yardley.

The meal began with a deceptive flourish. Toni, who favoured the festival by donning a bright green jacket and plum-coloured trousers, glided in with plates of pea soup. Whatever the circumstances under which it was concocted, it proved to be very tasty. Even Misery declared his satisfaction. Then Toni came in balancing plates of turkey and ham like a juggler, proud of his professional deftness. Unfortunately the fare that he ferried in was unequal to the grace with which it was delivered. The portions were hidden beneath a cow-pat of thick greasy gravy. When this substance was scraped away, it was found that the turkey had been only superficially singed. The ham, on the other hand, had apparently been parboiled to the point of squelchy disintegration. Mr Yardley, Misery and I picked dolefully at our plates, nibbling at wet strands of ham and a few slivers of turkey. Thompson, of course, wolfed his portion with great relish, grease and all, and asked for a second helping.

Misery picked up the menu, squinting at Ted's alcoholic scrawl. 'At least there's plum pudding and Christmas cake to survive on,' he said glumly.

He had hardly spoken when there was a yell of alarm from the galley. Toni came rushing in, head and shoulders arched back, arms extended full length, bearing a huge ball of blue flame on a platter. He deposited it in the centre of the table and then blew on his fingertips.

'Christ, he's drowned the bloody thing in spirits.' Mr Yardley pushed back his chair and peered from a safe distance at the black object at the centre of the conflagration that was our Christmas pudding. There was at least an inch of burning spirits swashing about on the platter, most probably some of the bountiful Vat 69 from the Number Two hold. Toni tried to put out the blaze engulfing the pudding by waving a napkin at it. This served only to fan the flames.

Then Captain Thompson took charge. He jumped up, seized the water-jug and poured its contents over the fire. With a sizzling sound the blue flames flickered and then went out. The sodden, smoking pudding looked like a cannonball come to rest after its explosive trajectory. A cloud of blue alcohol vapour rose over the table. Some of it entered the diseased lungs of Mr Yardley and set off a sickening bout of gurgling, heaving, scraping and coughing.

'Take the bugger away, steward,' ordered the captain. A few seconds later came a heavy thunk from the big metal wastebin in the galley.

I hesitate about recording the last episode of our Christmas dinner, simply because it seems like something out of a clichéd, jaded farce.

'Maybe we'll get a bit of Christmas cake, at least,' said Misery forlornly.

'If it's not dropped on the deck,' gasped Mr Yardley, eyes steaming, chest heaving, beads of perspiration on his forehead.

As if on cue, Toni appeared holding a cake, decoratively iced, with a frilly paper band about it. Just as he stepped over the coaming, the ship gave a slight lurch. For once Toni's balletic feet failed him. He pitched forward and fell full length on his face. The cake hit the deck and disintegrated, scattering pieces all over the floor. We sat there, nonplussed. Toni, recovering his composure quickly, gathered some of the larger fragments in a napkin and with a little gesture of apology, laid it on the table. None of the others felt like sampling any, but I was ravenous. I ate as much as I could and bundled the remainder in a napkin to take away.

'That's it,' said the Old Man, rising from the table with an amused grin. 'There's nowt more.'

'We thank Thee Lord for Thy bounteous gifts, of which we

have partaken this day,' murmured Mr Yardley savagely as we filed out.

I ate more of the cake in my cabin and finished the remaining morsels during the evening watch.

In the final few minutes of the last watch a familiar call came from a Swedish ship. 'Man overboard in position . . . all ships keep a look out.' The ship was two hundred miles away, following a different course to our own, so the matter did not concern us. I record this to make the observation that I never spent a Christmas at sea without hearing such a tragic call from a Scandinavian vessel. Many of their ships are dry except for special festivals. Then, it seems, some of the crew make up for enforced abstinence in a determined way. Inevitably some gloomy Nordic soul goes berserk and decides to mark the occasion by flinging himself over the side.

I signed off, spun the gyro of the auto-alarm, watched the little red light come into being, and then went out to the bridge for a word with Pete. He was by the window, a lumpy outline in his anorak, gazing into the distance.

The ship was rolling gently in a very moderate sea. There were silvery cloud-plains high in the sky. I imagined that a very faint glow was discernible on the horizon ahead.

'Your eyes don't deceive you, my lad,' said Pete. 'That's the reflection of the lights of New York on the clouds overhead.'

'But we're miles from New York.'

'Over three hundred – a-day-and-a-half sailing. But that's it alright.'

It was my first sight, if such it can be called, of the United States. That distant glow seemed an indication of the energy and vibrancy of that great city and country that we were shortly to grace with our presence.

7

New York Landfall

Flurries of snow moved across the black waves as the radar picked up the shoreline of Long Island and painted it as a kinked orange stripe on the edge of the 40-mile range.

'That fucking dot there is the Ambrose Light vessel,' said Captain Thompson with a grunt of satisfaction. His thick fingers hovered over the controls while I stood by in case he should wipe the picture away. A feeling of quiet celebration pervaded the bridge. We had made an accurate landfall at the end of a difficult voyage. Even Misery allowed himself a faint smile as he scanned the dim horizon through his binoculars.

Presently a grey smudge of land began to stretch out to starboard and we closed obliquely with it. Somewhere off the Ambrose, if memory serves me right, a big pilot boat nosed through the waves and drew alongside. The pilot was muffled and mackinawed against the biting cold as he stomped up to the bridge. Over the rim of his upturned collar a pair of wrinkled eyes surveyed the *Allenwell*. The ship had been tatty enough when we left Liverpool; now she was sea-scarred, salt-streaked, with patches of rust breaking out over her decks and superstructure. When tea and biscuits were brought up by Toni, the pilot politely declined. His American sense of hygiene may have recoiled at the prospect of picking up some nautical infection from the chipped mug.

As we passed by the impressive Statue of Liberty, holding aloft her torch towards the snow clouds, a rival spectacle presented itself on the *Allenwell*. Our crew stumbled about, clearing the decks, unfastening the hatch-covers, unlimbering the derricks, like leaden-footed troops at the end of a long and arduous campaign.

'There's a collective hangover if ever I saw one,' said Pete.

The commander of the deck force was the most pitiful sight of all. Our shaven-headed bosun was barely able to move, gripping the railings to hold himself upright. He croaked out orders unintelligibly. He tried to raise one arm authoritatively and then, overcome by the effort that this entailed, let it fall to his side. None of the men took the slightest heed of him.

The bedraggled state of the ship would have been less noticeable if we had been discreetly nudged into an unpretentious berth in one of the more dilapidated areas of the New York dockland. But the pilot headed the ship towards Manhattan, the looming skyscrapers increased in size and height, and we found ourselves going into the city's most famous and distinguished berthage, the Cunard piers. In no docks anywhere in the world had more newspaper photographers' flashbulbs popped, more newsreel cameras whirred, more impromptu press conferences been held on deck or on the quayside. Statesmen, filmstars, gangsters, opera singers, politicians, literary giants, ham-fisted pugilists, the famous and infamous had posed and postured before camera and battery of network microphones during the halcyon era of trans-Atlantic sea travel. The heyday was now drawing to a close and the majestic length of the *Queen Elizabeth* would not often be seen here again. But two of Cunard's medium-sized liners were there, deck upon deck of polished windows and portholes, immaculate monarchs dominated by the famous blood-red, black-topped funnels. The tugboats pushed us gently towards the quayside immediately in front of one of these. Its flared bow towered over us. We looked like a vagabond who had been inexplicably admitted into an exclusive club-room. Several officers in smart uniforms, accompanied by ladies, gathered on the bridge deck of the Cunarder to gaze down at us. Captain Thompson spotted them. This may well have prompted a notion to pay a call on our lofty neighbour; it was to prove a disastrous visitation, especially for the captain of the liner.

We tied up alongside. The telegraph rang 'finished with engines'. The gangway was lowered. We were now part of the New York dock scene. Alien footsteps resounded on stairways as customs and immigration officials, people from the Cunard agency, and longshoremen invaded the ship. Sharp adenoidal accents echoed strangely in foyer and alleyway. Every ship loses something of its character when it reaches port. The berthed vessel, secured by ropes, temporarily relinquishes its essential sea-challenging role. It is like an operatic baritone heard snoring in an hotel bedroom. Yet, for a few hours, the deep tremor of the engines still murmured somewhere in the inner ear; the automatic balancing reactions, so sharply activated during the North Atlantic crossing, still prompted the legs to adopt a wide gait, the arms to brace against bulkheads.

The customs and immigration men did not linger on board. They completed the formalities quickly and filed off the ship, reluctantly touching the grimy railings. I overheard one of them remark, 'This is a no-account tub.' They might have come upon a sizable haul of secreted whisky if they had bothered to search the vessel.

Proof of our self-sufficiency in spirits might have been deduced from the fact that hardly a soul put foot ashore that first night or indeed the second night. Admittedly the shore-side setting did not present an inviting prospect. Freezing winds howled down the immense concrete canyons, scattering the post-Christmas refuse over the mounds of dirty frozen snow on the pavements. Just the same, at least some of the men from a spirit-bereft ship would have bundled themselves up and hurried the few hundred yards to the cosy bars about the foot of Fifth Avenue. As it was, many on board were nursing hangovers, while others were stoking the embers of the afterglow. After our weary voyage, everyone, drinkers and sober-sided alike, wanted nothing more than a sound night's sleep in a steady bunk.

Most of the crew saw little or nothing of New York during

our 48-hour sojourn there. My memory of my first visit to the great metropolis is of trudging up Broadway, teeth chattering, huddled in inadequate clothing while the temperature fell to well below freezing. Water-filled eyes gave a psychedelic effect to the kaleidoscope of flashing, spiralling neon signs. Outside a theatre I heard people speaking Yiddish. On the way back, I came across two men, fur-hatted and heavily muffled, having a histrionic argument beside a steaming barrow of roasted chestnuts. 'OK, OK — so I'm a dumb Hungarian,' shouted one. What ethnic or social significance this remark may have held, I do not know.

New York in midwinter is no place for the stranger who is inclined to explore on foot, is reluctant to stand shivering at bus stops and is unwilling to spend any of his frugal funds on a taxi.

Misery went ashore briefly the next afternoon to post a letter to his wife. He felt that being English ought to evoke a respectful response from the inhabitants. 'Well, what do you know! All the way from the Old Country. That's nice, real nice.' When he returned, beak blue with the cold, he was in bad humour. The hurrying, manic populace of the polyglot city, spiky with abrasive wit, had apparently displayed little deference towards this visitor.

'Fucking Jews and Germans, Irish and Spaniards, niggers and wops of all sorts – all chewing gum,' he said, moving his long bony jaws up and down demonstratively.

Toni had a more warming experience of the city. He had gone ashore on our first night, hair coiffed, eyes shadowed, sporting gleaming ear-rings. Next morning he was somewhat less presentable as he tidied my cabin; his hair was frizzily askew, his sallow face bereft of all make-up. But he was in a reflective, happy mood.

'This is a great city, Sparks. Full of blacks, it is. I met one last night. A real muscle-man he were.'

He was probably the only person on board who engaged in any amorous activity. We had not been long enough at sea for any real flesh hunger to develop. Seasickness and weather weariness are effective dampers of desire.

'If I'm going to chase pussy, I'll wait until we get to New Orleans,' declared Pete, who was already adopting the American idiom.

The prospect of three weeks under balmy skies, by the banks of the Mississippi, was another very good reason for the disinterest our men displayed towards New York.

Our brief stay was not entirely without incident, however. On the evening of the second day Pete came bursting into my cabin, grinning from ear to ear. He had just come back from the big Cunard liner astern of us. Earlier in the day he had struck up an acquaintance with one of her several third mates when they were both out on the quay inspecting the ropes. Pete had been invited on board and had spent the evening there. Now he stretched himself on my settee and shook with laughter.

'You must have had a great time. Was there a party?'

'Oh there was a party alright. I wasn't at it, but you'll never guess who was? The Old Man!'

At lunchtime that day Thompson had remarked, 'I think I'll go over and see the captain of that Cunard bugger astern.' He was tickled, in a mischievous way, by the notion that our charter conferred on him some kind of kinship with our majestic neighbour, though his robust Geordie self-esteem would not allow him to feel in any way deferential.

'I know what's on his mind,' Mr Yardley had said, 'He's after as much free beer as he can guzzle and a bit of tail if he can get it. It doesn't matter if it's the Cunard chairman's wife or one of the lassies working in the laundry.'

Pete was now able to give a second-hand version of what had transpired. A story like this is inclined to gather colour and adornment with each retelling, but it was pretty much in keeping with our captain's style and character.

Thompson, in his best suit, had made his way along the quay in the early evening. He had presented himself to the quartermaster at the top of the gangway and had asked to see the captain. At that moment this distinguished mariner, resplendent in immaculate gold-braided uniform, was entertaining a large party of patrician New Yorkers in one of the tastefully decorated reception rooms. With admirable courtesy — which he was later to rue — he directed that this unexpected guest be conducted to the gathering. When he met Captain Thompson, he expressed regret that he would not be able to entertain him personally, but invited him to join the party and enjoy himself. In no time at all our captain was in the thick of things, quaffing much beer, wine and spirits, circulating easily among the evening-gowned ladies and their escorts.

At first, apparently, he was something of a success. His rotund jollity and roguish sallies, directed at the ladies, enlivened the occasion. Then he began to tell stories and anecdotes, ribald and Rabelaisian. Fortunately many of these were only barely understood by those in his company, for his accent got broader and his words became slurred. Pete said that the third mate had told him that any laughter began to change to uneasy chuckles, especially after our captain had made the eye-wiping gesture and delivered the punch line of his railway story.

It may well have been that the elegance and mannerisms of some of the guests aroused in Thompson his innate irreverence for the conventional. Soon he was seen going about slapping men on their shoulders and women on their bottoms. When he began to pop cocktail cherries down the cleavages of the ladies, the atmosphere about him turned very strained and frosty. Then he collided with a steward bearing a tray of drinks; the glasses toppled to the floor, spattering the clothes of those nearby.

Eventually the captain of the Cunarder came over and asked Thompson to be a little less boisterous. 'Fuck off, you bollocks' was our captain's reply, heard by many people in the room. Following this, the Cunard captain detailed one of his senior officers — the one who afterwards related the whole affair to Pete and others — to try to curb Thompson's gaiety. When this wily officer heard the Old Man ask, 'Where's the shithouse round here?' he immediately came forward and conducted him down corridors and stairways until they were at the head of the gangway. Thompson was given no option but to leave the vessel. He did not accept his expulsion with good grace. He shouted insults and innuendoes as he made his way down the gangway. When he reached the dockside, he revenged himself by relieving his swollen bladder against the side of the Cunarder.

Pete said that Captain Thompson's departure had caused a buzz of relief in that glittering soiree. The guests went about exchanging stories of their encounter with him. Some tried to retell a couple of his anecdotes. One man, somewhat the worse for drink, was seen to make the eye-wiping gesture associated with the captain's favourite story.

That was the only notable escapade during our New York stopover. It may have been a relief to some that the Number Two hold was not uncovered, although, as it transpired, the raiders had been so boldly efficient in the operation that there were no obvious signs of depredation that might arouse suspicion.

8

Towards the Land of Heart's Desire

New York had given us two days of rest and repose, a brief period of recuperation before we headed out once more into a heaving ocean. It was blowing hard, and scattered snowfalls were turning the crowded skyscrapers into a grey craggy mountainscape as the tugboats pulled us away from the haven of the Cunard pier. When we came abeam of the Cunarder, several faces appeared at the big windows of one of the upper decks to watch us, like snobbish neighbours gratefully watching the departure of people who had lowered the tone of the vicinity. Captain Thompson scowled in their direction.

'You'd think they never had to wipe their arses' was his comment.

As soon as we dropped the pilot and ploughed into the moderately rough sea, the *Allenwell* started to yaw and shift. After we had made a slow turn to the south, the wind was on our starboard beam and we began to roll uncomfortably. Wind-swept snow made little piles in corners of the decks. 'It'll be three days before we get out of this,' said Brad when I handed him the forecast; strong winds and low temperatures were predicted. As second mate, he had an assigned role in assessing weather, currents and tides.

Captain Thompson came in to watch him lay off our course. It would take us well out from the coastline until we came abreast of Cape Hatteras, where North Carolina reaches out into the sea. From there we would be out of the sight of land until we neared the tip of the Florida peninsula.

'Keep the bugger well out from Hatteras,' instructed the captain in his corncrake voice, bending over the chart and tapping the cape on the angle of an island which reached out into the ocean like a bony finger. This was a preamble to an inconsequential little scene which took place two nights later. Every mariner would be cautious about such a protuberant headland and the currents which surged about it. But Captain Thompson, uncharacteristically, seemed to regard it with a mixture of distaste and awe. He was not a man to hide the disasters of his life; indeed he took great pleasure in relating them. So, when he asked me to stand by the radar as we approached Hatteras in pitch darkness, I was all ears for the story he might tell. But he had nothing at all to say and for the only time in the voyage seemed tetchy about a navigational matter. He kept going out to the wing of the bridge, searching the darkness through his binoculars for the flash of the lighthouse and coming back into the wheelhouse.

'Any sign of it yet, Sparks? Don't let the third mate fuck about with that radar.'

We picked it up on the 40-mile range. Then the Old Man saw the first faint momentary twinkle of the light. He kept checking our position on the chart. Brad came on duty as we came abeam of the light and seemed to catch something of the captain's unease. The four of us stood on the wing staring into the blackness, waiting for each tiny pinpoint from twenty miles distant, until it became no more than the faintest glimmer on our starboard beam. We were like men on the trail, tiptoeing apprehensively past some dark cave of evil reputation.

'It would be just our luck to bash into some other ship while we were all concentrated on Cape Hatteras,' said Pete, cheerfully breaking the mood as we made our way down to our cabins.

We were not to see the United States for another three days. It gave one some idea of the size and length of that enormous country. Out of sight we may have been, but not out of hearing. The medium wave throbbed with the clamour of dozens of broadcast stations. They were like stall-owners in a crowded bazaar, shouting their wares at the tops of their voices, vying with one another for attention. They were caught up in a frenzy of post-Christmas sales, extolling rock-bottom bargains, giveaway prices, two for the price of one. In between the outpouring of temptation and blandishment, the top hits were played and played.

Sometimes the same voices, so lightly voluble pouring out cascades of commercials, suddenly turned dramatically solemn to deliver the news headlines. As we made our way southwards, the accents changed. The sharp, abrupt tones of Yankeedom began to give way to softer, slower voices as we came abreast of the old Confederate states. Further down came the sort of drawls that I thought existed only in Hollywood movies, spoken by lean men in dungarees liplulating at toothpicks or fat men in seersucker suits who were surrounded by halos of cigar smoke.

However, the change in the weather was the most memorable experience of our voyage southwards. We had grey and unpleasantly choppy seas all the way down until we reached the area between the island of Bermuda and the northerly region of Florida. Then one afternoon the waves began to subside, losing their rough bustle; for the first time since leaving Liverpool, the *Allenwell* chugged ahead evenly. A light balmy breeze replaced the flapping wind. The most rapturous event was the way the sky changed. For most of our voyage, it had been covered by endless masses of sodden cloud rolling overhead, monotonous and dour. Now it suddenly began to lighten, and the covering became suffused with strong yellow sunlight. Then, way ahead, like an oasis in the desert, we saw a patch of blue sky. The sea below it sparkled. Within an hour the cloud had dissolved into delightful little cotton balls floating tranquilly beneath the vast blue heavens.

The sun, warm and benign, beamed down on the sea-scoured *Allenwell*. It began to dry out the wooden decktimbers, to glisten on the railings, gently heating the rust-riddled iron deckplates around the holds, turning the canvas hatch-covers a light dry grey. A smell of iron, of warmed wood, of salt and oil began to waft about the ship.

This transformation evoked a remarkable change of spirits on board. Men smiled easily, walked about with a relaxed step, cleared foggy throats to hum, puckered lips to whistle awkwardly. Portholes, which had been tightly clamped for weeks, were energetically prised open. A warm draught ran through the ship, sweeping aft sour cooking smells, the musty odour of damp clothing, stale whisky fumes. If this miasma of rank smells could have manifested itself visually, it would have been seen as a sickly green streamer streeling in the air over our wake.

Pete and I stood on the wing in our shirtsleeves, faces upturned towards the sun. Its rays caressed skin that had long been creased protectively against gale, sleet and rain, soothing that place just below the eyes where weather-weariness gathers in folds.

All the off-duty men appeared on deck in singlets and trousers, lolling about the hatches, stretching and yawning in the sunlight. Most were pallid of face, bleary of eye, blinking, patting their bare arms as if to assure themselves that the sun was actually shining on them. They were like cave-dwellers who had emerged from the darkest recesses of the earth into the bright air. Ben the bosun was there, wan and shaky. Any impression of burly vigour had vanished by now. He sat alone on the corner of Number Two hatch, grey jaws chewing ruminatively. From the bridge Misery stared down at him, nodding his head with small movements, indulging in a bilious satisfaction that his predictions were being borne out.

The life-giving effect of the weather-change was best seen when Ted came out of his cabin and edged hesitantly into the sunlight. He stood immobile, as if stunned by the purity of the blue sky and the golden glitter of the sea to the west. He moved his head slowly, like a ponderous dim-witted turtle surveying the world about from leaden-lidded eyes.

'It's risky for a man to go out in the fresh air like that after he's existed for so long in an atmosphere of whisky fumes,' commented Mr Yardley, when he heard of this event. 'The shock could have a very bad effect on the metabolism.'

At last the low coastline of Florida came into distant view on the starboard beam as we took up a course parallel to the curving line of sandy islets on the tip of the peninsula called the Keys. This was an adventurous seascape, full of the images of gold-laden Spanish galleons and the French and English privateers who preyed on them; these waters had a continuing tradition of gun-running, bootlegging, drug-smuggling and boatloads of political opportunists or refugees. Here it was that men sat in harness in the sterns of fishing boats, battling with giant spine-nosed marlin which flung themselves out of the water in frantic attempts to break the line.

A shining white causeway linked the necklace of the Keys. One could catch the glint of sunlight on motor cars moving along it. Here and there stood clusters of tall hotels and apartment buildings, gleaming like salt pillars.

'Them big hotels are full of rich divorcees,' pronounced Captain Thompson, binoculars to eyes. 'Dead ringers for a screw.'

Minds and imaginations were beginning to dwell on the soft flesh of women — white, brown, black — whom we hoped would be encountered when we reached New Orleans. At table the Old Man said jocularly, 'Sparks will be off ashore after black ham as soon as the gangway goes down.'

'Black women are an acquired taste,' said Mr Yardley pointedly. The Old Man grinned but did not rise to the bait. He was reticent about his amorous activities. Mr Yardley maintained that this was because he had to pay for his pleasure. For love or money, I found it difficult to imagine our corpulent master locked in sexual embrace.

'Yes, it's a bit like an elderly Friar Tuck astride Maid Marion,' said Mr Yardley when we were discussing it later in private.

As the *Allenwell* traversed the northern perimeter of the Caribbean, the sound of Spanish came through on the medium wave. On the afternoon watch the voice of Fidel Castro, high-pitched and hoarse, delivered a political harangue on Havana radio. He rolled his 'r's with gusto; twangy syllables sprang back and forth; words were spat out like olive stones. Two hours later, when I came on watch again, he was still speaking, his tone more ragged and strident.

When darkness fell, the diverse clamour of the sound-world came into being. Moving the quivering black marker across the yellow window of the receiver was like taking a night stroll down a multilingual street full of chatter and music. Snatches of melody are heard from the doorways of cantinas and bistros; the strumming of guitars, the jingle of steel bands, the clack of castanets, the accordion writhing a sinuous tango, rhythmic palms beating on hand-drums. Sharp Hispanic voices cried out their songs, purring negroid tones lent a peculiar attractiveness to ordinary melodies. From Martinique came the nostalgic lyric tenor of Tino Rossi, sliding gracefully from one note to the next.

The Gulf of Mexico was as calm as a millpond on a summer's day as we headed north-west towards the mouth of the Mississippi. A warm sun shone down from dawn to dusk out of a cloudless sky. The throb of the engines could be heard clearly on this placid azure plain. Our bow waves swept outwards, creaming cleanly into long curves on either side of our straight and bubbling wake. This idyllic sailing further raised the spirits on board.

'You can only really appreciate it after you've busted your guts in the North Atlantic,' said Pete. 'Well — New Orleans here we come.'

An air of expectancy, of joyousness, pervaded the ship. Men who had been in New Orleans put the word about that many of the riverside berths were beside the French Quarter. 'We might be lucky. When I was there last time, you could spit over the side and hit a strip-tease joint or some lassie swinging her tits down the nearest street.'

Only with hindsight can I surmise that a very substantial amount of whisky was removed from the Number Two hold about this time. It was to be used to fuel a long fiesta, both as an item of sustenance and as a valuable unit of barter.

With the ship holding a steady, even keel, the character of the nightly darts games became less bizarre. Instead, they were now invested with a jocose sexuality.

'Way off target again, cooky,' shouted someone at Little Alex. 'Fat chance you'll have in New Orleans if that's the way you go about it.'

'Don't worry – I'm getting my eye in.'

'It's not your eye I'm talking about.'

When Rat planted a dart dead centre, people roared 'Bull's-eye!' and made a ramming upward-thrust motion with their forearms.

It occurred to me later that there might well be some relationship between the way a man played darts and how he pursued women. Little Alex always had a tensely anxious bearing as he flung the darts waywardly. John Wright, alias the Lambton Worm, faced the board with a relaxed smile. He had an engaging meekness about him and threw the darts gently, without any apparent effort.

'There's a man knows how it's done,' said the shrewd ones when he hit the treble twenty with two darts. The Worm just shook his head modestly. Darts players and others were going to enlist for the mating game just as soon as the ship reached New Orleans.

9

Up the Mississippi

A thin yellow mist, suffused by sunlight, hung over the
water as the *Allenwell* neared the mouth of the great
Mississippi. Captain Thompson rang 'half ahead' on the telegraph. He asked me to stand by the radar. Dotted about,
straddling the water like huge antediluvian spiders, were oil-
rigs sucking up the dark liquid from the shallow seabed.

'We don't want to run into one of them buggers or there'll
be no black ham for anyone in New Orleans,' the master said
as he peered into the viewer.

Captain Thompson did not need the radar to tell him that
we were closing with land, or the echo sounder to warn him
that the depth of water underneath the keel was decreasing.
He had an old sailor's well-developed instincts. He went out
to the wing of the bridge, thrust his hairy-nostrilled nose
upward and drew in a long breath. 'I can smell the land all
right – all them fucking swamps and bayous.' Through his
feet, planted squarely on the deck, he could sense the faint
bumpiness made by the shallowing seabed, feel the echoes
of the propeller over solid ground.

Pete called me out to the wing. 'Hey – look at that water,
will you?' The sea had turned from clean blue to muzzy
green. Here and there were bubbling brown patches. 'And
we're still thirty miles away from the delta. Some river, huh?'

The chart showed the great river debouching into the Gulf
of Mexico from the centre of a protruding stalk of land,
formed over millennia by the silt carried down on the current. On the small-scale chart, the Mississippi and its many
tributaries looked like an enormous winter-bare tree lying on

almost one-third of the huge land mass. Any images I had of this immense waterway had been largely derived from Hollywood productions: intrepid trappers and explorers paddling across its reaches; multi-decked paddle-steamers, like oblong wedding cakes, hooting whistles as they came alongside wooden wharves where bales of cotton had been piled by sweating black slaves; at the green baize table in the ornate saloon on the upper deck, Southern gentlemen played for stakes that often included the family homestead, life savings and property which they did not own at all; out on deck, belles in crinolines twirled sun-umbrellas as they awaited the outcome of the poker game. The pilots always had drooping moustaches, like Mark Twain; the captains were given to chewing tobacco and had brought spitting to a fine art. The music of the Mississippi was composed by Stephen Foster, and played on the banjo, with a black chorus led by Paul Robeson.

'Sparks, call up the pilot station and tell the bugger we're here,' ordered the captain.

When I returned to the bridge, the haze had almost disappeared. One could clearly see the powerful current moving against us, carrying twigs and branches and the occasional sodden tree trunk rolling slowly. Then in the near distance appeared the white finger of the lighthouse on the tip of the South Pass. Away across from it was the tall beacon marking the extremity of the opposite bank. 'This is it,' said Pete, pumping an imaginary trombone to denote that we were on the threshold of Dixieland.

Shortly afterwards a smart pilot cutter came surging towards us, made a graceful curve and slipped alongside, keeping pace with us. The pilot, a lanky man, leapt nimbly onto the rope ladder that the bosun had heaved over the side at the last minute. Unfortunately the top two wooden laths had caught unnoticed on the edge of the scuppers. These jerked free under the pilot's weight and his agile legs splashed into the water up to his knees. 'What the hell!' he yelled furiously as he clung on. He climbed up cautiously. His long-jawed face was purple with anger when he reached the bridge, his squelching shoes leaving wet footprints on the deck. His mood did not improve when he saw Captain Thompson's ruddy face creased with amusement.

'Goddamit! I could have fallen into the drink, captain.'

'Have a beer, pilot. That's the only drink worth bothering about.'

'No thanks. I never drink on the river,' the pilot said curtly. From his holdall he extracted a radio which he placed on the little shelf beside the window. He thrust several sticks of chewing gum into his mouth and began to ruminate dourly. Here was a man who wished for nothing more than to be left alone. Captain Thompson, ever eager for badinage, was put out by this and went below. When he reappeared, he was clutching a beer can.

As we moved through the wide river mouth, the banks, which from afar seemed so fragile, now acquired a more solid appearance. These levees had been heaped with enormous effort and persistence. My Uncle Jim had worked on them briefly in the nineteen thirties during an adventurous period of his life. 'Man, it was backbreaking work for a few dollars a day, down in a deep ditch throwing up shovelfuls of mud onto the bank above,' he told me years later.

Pete and I moved from side to side on the bridge, looking out over the narrowing banks to the land beyond. We could see clumps of trees, lush vegetation, the glimmer of sunlight on patches of swampy water almost hidden by dense sedge grass. This was bayou country — a maze of coastal marshes and shallow lagoons where trees were draped with Spanish moss, mists and fetid vapours drifted about, alligators and spiny crayfish crawled, owls hooted and herons flapped. It was the haunt of French-speaking fishermen and wildfowlers. As we went further upriver, we caught glimpses of white-painted wooden houses sunk in the strange landscape.

In the radio room I tuned in to the local stations, listening to the languid Louisiana accents extolling the virtues of hot-dog restaurants, bed sheets, barbecues and second-hand automobiles, 'almost new'. The top-selling records of the day were interspersed with an outpouring of country and ·vestern music. One station had an unfamiliar melange of folk music, played on fiddle and accordion. When the announcer spoke, it was in slow Louisiana French, devoid of the nasal and lip-pursing emphasis of the smattering of French that I had picked up in the Indian Ocean listening to broadcasts from Réunion and Madagascar.

The sour feeling between Captain Thompson and the pilot did not subside. As the Old Man drank one can of beer after another, he became merrily boisterous and sought to impose himself on the pilot, making facetious remarks.

'Pilot, what's the price of a short time in New Orleans?'

'I guess that depends on the quality of the merchandise,' the pilot replied indifferently, keeping his eyes on the river, on the market buoys and on the occasional ship which passed on its way towards the Gulf.

'How much for a black woman, pilot?'

'Now that's something I wouldn't know anything about, captain.'

When Thompson tried to talk about his amorous adventures in New Orleans before World War II, the pilot responded by turning up the volume of his radio, from which a ball-game was being broadcast. The exclamatory commentary of the sportscaster, the roar of the crowd, like a huge flock of starlings taking off, filled the wheelhouse. Thompson retaliated by singing music hall songs in his harsh echo-chamber baritone. He had a considerable repertoire; like most Geordies of his generation, he had a fond nostalgic love for the great performers. Nowhere had the music hall a more devoted following than in the Tyne-Tees area of England, and many of its stars had come from there.

The pilot had brought some good news. Our berthage was cheek by jowl with the French Quarter. Word of this went around the ship quickly. It gladdened the hearts of the crew. Everyone had had the utterly deflating experience of heading towards a port which held out promise of multifarious diversion and then finding the ship shunted away to the far end of some dockland, miles from the epicentre of entertainment. Shoregoing then would have taken on the dimensions of an expedition; waiting at a bus stop, trying to thumb lifts on lorries, or hiring a taxi. Distance tended to diminish the sense of enjoyment; at the back of the carouser's mind was the nagging thought that if he missed the last bus, he had better have enough money left over for a taxi. Otherwise it would entail a weary, staggering walk back to the ship along strange streets and roadways in the dead of night.

The men were out on deck, leaning over the railings, standing on the hatch, lolling about enjoying the passing scene and the warm sunshine. Banter was flung about like a multicoloured beach ball. Two men did a sailor's hornpipe, while another attempted cartwheels. Every now and then one went forward to the prow, gazing ahead at the broad gleaming river for the first sight of the city.

Meanwhile, on the bridge, the contest between the captain and the ball-game had degenerated. Thompson began substituting obscene versions of the songs and ditties. Ignored by the pilot, he looked to the quartermaster, to myself and to Brad, who had come on watch at noon, as audience. Even the placid Brad was slightly embarrassed.

Fortunately the first distant sight of New Orleans put paid to this charade. The river curved round in a long sweep and along its right bank the low buildings of the city began to appear: a blur of white woodwork, brown brick, interspersed with trees and shrubbery in the afternoon haze. The city has probably changed since then, but at the time of which I write, only to the north of the main thoroughfare, Canal Street, were there any of the high buildings that tend to depersonalise American cities.

'It's up ahead,' came the cry from the lookout on the fo'castle. The decks and companionways rang with footsteps as our men raced up and stood bunched there, hands shading eyes. There was a spontaneous cheer, like that of Xenophon's foot-sore soldiers sighting the sea from the mountain top.

As we drew near, we could see a row of ships tied up alongside the low cargo sheds; more lay at anchor in midstream. A full size replica of a Mississippi riverboat, thin tall smokestacks high over the tiered decks, was berthed at a jetty at the foot of Canal Street.

At this juncture Captain Thompson ceased his buffoonery. The show was over. His beery jocularity subsided and he assumed the proper mien of captain. He ordered Misery and Brad to their stations fore and aft. His eyes still twinkled, but they missed little as he moved nimbly from one side of the bridge to the other, looking down on the tubby tugboat nosing against our port beam and at the slowly approaching wharf. He largely ignored the pilot; but he did perform a little act of vengeance on the radio which had rivalled him for the sixty-mile journey upriver. While the pilot's attention was elsewhere engaged, Thompson elbowed the radio off the shelf. It clattered to the deck. Pete was left to pick it up and replace it.

So absorbed was I with all that was happening that I almost forgot about notifying the Commonwealth high-frequency network and the local station that we had arrived. We had tied up by the time I raised Halifax, Nova Scotia. The New Orleans station tapped out 'Have a good time' at the end of our exchange of signals. This friendly injunction was hardly necessary to a ship of the *Allenwell*'s character.

10

'Lively Place, This'

No one was more eager to put foot ashore than our pilot. He scampered off the vessel without a word of good-bye. If one reason for his hasty departure was to resume listening to the ball-game, he had a disappointment in store. He was last seen standing on the dockside, shaking the radio vigorously, putting it to his ear and frowning.

Then the gangway shuddered and rattled as a troupe of corpulent customs officials climbed on board; bellies bulged over belts that held up floppy trousers, jackets hung loose on fatty bodies. These worthies were greeted with some warmth by the Old Man. He did not want any trouble and invited them to his cabin to ply them with beer. Soon blubbery bursts of laughter came from his quarters, while below in the foyer several of us waited impatiently for the arrival of the agent with our mail.

Presently the customs men came heavily down the stairs, full of burping cheer, and picked their way down the gang-way. In hindsight it can be said that there must have been a collective sigh of relief at their disinterest in the *Allenwell*. Even a cursory search most likely would have revealed caches of stolen whisky all over the vessel. For a few moments the fat men stood on the dockside in a group, held together by laughter. Pete nudged me when one fellow made an eye-wiping gesture with the cupped fingers of one hand while the others were convulsed with glee. Pete imagined a visual representation of the circulation of the captain's favourite story, such as one sees on television or on film depicting the spread of an epidemic. A small stain, coloured an appropriate brown, appears on the map of Louisiana in the dock area of New Orleans, expands to cover the entire city, edges out into the hinterland, enveloping the state until it reaches the capital of Baton Rouge. Perhaps the story would even be translated into Acadian French for the benefit of dark-browed wild-fowlers skulking in the marshlands and bayous.

The agent, a dignified silvery-haired man, came on board bearing a bulging briefcase and went up to see the captain. The distribution of the awaited mail showed Misery at his most characteristic. He fetched the bundle from the captain's quarters, sneaked down the outside stairway and gained his cabin unseen. When an annoyed group of men eventually knocked on his door, he was seen sitting reading his own letters while everybody else's lay in a pile on his desk. Possession of other peoples' mail conferred on him a transitory importance. He parted reluctantly with the letters, handing them over to outstretched hands like a Dickensian workhouse master doling out dollops of gruel. He had only a few letters left when I came up to him. I recognised immediately the distinctive green and orange edging of the Irish airmail envelope among the red and blue British ones.

'That looks like mine,' I said eagerly.

'Give us a chance to sort them out, will you?' he replied, with a pained expression.

He was in bad form. The air of ebullience, the whistling, the light footsteps tripping along the alleyways grated against his cheerlessness. The prospect of two or three weeks late-night rowdiness did not appeal to him. Within an hour of tying up, he had a foretaste of the torments that lay ahead. Pete, an indiscriminate lover of Dixieland, was visibly excited at having arrived at its fountainhead. He turned up the volume of his radio; the intertwined harmonies of trumpet, trombone, piano, clarinet and drums reverberated against the bulkheads of his cabin, boomed out into the alleyway and assailed Misery's sensitive ears. In no time he was standing in Pete's doorway, balefully watching the third mate stomping his feet and clicking his fingers.

'Could we have a little quiet, please?' he shouted above the din. Pete made a show of turning down the radio; but his cabin was to be a high decibel temple of ragtime and Dixieland.

That evening the saloon was the scene of one of the great set-pieces on board the *Allenwell*. Word had got around that an advance of wages would be paid out at seven. Men began to assemble in the foyer. Faces and hands had been scrubbed, hair brushed and combed, shoes polished, trousers pressed.

'A good meal is what I'm looking for ashore; I've had enough of the slop on this ship.'

'I'm after a bit more than that, and I don't mean pumpkin pie.'

'Hands up all who are going to dip their wicks tonight?' Several comedians raised both hands.

Then Captain Thompson appeared, carrying a ledger and a satchel of US currency notes. He sat down ceremoniously at the top of the table. Every man was entitled to draw a 'sub', but Thompson had the demeanour of a lord of the manor dispensing largesse to his vassals.

'All right now — who wants money?' he called out. A queue formed and shuffled forward. With a great licking of thumb and forefinger, the captain counted out the notes, entered the amount in the ledger and had the recipient sign his name against it. He revelled in his role, chuckling as he tossed off supposed witticisms.

'Fifty dollars, eh? Don't spend it all in the one whorehouse.'

'Twenty dollars — enough to get a good dose of V.D.'

When Alasdair, the sandy-haired Scottish steward, asked for ten dollars, Thompson burst out, 'You'll be lucky to get any more than a knee-trembler for that in this city.' Alasdair made a Glaswegian riposte. 'Well captain — I heard there's a special January sale on in town.'

Toni, decked out in red shirt, silk cravat and emerald trousers, came forward. As he bent over to sign his name, Thompson made a show of recoiling from the aura of perfume that surrounded Toni's frizzed hair-do and rouged face. When he minced out of earshot, Thompson laughed, 'If he doesn't get done tonight, he never will.'

It was the observant Pete who later pointed out a slightly puzzling aspect of the pay-out. There would not be another 'sub' for a week, but a good many men, the very types who seemed to be bursting with eagerness to sample the flesh-pots, drew only the most modest advances.

'I have an idea that bottles of Vat 69 are going to rival the dollar as currency in this town,' he murmured.

Men were going down the gangway speedily as the evening light faded and the neon signs ashore began to ripple and flicker.

'We'll give this place the once over, eh Sparks?' Pete's large ears and lumpy face were aglow after a vigorous shower.

'A reconnaissance is in order.'

'Yes. It's always a bad thing to run amok the first night in port.'

Our avoidance of any commitment to seek out women meant that we could have a more relaxed shoregoing. It skirted the prospect of coming back on board feeling that we had failed some kind of test. I sensed that Pete was as woman-shy as myself. Inhibitive bonds might have been loosened if we had had recourse to alcohol, but whatever about Pete, I was as uneasy about drink as I was of carnal encounter. Those who fear that they may stumble and fall, to the scornful amusement of some sex-hardened partner in a seedy back room, often decide not to enter the lists at all. Nothing attempted, nothing lost is the motto.

Just the same, the two of us swaggered off the ship with a simulated air of bold adventure. Several men leaning over the side shouted down at us, 'There's two fellows with only one thing on their mind.' We grinned in acknowledgment, waved back in confirmation.

The *Allenwell* was berthed on the southern perimeter of the Old Quarter. Immediately behind the cargo sheds were a few streets of bars and shady places which catered for sailors, stevedores and all the flotsam and jetsam that washes up on the shore of every big port. Even at that hour a few drunks and derelicts were stumbling about. From within the bars came the sound of loud voices and the musical thump of jukeboxes. The gaudy neon signs flashed a tatty welcome. Those were the kind of places where you would need to watch your wallet, and know where the door was when violent arguments began to rumble.

We ambled further on through an old residential area. Behind walls of mellowed brick, guarded by high gateways of ornamental ironwork, were houses in which French and Spanish merchants and administrators had lived in. We gazed in at paved courtyards and patios, trickling iron fountains, tubs of subtropical flowers. The pillared verandas and arched doorways were hung with flower baskets trailing long leafy tendrils. High over the pavements were slatted windows, open to the evening air. At one corner we passed two old ladies in flowered frocks, bare arms age-mottled, conversing in Louisiana French. This placid, harmonious place slowed down one's footsteps to its own gentle pace, induced pleasant feelings.

We turned a corner and found ourselves looking down a long street, twinkling with light, full of strolling people. Tiered balconies of hand-wrought lace-iron overhung the pavements, supported on narrow iron stalks.

'This is it — Bourbon Street!' Pete said, rubbing his hands.

Every doorway led in to a bistro, restaurant, nightclub or music hall. The smells of strange, exotic cooking wafted across the pavements from gently lit places where waiters went about the tables to the clink of cutlery and glasses and the hum of talk in several languages. The sounds of Dixieland echoed from within the music places. Outside the cabarets, the walls were embellished with blown-up coloured photographs and garish paintings of the female performers — mouths open to show a sliver of inviting tongue, tasselled breasts, a creamy area of thigh, buttock and torso. The bold captions emphasised the acrobatic and erotic accomplishments of the entertainers. Before the slatted swing-doors stood burly fellows who tried to entice passersby, opening the doors briefly to allow a glimpse of women gyrating on spot-lit stages to the sound of saxophone and the thump of drums.

'Come on, you guys. Plenty of pussy inside.'

Pete and I crossed and recrossed the crowded streets like two children let loose in a toyshop. We shouted to one another.

'Over here — have a look.'

'Listen to this.'

'Hey Sparks, we just might take a look at Mademoiselle Mouchette when we've looked around some more. I want to hear some Dixieland first.'

The streets running parallel were part of the entertainment area, connected by small laneways and cobbled alleys. Here and there were souvenir shops crammed with antiques, genuine or mass-produced, redolent of the city's history: muskets and powder-horns, coonskin hats, telescopes, ships' bells, French royalist fleur-de-lys emblems, Spanish cockades, Napoleonic pistols, piratical cutlasses, Confederate uniforms. The names over the shops, bars and nightclubs sought to evoke the memory of the famous — de Soto, the early explorer in the region, Pierre Lafitte, leader of the Barataria pirates, Andrew Jackson, who repulsed a British attack in 1815, Mark Twain, one-time riverboat pilot, and General Pierre Beauregard, who had ordered the cannonade that began the American Civil War.

Moving about, one felt an affinity with all those evening strollers from the past: trappers toting long-barrelled squirrel guns, bow-legged buccaneers, war veterans, Spanish artisans and grandees, riverboat men, cotton traders, aristocrats and levee labourers, the slavers and the enslaved, heroes and scoundrels and all those, like ourselves, neither saintly nor wicked.

Pete stopped outside the door of a capacious hall, captivated by the fascinating interplay of a band thumping out Dixieland. We entered and found a place amongst the crowded tables. The sound boomed off the walls and ceiling, vibrated in the ears and against the breastbone and made one's feet tap out the rhythm. The black players delighted in their own pleasure-giving dexterity, proud of this love child of European instrumentality and African spontaneity.

Pete was greatly taken by the style and verve of the trombone player. When we got outside, he declared his intention of buying a trombone and learning to play it. As the occupant of the next door cabin, I was less than enthusiastic about this project.

After further wandering about, shirt-sleeved in the balmy air, we eventually came again to the poster advertising the act of Mademoiselle Mouchette. 'Sensational!' shouted the blurb. This buxom blonde was depicted standing with legs apart, breasts and pelvis thrust forward, like an Amazon warrior surveying the enemy from a hill top.

'You'll just make the next show, you guys,' said the muscular tout. 'This is really something.'

We entered hesitantly and sidled up to the bar, where we paid very dearly for glasses of Coca-Cola. From the small stage a ramp extended amongst the tables; I noticed that the subdued lighting reflected off the bald pates of men who had strategically placed themselves beside it.

A clatter of drums, a circle of spotlight on the centre of the curtain and a man in evening dress, with oiled black hair and Hitlerian moustache, appeared. In a tired drawl he said something about the greatest stripper south of the Mason-Dixon line. There was a scattering of hand claps and the curtains parted to reveal an All-American girl in diaphanous fronds. To drum and saxophone she began to weave about clumsily, advancing down the ramp to cast a wink or a slight heave of breast at some intent spectator, then returning to the stage limply to discard a veil. There was something sad about this wholesome open-faced girl trying to invest her movements with sly, sensual allure.

'I see her as a milkmaid, churning butter,' Pete observed.

One was afraid that some half-drunk patron would guffaw derisively. Some were indeed grinning, but many of the middle-aged voyeurs near the ramp watched her with frowning concentration, as if listening to a complicated lecture on the internal combustion engine.

The last veil was cast aside and the plump body was clothed in nothing more than nipple-tassels and a g-string. Total nudity was prohibited at that time and the more anatomically inquisitive had to rely on their imaginations. Mademoiselle Mouchette made her exit with pouting movements of almost bare buttocks, as if inviting a kiss.

'Just the same, I wouldn't mind a bit of that at all,' laughed Pete. Next thing a woman beside us turned and placed a hand on his inner thigh, saying, 'Hi, honey.' Pete pulled away.

'Something wrong, honey?'

'I just don't like people to touch me.'

'You'd best go home to Mamma, child. Way past your bedtime.' We beat a retreat into the street.

'Not my type at all, Sparks.'

'She could be a pickpocket for all we know.'

At the next corner someone said, 'Lookin' for business?' A handsome dark-skinned woman thrust out a shapely leg from her split skirt. She swung a latch-key from a dazzlingly ringed finger. I moved away with the air of a world-weary mariner not easily impressed by female allure. Pete stood his ground.

'What kind of business?'

'Lovin' business.'

'How much?'

'Twenty dollars for a short time.'

'Twenty dollars! I only want to use it – not buy it.'

'Then fuck off, Limey.'

Pete rejoined me, shifting his shoulders insouciantly, a slightly heroic grin on his pustule-pitted face.

'I haven't much time for whores, Sparks, unless they are really good.'

'It's fear of catching a dose that puts me off.' As we headed back to the ship, he told me that he had a girlfriend back home.

'You never mentioned her before.'

'Well — she's not exactly a girlfriend. I just met her at a

party. We didn't speak much. She was a lovely bird. I might write to her tonight.'

The sleazy dockside bars and clubs were throbbing with noise. Groups of sailors went in and out. The clamour of raucous song, jukeboxes, fiddle and banjo came from within. A crowd of our men stumbled out onto the pavement. 'You two fellows look as if you got your ends away already, right?' said one. We laughed. They shouted after us, 'Where are all the good women?'

'Plenty up in the French Quarter,' called back Pete, 'Twenty dollars for a short time.'

Someone said 'Twenty dollars! Those two must have money to burn.'

We had been walking and wandering about for almost three hours. Legs unused to exercise and feet unaccustomed to concrete pavements were beginning to drag. The sights, sounds, smells and impressions of this effervescent port siphoned off a good deal of energy. The shabby old *Allenwell*, seemingly deserted, was home from home and I climbed the gangway thankfully towards the cosy roost of my cabin. Leaning over the railings was the lone figure of Mr Yardley, gazing out towards the reflected lights and pulsing life on the other side of the cargo sheds. 'Had a good time, then?' he asked.

'Great,' Pete answered emphatically. Mr Yardley nodded his big bushy head approvingly, as if he somehow shared a morsel of our shoregoing.

As we went to our respective cabins, we both expressed a vague promise that subsequent forays ashore might be more adventurous. But Pete probably knew, as I certainly did, that shoregoing for either one of us was going to be sober, celibate and subdued. We were just quiet types. At least my inhibitions and innate timidity resulted in a heightened interest in the more zestful doings of others, much of which I noted down.

11

Roistering in New Orleans

If people like Pete and me, Misery and Mr Yardley, did not take our places in the carnival cavalcade, we were certainly the exceptions. Every evening the showers gushed and steamed, the smell of carbolic soap hung in the alleyways as towel-clad men strode about. The sounds came from the cabins of hands being scrubbed, of drawers being opened and shut, of cheerful banter. 'Away man — if you comb your hair again there'll be nowt left soon.' 'Hurry up or we'll miss that big lassie on the trapeze.'

From eight o'clock onwards men clattered down the gangway in good-humoured groups and paced away purposefully towards the neon lights. As soon as cargo-working was over, the men on deck duty replaced the hatch covers with an unaccustomed efficiency and raced towards their cabins to get changed. They were often on their way ashore while the last of the longshoremen were still lumbering about the decks.

'Notice anything about those fellows?' asked Pete as we leaned over the railings on our second evening there.

'Some are half seas over, that's clear.'

'Anything else?'

'All those raincoats. Is rain forecast?' The men presented bulky, bundled figures as they went out between the cargo sheds. It was a warm night with clear skies.

'Rain my arse. The barter business is under way. Two bottles for a short time, five for all night.'

There were no gates or barriers where port police or

customs officers might lurk to make the occasional inspection. Later when the whisky merchants had grown in confidence, they left the ship in shirtsleeves, carrying handgrips and even sea bags.

From midnight onwards, until the sky began to lighten in the east, the dockside echoed to the sound of the merrymakers returning. As I sat reading into the small hours, I could hear the shouts and laughter, drunken mumblings, and loud incoherent conversation as the men stumbled towards the gangway. They climbed it hand over hand like exhausted mountaineers using their last reserves of energy to reach the summit. The chains rattled and the aluminium steps banged. The wonder is that nobody fell off and maimed themselves on the concrete dock or plunged between ship and wharf, ending up in the Mississippi. Men floundered about the alleyways, burping and muttering. Some were so far gone in drink that they wandered about seeking their cabins on both accommodation decks, groping at every door handle. I soon took the precaution of locking my door at night.

There were hardy, lively fellows who felt that the long uproarious night ought not to end tamely by tumbling into their bunks; drinking sessions flared into being at 3 or 4 am, accompanied by roaring choruses, storytelling and, now and then, noisy arguments. There were a few scuffles but nobody came to any harm; knuckles were bruised on bulkheads rather than on the blurred wavering faces of opponents.

Several men tumbled down stairways, but sustained no more than a few bruises. 'God looks after babies and drunkards,' said Pete. 'On most ships men go ashore sober and come back drunk. Here, fellows go ashore pissed and come back stocious!'

There were a number of dedicated topers, the bosun among them, who did not overindulge in shoreside jollity. The caches of pilfered whisky, secreted in cabins, murky stores lockers and hidey holes, enabled them to drink determinedly without the distractions of soliciting hookers, tiresomely repetitive strip acts and blaring Dixieland bands. These devotees could drink all night and simply collapse into their bunks or even onto the floor; they thought this much more sensible than having to make their way back on board, inhaling the dank night air of the river, running the risk of walking into a malevolent lamp-post or being run over by some careless motorist.

After a few nights our men got the run of New Orleans, settled on favourites bars and nightclubs, and began to make friends with some of the denizens of the night-world, male and female. The sailor, without pretence or snobbery, readily accepts proffered friendship, has an openness about him that shoresiders find appealing. Who but a sailor will tell a new-found friend that he is not quite sure who his own father is, has just got over a dose of the pox and is willing to carry his companion home drunk through the streets?

Stories of riotous escapades, of hilariously vulgar acts in the shadier nightclubs off the French Quarter, of all-night gambling dens, of women wooed and won, began to circulate. There was a certain amount of boasting and embellishment in tales of fleshly encounter. Nobody wanted to say that he had merely gone ashore, picked up a woman, paid for his pleasure and plodded back on board again.

'She's taken a shine to me – no doubt about it. I get it at cut-price rates and completely free on Saturday nights. There's a lot to be said for sticking to one woman.'

Some braggarts told of acrobatic grapplings with women who looked for no other reward than the vigour and staying power of her partner. Others claimed ecstatic experiences with women who practised unusual forms of titillation. Several men claimed that their women had paid them the ultimate compliment of inviting them to meet members of their families.

'I got on great with the granny. She doesn't know her lady-ship is on the game, thinks she works as an all-night telephone operator. After the Sunday lunch we went for a trip along the river. I carried her little fellow on my back.'

Little Alex maintained that he had laid one of the most statuesque strippers in the Quarter. This lady was noted for gymnastic rather than choreographic ability. When this story reached the ears of Mr Yardley, he snorted, 'Bloody rot, that little cockroach! She'd suck him in and blow him out in bubbles.'

There was one member of the ship's company who had the most extraordinary good luck to find an ideal niche. On our second night in port, Taffy, the wiry little Welshman with the mellifluous tenor voice, had taken his chiming mandolin ashore and wandered into a bistro in one of the more obscure corners of the Quarter. He got chatting with the manager who, after a while, asked him to sing a song. As soon as the applause died down, the manager engaged him to sing there every night until 3 am.

I went to hear him on several nights. He was perched on a tall stool in a corner, lit by a single spotlight. His none-too-clean fingers moved deftly about the strings of his battered instrument, his dark face radiant with passion and joy as the notes poured from his throat like a blackbird in springtime. He sang with such quivering intensity, mostly in his own language, that the audience was enthralled. Whenever I hear a Welsh folk song, I think of that scene.

'It's great, mun. I get twenty dollars a night and all the free beer I can get down my gullet. And there's no shortage of women either.'

He was an ardent womaniser and said that he had six different women within a fortnight of his engagement. At seven or eight each morning he was to be seen hauling himself up the gangway, utterly drained after a night of emotional song, beer-swilling and the amorous exertions with which he concluded his nocturnal activities. By that stage, his respect for his mandolin had diminished and he held it by the stock the way a weary poulterer holds the last plucked turkey on Christmas Eve. That mandolin, scarred and scratched, bore a charmed life. It survived punchings-up and fallings-down, deluges of wine and beer, the impact of backsides, male and female, which sat upon it in dark corners of bistro and bedroom, and the irresistible desire of melody-makers to pluck its strings as soon as Taffy's back was turned.

The all-night carousers on the *Allenwell* were less than

enthusiastic about rising each morning to face the working day. Even the few quiet types were drawn into the revelry, if only by the fact that they were kept awake at night when their shipmates returned.

Misery, with a dour sense of duty and a puritan work-ethic entirely at odds with the prevailing spirit of wassail, had conceived an ambitious programme of scaling, chipping and red-leading which, when completed, would be followed by painting. He was disgusted at the sight of the rust-ridden, sea-scarred decks and superstructure. He was also impelled by a desire to punish those who had kept him awake half the night.

Chipping hammers, scalers and pots of red lead were brought out of the stores' lockers. All that was required was a will to work. Men, bleary-eyed, unsteady of hand, leaden of foot, emerged on deck, crinkling their haggard faces under the unwelcome glare of the morning sun. They knelt on deck, chipping slowly and painfully at the rust-bubbles. Each hammer blow jarred the fragile nerve-ends of drink-bruised crania. Ben Jennings, the bosun, was meant to be in charge. He was far from being an inspirational or authoritative figure. He had to be pulled from his bunk by Tommy Carey, the gap-toothed Liverpudlian lamptrimmer, who was one of the few work-inclined on board. Our bosun would then make his way out on deck, looking about uncertainly. When Misery appeared, picking his pigeon-toed way vindictively about the dirty decks, Ben would attempt an impression of dedication. 'Aye, aye sir. That will be done. You can depend on it, sir.' As soon as the mate was out of the way, Ben stumbled back to his cabin. The deck crew, exhausted after an hour's work, sneaked away to find little corners of repose. It was common to find them dozing down by the stern in the midday sun.

'That bosun is a liability,' said Misery to the captain, with rare directness, when we were sitting at table one day. The Old Man merely grunted.

Mr Yardley was incensed about the state of the engine-room. He had taken to standing on the platform inside the

104

door leading down to the engine room, chest heaving in the oily warmth that rose from below. Infirm he may have been, but his sight was good; he was able to see the grease and oil dangerously coated on the handrails, the discarded hand-rags littering the working spaces between the engines and on the platform before the control board. Each day, when Rat brought him up the big canvas-covered engine room log-book, there was a bitter confrontation. Mr Yardley demanded a thorough clean-up, in addition to the normal maintenance work carried out in port after a three-week voyage. Rat, who had given himself over to what he described as a final pre-marriage fling, ignored the chief engineer's wishes. Since he would be leaving at the end of the voyage, he had no intention of making himself unpopular with the other pleasure-bent men in the engine room. There were several angry shouting matches between the two, all the more savage because of Mr Yardley's helplessness.

On a number of occasions the chief engineer had emerged from his cabin in the small hours and had wheezed his way down the alleyway to Rat's cabin, where a noisy party was in progress.

'They're tough when it comes to boozing and kicking up a row in the middle of the night,' he said at table. 'They wouldn't be so lively if something went wrong down below. God knows, when I was their age, I drank hard and I played hard — but I worked hard too. They've got no pride in their job — that's their trouble.'

Much of the spleen of Mr Yardley and Misery was directed at the person of the captain, whom they saw as the supreme exemplar of the spirit of wassail that dominated the ship to the detriment of good order. He went ashore almost every evening, usually in the company of the cooks, with Ted and Brad and sometimes Rat. He rarely returned before midnight. Nothing pleased him more on his return than to round off the night's jollity with a rowdy game of darts. Anybody in his company or indeed hanging about the foyer was persuaded or dragooned into the recreation room. Roars, peals of sodden laughter and burping banter echoed in the foyer. I was thankful that my cabin was well down the starboard alleyway.

Yet one thing could be said about our resilient captain: he faithfully followed the British seafaring tradition that no matter how late or how drunk you were getting into your bunk, you must appear for breakfast next morning. More than that, he would come into the saloon in great good humour, as if remembering the more colourful incidents of the night before. He was amused by the bleak looks of Mr Yardley and Misery, whose sleep had been disturbed by the uproar attending the post-midnight games of darts.

There was a rumour that the captain had become friendly with a middle-aged hostess in one of the strip joints and occasionally slept with her. Nobody knew for certain; he was inclined to be secretive about such matters.

On our second night in New Orleans he had been asked out to dinner by one of the senior members of the shipping agency, a portly Southern gentleman. We were surprised therefore when, that evening, he appeared at table and wolfed down a plateful of greasy stew.

'That will put a lining on my belly.'

'It's the only way to make a fair comparison between two great culinary traditions — have one meal not long after the other,' said Mr Yardley.

Misery was seething. He was aware that he had been included in the dinner invitation, but the captain had not chosen to inform him about it. When Thompson had departed, the mate said acidly, 'That agent doesn't know what he's letting himself in for.'

We were never to hear how the captain had behaved during the dinner, held in one of the city's exclusive restaurants. When, next day, Mr Yardley asked him how it had gone, the Old Man merely harrumphed and puffed out his cheeks like a bilious owl. It may have been significant that the portly Southern gentleman never set foot on board again; nor was Captain Thompson ever afterwards invited ashore by anyone from the agency, either in New Orleans or in the other ports at which we called on this voyage.

Apart from seeing him perform at the 'Windjammer' in Liverpool, all the accounts I had of the captain's shore-side forrays were second hand. Most came from Mr Yardley, who regarded the master as a contemptible rogue. I had an affection for the Old Man and felt that Mr Yardley took a certain malicious delight in exaggeration. I was soon to have an opportunity to make my own judgment.

12

A Night out with Captain Thompson

Almost every afternoon, I ambled ashore and wandered about the French Quarter. It was a quiet time of the day. The sun was pleasantly warm on the streets; it shone down on the delicate lace ironwork of the balconies and gateways, throwing patterns of compressed tracery on the pavements and flagstones. The nightclubs and band halls were shuttered, but from the little restaurants came the whiff of bouillabaisse, café brulot and spices. Around Brulatour Courtyard and the Rue Royale were antique shops and bookstores, where I browsed happily for hours on end.

New Orleans was full of sleepy little corners of repose where wooden benches warmed themselves in the sun against old walls. In patios of brick cobblestones one could drink coffee and daydream all afternoon. I discovered a little haven, a restaurant behind beautiful wrought-iron gates, where the tables in the courtyard were placed amongst tubs and urns of blossoms, and a fountain trickled and glittered in the sunlight. It was an ideal place to go to in the late afternoon to read and drink superb coffee and nod off to the hum of bees and insects flitting about the flowers. I favoured a seat in one corner, beside the old end-wall encrusted with ancient vines. My life at that period was full of discontent; I was always feeling I should be doing something else, be somewhere else, be a different kind of person. Those idylls in that corner, sitting in quietude, were like small peaceful clearings in a tangled bushland.

I was in that patio early one evening, had a light meal and

then sat watching the yellow sunlight moving upwards to the top balcony and its pendant flower baskets. The courtyard became suffused with a soft blue light. Presently the ornamental lanterns lit up. People began to come in from the street, sitting at the tables outside or entering the restaurant proper.

Suddenly there came loud and familiar voices from the gateway. In marched Captain Thompson, with Little Alex swinging jauntily at his heels, followed by the shambling figure of Brad. Bringing up the rearguard was Ted, smiling vaguely about him. I hunched at my corner table, but the sharp shifty eyes of Little Alex spotted me.

'Hey, look at Sparks. On the lookout for a bit of nooky, eh Sparks?'

That was it. They came over, took chairs from nearby tables and sat down.

'Out for a night on the town, eh Sparks?' Captain Thompson's russet face was flushed. 'Let's have a beer then. Where's the fucking waiter?' He looked about impatiently. There was no waiter in sight, so he stuck the big and little fingers of one hand into his mouth. His jowly cheeks ballooned like a trumpet player's. The piercing whistle startled people even at the farthest tables.

A waiter strode forward, surly at being summoned in this way. The Old Man addressed him in pidgin English.

'Beer, savvy? Si, si — four beers. Savvy?' He held up four stout fingers.

The waiter, puzzled and irritable, likewise held up four fingers. For a moment they confronted one another like rival sorcerers casting spells. Then the waiter growled, 'Ya want four beers, that it?'

'Well we don't want horse-piss.'

'We don't sell horse-piss here.'

'I'll tell you that when we taste your beer.'

When the waiter returned, he plonked the glasses down truculently and snapped the proffered note from Thompson's hand. This unpleasantness caused the captain to view the establishment with a very critical eye. He sniffed the air disapprovingly, as if the scent of flowers and magnolia blossoms was offensive to his snub, hairy-nostriled nose.

'All them shrubs and vines bring bugs and wasps about.'

The air was indeed full of moths and midges, and the most peculiar feature of their presence was that they seemed to have a particular attraction for Ted. He sat there in a state of alcoholic tranquillity, completely unaware of the insects buzzing around his head in circles and erratic configurations, like atoms going out of control about a central core. Perhaps they were attracted by his brilliantined hair or by some emanation of ingested alcohol issuing from his pores.

Captain Thompson ordered more beer. He would allow nobody else to pay for a round. He was a generous man; but he also seemed to regard this as an obligation of the one who was in command for the evening, who decided where and when to go, who dominated the conversation. Little Alex played a fawning role, laughing loudly at his master's witticisms. Brad sat at ease, his round brown face full of inner peace, as he rolled cigarettes slowly and delicately, putting the finished products into a tin box.

From inside come the sound of Louisiana folkmusic on accordion and fiddle. Captain Thompson was not at all impressed. His mind turned to the bars of South Shields and Blyth, with their battered pianos, dartboards, mounds of meat pies and bottles of Newcastle Brown Ale.

'I'll bet the whores of New Orleans wouldn't stand up to the whores of Tyneside,' he declared. To illustrate the doughty qualities of the ladies of North-east England, he related a story of a shipboard fight in Blyth.

'Two of these lassies got pissed on board and began to kick up a racket. I couldn't get them off the bloody ship, so I sent for the shore bosun in the pub across the way.' This was the woman who, by strength of arm and character, was the tribal chieftain of the dockside prostitutes. 'She gave one of them a punch in the belly, knocked her flat on her arse. Then she grabbed the other one by her hair and dragged her down the alleyway to the shithouse — pushed her head into the bowl and pulled the chain. Nearly drowned her, she did.'

The watery ending to this story may have stimulated Captain Thompson's kidneys. He pushed himself to his feet and went inside to look for a toilet. A few minutes later he emerged from a door set in the side-wall, looking about with a frown.

'I've been all round the place looking for the bloody jacks. Those fools sent me on a wild-goose chase. Well, I can't hold it any longer.' With that he went over to the corner where stood a big stone urn resplendent with a profusion of flowers. He was only partially hidden from the nearest tables as he proceeded to urinate powerfully. Several large moths flew up in alarm.

'Hey! hey!' came an angry shout. The surly waiter came rushing forward, brandishing a napkin as if he might take a swipe at the captain's exposed member. He grabbed Thompson by the arm. Our captain rounded on him. 'Stand off, you twat, or I'll piss all over your shoes.'

That waiter retreated and ran off. He soon reappeared, accompanied by several others; they closed on the captain. Wily old battler that he was, Thompson knew that the best option was to retire with grace.

'Come on lads, we've had enough of this kip.'

We were roughly ushered out, with all heads turned in our direction. Outside the big iron gates Thompson stood grinning. Lesser souls like myself might be cringing with embarrassment, but this kind of incident was the very stuff of life to him.

'Come on then. Let's see some of them nightclubs,' he commanded and led the way forward. I had not it in me to excuse myself and go on my own quiet way. I was to regret this lack of character.

When we turned a corner and found ourselves facing up Bourbon Street, thronged with people and ablaze with flickering neon signs, the captain stopped abruptly. Here it was that a most unfortunate memory rose like a beery bubble to the surface of his mind.

'I remember this very spot. 1938. There used to be a lassie pulled nails out of a cork board with her arsehole in one of the halls somewhere about here. I wonder if some lassie is still doing that act?'

He brushed aside our mumbled doubts. The recollection of bizarre anal dexterity had fixed itself in his mind like one of the nails in the cork board. 'Let's find out then,' he said determinedly and rolled ahead on his bandy legs while we shuffled along in his wake.

Thus began a search which took us all over the Vieux Carré, up one street and down another, pausing at each doorway while Captain Thompson questioned the doorman or went inside to enquire of the manager. No detective searching for clues could have been more diligent than our captain. At the first nightclub he went straight up to the greasy tout. This fellow, thinking we were prospective customers, released a ritual smile of welcome.

'We got plenty of lovely girls inside, gentlemen.'

'Any girl that pulls nails out of a board with her arse?'

The man's eyes narrowed; he imagined that he was being made fun of and, besides, he barely understood Thompson's Geordie accent. He regarded us with some hostility. 'No – we got nobody that does that,' he said flatly and slammed shut the door that he had been holding open. Several other doormen were equally unfriendly. Others were puzzled, while more roared with laughter. One, with typical American enterprise and opportunism, said, 'Now that just might be a good kind of act. It might go down real big. I must talk to the boss about it.'

On and on we went, pushing along the crowded pavements, glimpsing lavish floor shows and exotic striptease acts as we paused briefly outside, hearing snatches of Dixieland, ragtime and more modern jazz played by famous exponents, inhaling the aroma of Creole cuisine as we trudged by bars and restaurants. All the while Captain Thompson plodded ahead doggedly. We trailed along behind, our initial amusement now turned to irritation.

The odyssey came to an end after the captain had called on a renowned musical establishment called 'The Famous Doors.' Here the names of all the great musicians who had performed there were engraved on brass tablets affixed to the doorposts. It seemed most unlikely that the sought-after performance might take place in the intervals, for the diversion of music-sated patrons. But Captain Thompson was not to be deterred. In he went while we hung about outside, foot-sore and drooping. Suddenly our captain was propelled through the famous doors by the arm of a furious attendant. 'Go on — scram,' the man shouted.

To our immense relief this ended the search. 'All right, then,' the Old Man said finally, 'That's it. There's no lassie in this city pulls nails out with her arse. New Orleans has changed for the worse since the war. Let's have a beer.'

Some distance along the pavement he led us into a small, subdued hall; drinks were served at tables while a band of black musicians played a slow blues. We sat down wearily, thankful that the captain's obsession had evaporated at last. To make up for lost drinking time, he ordered three rounds of beer and began to guzzle with gusto, looking about as if to attract the attention of the other customers. He cast critical frowns at the players. They were all corpulent and elderly, with wiry grey hair, fat thighs spread apart to allow their bellies to flop forward. They were playing some rueful, lingering melody, redolent of the deprivation that their race had endured — of menial jobs, slum housing, garbage in fetid alleyways, seedy hotdog stands and fried chicken in brown paper bags.

'Thank God that's over — it's like the song the old cow died on,' said Thompson when the performance ended. He showed little enthusiasm when the clarinet player stood up, came forward and, to the gentle accompaniment of the others, began to play. Brad told me later that this man was one of the great maestros of this instrument. Completely relaxed, in a simple and unaffected way, he produced a sweet melody of marvellous clarity which unwound like a silken ribbon. When he had finished, there was a spontaneous burst of applause from all but Captain Thompson. 'Thought the old bugger would never finish,' he grunted. For him the cymbals and drums, the clarinet, trumpet, trombone

113

and, most of all the piano, were there to be played with vigour and verve, like in 'The Crown and Anchor' back home. But there was another reason for his grumpiness; he was a performer himself who wanted to be in the spotlight rather than a mere member of the audience.

Unfortunately, at this juncture the band took a break. They lumbered off the stage, their flabby, ponderous movements in contrast to the nimble grace of their playing. The spotlit stage was now empty. Thompson's mischievous little eyes glinted and an impish grin appeared on his chubby mouth. He got to his feet and approached the stage circuitously, like a big crab crawling sideways towards its victim, giving the impression of going elsewhere, but inexorably closing the distance. Then, with the surprising agility of fat, round people, he sprang onto the stage, smothered the piano stool with his posterior and, without any preliminaries, began to thump out 'The Galloping Major'.

The audience was taken by surprise. Some imagined it to be a clownish interlude and nodded with amusement. Others were puzzled and asked, 'Who is that guy?' The manager came striding forward. For a moment he stood uncertainly by the piano. Our captain ignored him, hammering away for all he was worth, his thick fingers often striking two notes together, while he stamped his feet in time.

The escapade might have ended amicably had Thompson the good sense to take his bow after the last chorus of 'The Galloping Major', but the delight of being centre stage, the focus of everyone's attention, had gone to his head. With a wave to the audience he launched into 'Knees up, Mother Brown'. The notes came crashing out thunderously. This brought the black pianist on the scene, his old face wrinkled with anxiety. The manager tapped Thompson vigorously on the shoulder. 'Okay, okay — the show's over,' he shouted.

'What's the matter with you?' asked Thompson aggressively as he came to a sudden stop.

'Know what it costs to buy a piano like that?'

'Keep your hands off me. You can stick your piano up your arse.' There was a titter of laughter from the onlookers, some of whom had stood up to see what was going on.

'Come on — git!' said the manager. Thompson backed away with the intention of making a dignified exit. Unluckily he backed into the drum ensemble and fell in a clamour of drums and cymbals. The manager bounced forward to see if any damage had been done. Satisfied that nothing had been broken, he hauled Captain Thompson to his feet and pushed him towards the door.

'Come on lads — this is only a dive,' shouted the captain over his shoulder. So we made another cringing exit, under the audience's curious gaze. Out on the pavement it was discovered that Ted was not with us. Malicious Little Alex proposed that I — as the non-drinker in the company – go back in to fetch him. When I re-entered, very reluctantly and cautiously, I found Ted still sitting at our table, gazing about dreamily. He was apparently unaware that anything untoward had happened. He followed me out, sucking away at his teeth.

We caught sight of the others ahead, just as they were turning into a strip show. This was my chance to cut and run, even though I knew the captain would not be pleased. I hit on the abject stratagem of feigning illness and asked Ted to convey this to the captain. He promised to do so and went zombie-like through the swing doors while I scurried along the pavements towards the sanctuary of the *Allenwell.*

Next morning at table Captain Thompson asked me how I was feeling. I said that I had been a bit out of sorts for some days.

'A bit of black ham would put you right,' he offered as remedy.

Brad told me that there had been another rumpus at the strip show when Thompson had tried to engage a performer in salacious banter while she was doing her act.

'Well, all that kind of thing is to be expected when you go ashore for a night with him,' Brad said with a tolerant smile.

13

'Dinner at Antoines, no less'

When the hatch-boards were lifted off to uncover Number Two hold for the unloading of cargo, many eyes were cast furtively, if not guiltily, towards the scene. The tremor of unease must have disturbed many on board as the rich lode that had already been partially mined in stealthy darkness was now revealed to the light of day and glaring cargo lamps.

Misery was out on deck long before the uncovering began, walking watchfully about. At breakfast that morning, after the captain had left the table, he said 'The day of reckoning may be at hand,' in the manner of a scorned prophet who ardently prays that retribution will fall on the heads of the mocking mob.

Now he leaned over the hold, bitter blue eyes full of vengeance. Then he climbed down the footholds and, torch in hand, insinuated his thin body into the narrow spaces between the crates of whisky and the other items of cargo. If our predators had been mean-spirited in their operations, broken open a crate here and there to extract a few bottles, Misery would have been able to report this evidence of pilferage to the captain, the agents and in turn, to the police. But our jolly fellows had been grandiose in their larceny, removing whole sections in an admirably ambitious and tidy manner.

Misery's sleuthing was further frustrated by the fact that somebody had neglected to stencil the destination on the crates, half of which were for New Orleans and half for

116

Houston. He would stand for long periods by the greasy winches as the slingloads came up and were swung out onto the dockside, patient as a heron at the water's edge. Having made the occasional note, he then repaired to his cabin, where the cargo plan was spread out on his desk. He pored over it, consulting the ship's manifest with a bony forefinger. I peeped in at him several times while he was thus occupied: one got the impression that his prime motivation lay in the pleasure to be derived from putting the wrongdoers behind bars. His detective work was further hampered by the way the cargo had been haphazardly stowed.

'That's what happens when the third mate fucks off ashore to the pictures and the second mate to the boozer when they are meant to be supervising the stowage,' he said biliously to Mr Yardley, in an oblique reference to the touchy subject of the missing cargo. He had words with Pete about this negligence, though he had not the courage to confront Brad about it.

'Sherlock Holmes has found fuck-all clues,' laughed Pete. 'We won't know how much is missing until the last slingload goes onto the dockside in Houston.'

Pete told me that, late at night, long after cargo-working had ceased and the dock was deserted, he had seen whole cases being carried down the gangway to cars and vans waiting below. 'I wasn't going to stick my neck out. I don't want to end up floating down the Mississippi with a marlin spike in my back.' Apparently the entrepreneurs amongst the whisky-raiders had done deals with the proprietors of the more disreputable drinking dens and nightclubs. 'This is big business,' said Pete, with the air of one impressed by the audacity and opportunism of those with a commercial instinct. It never occurred to me that Pete, the least mercenary of persons, might himself be tempted to embark on a similar enterprise.

All our men were careful to queue up for the weekly 'subs'. Perhaps they regarded it as a precautionary measure to record drawing money in case the 'subs' sheet might ever be scrutinised as part of some subsequent shipboard or police investigation. Just the same, it was rather telling to see men come forward to request a 'sub' of thirty or forty dollars, clad in American suits and shiny patent-leather shoes. Many signed the book with unsteady hands and stuffed their derisory sums into genuine crocodile-skin wallets which had cost almost as much. It was hard to believe that the material well-being, if not ostentation, of so many passed unnoticed by Captain Thompson as he doled out the notes.

The most conspicuous of the well-heeled were Little Alex, Old Charlie and Ted. They had gone ashore and outfitted themselves in a haberdashery. They had a very special occasion in mind. Their ill-gotten gains would enable them to fulfil what was surely the ultimate dream of two galley-toilers and their despised chief steward – dinner at Antoine's, one of the most exclusive and famous restaurants on the American continent. Their own insobriety and some confusion between the British and American size-scales resulted in their buying bright seersucker suits that were several sizes too large. When they decked themselves out in this apparel, preparatory to going ashore for the great event, they looked for all the world like extras from the male chorus line of some brash American musical.

Word of their momentous expedition went round the ship. A crowd of men gathered at the railings to see them off. There were some catcalls and derisory remarks from those who did not take kindly to the staple diet of greasy stews and oily soups.

Off went the three for what was to be one of the most memorable meals of their lives. In Antoine's they would be shown a respect and deference never accorded them on the *Allenwell.* The maître d'hôtel would usher them to their table, bow, and present them with huge menus in embossed leather covers. The wine-waiter in this opulent establishment would hover solicitously about while they studied the wine list. In the gracious ambience of Antoine's they would find themselves in the company of epicures and fastidious connoisseurs, for whom a visit to this restaurant was a grand occasion.

118

All this certainly happened, but it transpired that the evening was not without incident. They afterwards related the details to Brad, who in turn told me. I supplemented this with some subtle probing of Little Alex and Ted and was able to compile a hearsay account of their night out.

It appears that the trio were a little overcome by the effusive courtesy given them at Antoine's. As a mark of approval, they ordered several bottles of the best wine and drank them without waiting for the accompanying food. They were in splendid form before the first course arrived. Then they consumed large quantities of oysters, followed by thick okra soup and, as a main course, what Little Alex described as 'huge fucking lobsters'. Sated with food and drink, they were exuding a spirit of goodwill to all. Little Alex thought that it would be a capital idea to compliment the chef personally. The maître d'hôtel tried to dissuade him, saying the chef was busy. But Little Alex insisted, rising from his seat to press the point. Eventually a portly figure in chef's garb emerged from the kitchen. He bowed to acknowledge their accolades. Little Alex, in the manner of one chef to another, began to deliver an eulogy. Just as the impatient chef was about to detach himself, Little Alex, in an excess of fellowship, snatched the tall white hat from the man's head and placed it on his own. Just as quickly the chef snatched it back and strode away angrily.

It was when they began to sing that the maître d'hôtel appeared and politely explained that their table was now required for some other guests. He presented them with the bill on a silver salver and hung about anxiously while they fumbled with their well-filled wallets. Little Alex tucked a ten-dollar bill into the top pocket of the waiter who had served them.

They were hardly outside the door when Old Charlie's face turned an unhealthy green. He began to get wretchedly ill.

'Spewed his ring all over the pavement, he did' was Little Alex's picturesque description. Several people about to enter the restaurant scattered in alarm and disgust.

The trio walked unsteadily back to the ship. Ted began to

lag behind. When his two fellow diners reached the gang-way, he was nowhere to be seen. He did not return until eight o'clock the following morning. He was vague about his movements, except to say that he had lost his way and had wandered about until weariness overcame him.

'I dossed down in the bushes in a kind of square, near the statue of a bloke on a horse.' Pete and I reckoned that he must have spent the night in Jackson Square, in the shadow of the equestrian statue of General Andrew Jackson, saviour of the city when he defeated a superior British force at Chalmette, a few miles downriver.

It was difficult to glean any more than indistinct scraps of information from Ted. He lived in his own drink-happy world. But sometimes his eyebrows would arch and an expression of sad desperation would rest momentarily on his yellowed eyes. This had always touched some unknown, yet distantly familiar, chord in me. That morning in New Orleans it suddenly struck me: it was the same hopelessly pleading look of the trapped alcoholic that I had often seen on the face of my father. From that day on, I never joined in the amusement evoked by Ted's small misadventures.

The news of the extravagant outing aroused great resent-ment in Misery and Mr Yardley.

'Dinner at Antoine's, no less,' said the chief engineer, as he hacked at a piece of hard, singed beef. 'There's money being made somewhere.'

'The day of reckoning will come, sooner or later,' Misery said, absorbed in contemplating the distress that he hoped would be visited upon the lavish spenders when the whisky theft was revealed. This prospect was a source of consolation to a man whose authority had been so undermined by the captain's cheerful tolerance that people almost ignored him. He would sit at table after meals, slowly moving his dentures against his gums; perhaps he derived some obscure pleasure from the slight soreness this must have caused him. After the captain had left the table, Misery was wont to nod his head in little jerky movements, as if imagining the reverberations in Houston when the gaping hole was discovered; the

120

frowns, raised eyebrows, urgent consultations in the captain's cabin, with the agents crowded round the cargo plan, talking in loud accusatory voices.

Misery professed to be without enthusiasm for anything he might encounter in New Orleans. 'Them old balconies are dangerous — the whole place should be knocked down. It's only a tourist trap.'

He was prone to little accidents that earned him small sympathy. One evening when Mr Yardley and I were leaning over the rails, he appeared in his sober grey suit: 'Ah'll just go ashore for a stroll; get off this bloody ship for a while.' He went along the dockside with the reluctant gait of someone heading for a boring wasteland. Not five minutes later we were surprised to see him come limping back, his suit powdered with dust. As he made his way painfully up the gangway, Mr Yardley called out, 'Had a nice stroll, then?'

'Nice stroll be damned. I nearly broke my neck round the back of the cargo sheds. Slipped on a loaded French letter.'

Mr Yardley shook his big fuzzy head with an air of philosophic sadness.

'Yes indeed — that's the age we are living in. You can't go ashore these days without running the risk of maiming yourself on discarded condoms. The litter of licentiousness is strewn on the ground, waiting for the unwary foot. Someone's joy was your misfortune. Oh, indeed it's one of the reasons I don't venture ashore at all now.'

Mr Yardley sat reading in his cabin for most of the day. The door was always closed, but passersby winced at the scraping, wheezing coughing that was often heard from within. At about ten each evening he came out and shuffled on slippered feet to the starboard railings outside the foyer door. This was the quiet time; the rattling winches had stopped, the loud-voiced longshoremen had departed, the cargo sheds had been locked and our own determined merrymakers had rumbled ashore. There would be hardly anyone left on board.

He leaned over the railings, looking towards the rooftops over the top of the cargo sheds. Chained to the ship by his infirmity, he knew that he would never savour the delights of New Orleans or anywhere else. Sometimes he was racked by whistling, gurgling spasms, and gripped the railings tightly; when they had subsided, he would bow his head like a long distance runner. His spirit was unbowed, however. He was sustained by a tough Yorkshire stoicism. I suspected that he was also sustained by occasional nips of gin, even though alcohol was strictly forbidden by his doctor and he made some pretence of adhering rigorously to this injunction. At table he would sip water distastefully. 'Water. To think I've sunk so low. Once I was amongst the elite of British gin-drinkers.'

Yet whenever I joined him at the railings in the evening, his veined nose had acquired a dull glow. Once, in an attempt at awkward sympathy, I suggested that drink in moderation did no harm.

'Moderation. Yes indeed, Sparks. Moderation has always been my motto. That's how I've lived to this great age in this excellent state of health. People ask me how I achieved it and I always answer with the word 'moderation'. The ancient Greeks had a wise saying; "Moderation is the highest form of dissipation".'

Mr Yardley's dour humour, his caustic wit and satire rested on the mealtime table like a bottle of pungent sauce. His beady eyes roved about, focused on the fat face of the captain chewing with billowing jowls, noted Misery's unspoken spleen as he nibbled parsimoniously on morsels of food. The enmity between master and mate would have been discomfiting had it not been for Mr Yardley's presence. Every now and then, our eyes met momentarily and it was hard to suppress a smile.

Sitting down to table three times a day with this trio was like attending an entertainment. The captain played the role of the jolly, life-loving buffoon; the mate was the sour, embittered foil; while Mr Yardley regularly delivered lines of acid, worldly-wise commentary.

I had become obsessed by the characters and quirks of these three Englishmen. In my cabin and in the radio room, I used to draw their facial features over and over again; Captain Thompson's beer-bloated face, flat jutting lower lip and brambly eyebrows; Misery's narrow skull, resentful eyes and thin peevish mouth; Mr Yardley's rising steps of bushy hair, his florid nose and watery, piercing eyes. Even now, thirty years on, I can make a drawing of them that their families and friends would recognise.

Sometimes I wrote down scraps of conversation, dialogue and anecdotes while actually sitting at the saloon table. As a cover for this surreptitious annotation, I carried a book on electrical theory, letting it be known that I was studying for a higher qualification. Misery would sometimes give a faint smile of disparagement when he saw me jotting, as if doubting my ability to make any progress. Captain Thompson regarded my activity with amusement, something to be expected of a studious bookworm, who abstained from drink and 'black ham'.

But wily old Mr Yardley was not so easily deceived. One evening, after the tipsy captain had repeated his railway story before stumbling away from the table, Mr Yardley fixed a watery eye on me. 'At least there's one advantage in hearing the oft-told gem again; you don't have to bother writing it into your notebook, Sparks.'

14

Success on Stage and in Bedroom

One morning, about halfway through our stay in New Orleans, Toni entered the saloon humming joyfully. His small sallow face was bright with an expression of ecstasy. He served the breakfast with heightened flamboyance and style.

'What's the matter with the bugger?' queried Captain Thompson.

'Exhibitionism is part and parcel of this ship,' replied Mr Yardley tartly, turning meaningful eyes towards the master.

By mid-morning the news was all round the *Allenwell*. Toni had performed on stage the previous night in a dockside nightclub and, apparently, had received several standing ovations.

'I've been engaged to perform there twice nightly, Sparks,' he said excitedly, as he bustled about my cabin. 'This is the big breakthrough for me, it is.'

Pete and I decided to go and watch his act that night. We were puzzled.

'What you need most of all in those sort of clubs is a strong pair of lungs — and he certainly hasn't that', Pete said.

I heard Toni singing as he went about his tasks; he had a small husky voice of limited range. He favoured banal songs of sexual invitation, such as 'Take All of Me', and, if he thought anyone was looking, accompanied them with saucy smirks and fluttering eyelids.

However, Toni did have one remarkable accomplishment.

By furling his small tongue into a funnel, he could produce a burbling, melodic whistle. Not alone that, but he was able to cast this whistle across a room, his tongue-tip barely visible at the side of his mouth. He made mischievous use of this ventriloquistic talent. Several times during the North Atlantic crossing, while serving at table, a short piping whistle would be repeatedly heard. Captain Thompson would look about; Misery reckoned it came from creaking woodwork. On one occasion the master jumped up in some irritation and examined all the portholes in the saloon, imagining the sound had come from the wind pressing down through a loose one. After that Toni ceased this mealtime gambit; but it was a tribute to his expertise that he was never suspected by my three table companions.

He told me that he had once travelled on a tram in a South American port where the conductor signalled to the driver by means of a brass whistle attached to his uniform by a chain. The tram had halted momentarily and the conductor alighted to chat to a girl on the street. On playful impulse Toni simulated the conductor's whistle. The tram had taken off, with the conductor racing after it, yelling and waving. The passengers grinned; they were convulsed with laughter when the conductor was knocked down by an elderly lady riding a bicycle.

It was never clear how Toni got his chance in the nightclub, which I think was called 'The Riverboat'. Some suggested unkindly that he got on stage only because the proprietor, a tall, cadaverous individual, found him sexually endearing. The club was a big noisy cavern, with bar-counters along two sides, heavy wooden tables on the floor and a motheaten curtain hanging over the stage. This was a boisterous place where few tourists ventured; the haunt of hard-drinking sailors, bulky longshoremen, truckers, predatory homosexuals and hard-bitten prostitutes. When Pete and I arrived, we found that many members of our crew were already occupying the tables nearest the stage and so we had to perch on barstools midway down one counter.

The show opened with the five-piece band playing a few

numbers. The principal virtue of this ensemble was its ability to make itself heard above the multilingual din. Then a weighty stripper did a turn. Sweaty faces turned towards her; a few heavy hands tried to keep time with the drum-beat. There was a sporadic outburst of cheering as she discarded flimsy clothing. This was a place for brazen raunchiness rather than choreographic grace. Yet the loudest bouts of applause came when, near the end of her act, some of the fog of American, Dutch and English tobacco-smoke caught in her nose and she began to sneeze violently. Each sneeze brought a thunderous roar of applause. The curtain came down on her still sneezing.

She was followed by a wizened old man who played American and Cajun folkmusic on the fiddle. I thought he was marvellous, as dexterous and tuneful as any Irish fiddler I had ever heard, but few took any notice of him in this rough-house. When he finished, he bowed and left the stage unheeded.

Then came a roll of drums. The sinister proprietor appeared on the stage. He held up both arms in a Mosaic gesture to momentarily quell the hubbub.

'Ladies and gentlemen, mes amis, mein dammen und herren — for your entertainment, straight from London, England, where he has been starring in all the big shows, the one and only Toni.'

Toni came gliding onto the stage, moving hands and elbows like a Balinese dancer. He was clad in pink silk shirt and tight pastel-green trousers; a maroon cummerbund emphasised his wasp waist; the make-up round his eyes glittered in the spotlight. There were distinct notes of derision in the shouts which greeted him, but he was unconcerned, revelling at being the centre of attention.

He launched into one of his 'take me' songs, purring into the microphone which he held against his lipsticked mouth, wagging his hips about. I thought his performance mildly entertaining and no more; yet, for some reason which I have often pondered on since, he held the attention of that coarse-grained mob. Perhaps it was a self-assurance bordering on effrontery which temporarily subdued the onlookers. He finished his song to a hefty cheer, especially from our fellows in the forward tables.

But this was only a prelude to what was, by any standards, a remarkable tour de force. He licked his lips, made a few comic facial contortions, signalled to the band and began to whistle 'The Shepherd and his Dog'. This was a virtuoso display of accurate, melodic whistling, interlaced with variations and grace-notes, like fast intricate needlework. The whole place shook to the sound of feet stomping out the rhythm; the proprietor stood to one side, smiling. A huge roar burst out at the end, especially from the Germans and Scandinavians in the audience, who seemed particularly appreciative of his act. There were shouts of 'encore'. Toni responded with a marvellously masterful version of 'Whistling Rufus'. He united that international audience in a happy spirit of delight; men nodded to one another in elation. The entire audience rose to its feet, clapping and yelling, when he had finished. Toni would have carried on had not the proprietor leapt on the stage and shouted 'That's all for tonight, folks. Come again tomorrow and bring your friends.'

The unfortunate stripper who followed was met by disappointed groans. Her act seemed tawdry and boring and the audience returned to drinking and conversing; many were seen to purse their lips, as if attempting to emulate the star performer.

When, next day, I congratulated Toni, he glowed like an ember. 'I'm earning more as a cabaret artist than as steward on this old tub. The boss wants me to jump ship – says he'll fix me up with false papers and a work-permit. Wants to give me a contract. I've got to make my mind up by the time we come back from Houston.'

When he served at table, the accolades of the previous night still rang in his ears. He smiled to himself as he glided euphorically in and out of the saloon, setting down and removing plates with elaborate flourishes.

'That bugger is getting above himself,' said Captain

Thompson sullenly.

'Oh, I don't know,' contradicted Mr Yardley. 'He may have a brilliant career ahead of him in the world of entertainment. Why, in time, all of us sitting here at this table may be remembered principally because a famous artiste once served us our meals.'

'Bollocks.'

'Jealousy will get your nowhere,' replied Mr Yardley perceptively.

'He'll over-reach himself yet, you mark my words,' pouted the master.

Quite often, early in the morning before cargo-work began, a limousine of one kind or another would glide onto the dockside. From it would emerge the Lambton Worm, looking fresh and composed, his slacks without wrinkle, silk cravat about his neck. Few were around to witness his return on board or the undemonstrative waves of farewell he gave to the various sophisticated ladies at the wheels of their cars.

If he had the reputation of being an accomplished womaniser, it was not because he boasted of his conquests or indeed mentioned that he had any truck with women at all. This quiet, homely fellow, whom you imagined would prefer a rousing game of darts to the exertions of lovemaking, strolled off the ship in the afternoon. He always went alone and was casually, but carefully, dressed. Anyone watching him depart might think his purpose was to buy presents for his nieces and nephews back home.

'You won't find him hanging around any joints or nightclubs trying to pick up whores or strippers. He only goes to the best places' said Pete. 'But he never fails. I wish he'd tell me how he does it.'

One afternoon I went down the port alleyway to his cabin. He had the New Orleans *Times Picayune* spread out on his desk. I was surprised to see him combing through the pages devoted to cultural events. With a red pencil he circled notices and advertisements for art exhibitions, musical soirees, poetry readings, displays of sculpture.

'There's a big exhibition of modern paintings just opened in one of the art galleries,' he said, tapping the notice gently.

'I didn't know you were interested in modern art?'

'Not really — but they're great places to meet nice women.'

He explained that a picture, a piece of sculpture, a poem, or artefact of historical or cultural significance tended to exude an aura which created something of a bond amongst those gazing upon it or listening to it. Americans are invariably friendly and talkative, and in these favourable environments it was easy to strike up conversation with selected women whose dress and deportment indicated a certain opulence and graciousness. I have no doubt that his open, relaxed manner was a great asset. He chatted amiably and easily. His lack of facial attractiveness evoked trust. He told me that his invitations for a cup of coffee in the gallery or museum restaurant were rarely refused.

'I would never suggest a drink. That would be too pushy.'

I gathered that he had already had liaisons with two women, one a tourist from New York, the other a visiting businesswoman. Both of them had now left the city.

'That's really the best. A few days and they're gone. No regrets on either side.'

The exhibition of modern art must have created the kind of ambience in which he best operated. Pete told me that he had seen the Worm disembark next morning from a chauffeur-driven saloon.

The Lambton Worm seemed to contradict the commonly held belief that inveterate womanisers have a gaunt restiveness about them, ever hungry for conquests to assuage some insecurity in their personalities. In him there was a genial tranquillity. It put women at their ease at first encounter. Perhaps this was part of the secret of his success, together with a well-developed instinct for detecting love-hunger. Whether he left any wreckage in his wake, pregnancy or emotional trauma, I do not know, but somehow it seemed unlikely. Any envy his success may have evoked on board was diffused by his modesty and reticence.

Two or three of the younger, more presentable fellows had

embarked on affairs with what might be termed respectable women. Into the periphery of the entertainment area of every big port sidle love-lorn women from the staid residential suburbs. Neglected or deserted by husbands, divorced or with no men in their lives, they usually come quietly into the better bars, often in pairs for mutual support and encouragement. They might be coy at first contact, but if a man was friendly they opened up like flowers. It often led to a short but passionate love affair.

Some of these women had a vision of sailors as muscular, weathered fellows, hard with virility after weeks on the high seas. There were practical advantages in teaming up with a suitable seafarer. These housewives, plain secretaries, overlooked ones, did not want to have it off with the eager young man selling encyclopaedias door to door or the friendly neighbourhood postman. All kinds of complications might ensue, especially if passion flowered to deep attachment or love. But a sailor was here today and gone tomorrow; the affair had the attraction of being of limited duration, brought to a close by the blare of the ship's siren as it pulled away from the quay. The moment of parting might be one of regret but rarely one of anguish. There was neither time for the affair to deepen or to become soured by satiation. Both parties knew they were unlikely ever again to set eyes on one another.

In the case of the *Allenwell*, we were due to return to New Orleans for a week's loading. This would provide an opportunity for those who felt like going a second round. But the brevity and impermanence of the relationship remained. Letters might be promised when saying good-bye, but as often as not were never written or, indeed, expected. A brief encounter of passionate love was what both partners desired.

The scenes of such encounters were neat houses behind well-kept lawns or modest apartments in tree-lined suburbia. The women had motor cars which drew up unobtrusively at the back of the cargo sheds in the early morning to debauch the love-weary swains for their day's work on the *Allenwell*.

15

The Party Wanes

By the end of the second week in New Orleans many of our men were dragging themselves about the ship during the working day, dark pouches beneath bloodshot eyes. Misery's great scheme of restoration was marked by the sound of slow, reluctant chipping and the slovenly daubing of red lead on patches of rust which had been no more than cursorily scaled. The painting programme had not even begun. Rat reported to Mr Yardley that the clean-up of the engine room was well under way, but from the top of the stairway the chief engineer could see the piles of oil-rags merely swept into corners.

Misery picked his way peevishly about the decks, poking at undisturbed rust-bubbles with the toe of his shoe, bad-temperedly kicking scraps of dunnage out of his way. 'We'll set sail with the ship looking like a spotted wonder,' he seethed, surveying the measled superstructure.

The man meant to control and rouse to action the recalcitrant crew only stumbled out on deck at intervals. The bosun was in a constant state of alcoholic stupor.

'He should be replaced,' said Misery one day at table, directing his remark to a point in the air midway between Mr Yardley and the captain.

'I'll see about it,' said Captain Thompson gruffly. The very fact that this course was suggested by Misery made him reluctant to entertain it.

Ben Jennings was not the only casualty. A number of men had succumbed to successive nights of drinking, night-

131

clubbing and lovemaking. They were unable to rise from their bunks in the mornings and reported sick to Tommy Carey, the conscientious lamptrimmer, on whom some of the bosun's duties had fallen.

'Sick, my arse,' burst out the sturdy Thompson, who had no time for this kind of weakness and self-indulgence. 'If they don't get up and go about their work, I'll stop their wages.'

'Try to stop them going ashore tonight and see what happens,' Mr Yardley challenged.

The captain's threat prodded the lay-abeds onto their feet but, when one or two relapsed a day later, the captain, true to form, did nothing about it.

The standard of food deteriorated further, if that were possible. Breakfast, the only meal one could approach with modest expectations, began to lose its appeal. The rashers were burned black at the edges and the fried eggs had contracted into small brown discs. Even Captain Thompson began to complain.

'Steward,' he called to Toni, 'this bacon is as hard as a whore's heart.'

'Sorry, captain. Alex and Charlie is fighting like cats and dogs,' replied Toni, unnecessarily, for the uproar from the galley often overshadowed conversation at table. The bellows and obscenities were always accompanied by the banging of pots and pans. 'That kind of thing is always part of tribal war rituals,' explained Mr Yardley. On one occasion a shouting match was climaxed by a cascade of crockery falling to the galley floor.

'We'll be eating out of our hands before the voyage is over,' Misery murmured hatefully.

'How do you imagine people ate before plates, knives and forks came into being?' admonished Mr Yardley. 'Eating with one's fingers goes back into antiquity. The world has become too civilised.'

One lunch-time the row in the galley took a distinctly uncivilised turn. The combatants emerged into the foyer. Old Charlie, brandishing a long-handled pot like a medieval mace, confronted Little Alex, who was armed with an iron ladle. Captain Thompson, hungrily awaiting his meal, rose from his seat and advanced with some menace towards the pair. They backed off into the galley and went about their duties. Thompson stood in the doorway for a moment and then, with a grunt, resumed his seat. Mr Yardley eyed him contemptuously. The incident epitomised the disorder on board and the master's tolerance of it. Any man worthy of his stripes would have had the cooks summoned to his cabin later, and would have docked them a week's wages if they did not behave in future. When the captain had left the table, Mr Yardley said, 'He can't take action because he's boozing with those grub-spoilers and piss-pot jerkers night and day.'

'The day of reckoning will come,' said Misery.

By this time there could be no doubt that the captain was aware of the wholesale theft on board but had chosen to turn a blind eye to the matter. He himself, however, was not in any way involved in the criminal activity.

'Don't worry — he's too cunning to be mixed up in it,' said Mr Yardley. 'It would be more than his master's certificate is worth if it came to light. Oh, he knows what's happening all right, but he's run away from it. Wants to be popular with one and all.'

Misery never joined in any discussion of this kind. He kept his intense dislike of the captain to himself. One sometimes got the impression that he obtained some kind of perverse enjoyment from chewing silently on his own bile, poisonous and corrosive though it was to his personality.

The mate had a number of consolations to help him endure the nights of disturbed sleep, the execrable food and the work-shy deck crew. The unloading of cargo on our 6,000-ton ship was ahead of schedule, thanks to the efficient American stevedoring; it looked as if we would be away before the middle of our third week. This would put an end to the era of gaiety and abandon; it would bring closer the day of revelation.

Misery could barely hide his pleasure when one of the deckhands, a cheeky fellow who once had laughed in his face, met with an accident. Apparently this reveller had been expelled from a nightclub when he had burst into song during a striptease act. Continuing to sing, he had stepped out into the street so that his voice might reach a wider audience and had been run over by a truck laden, rather fittingly, with cases of liquor.

This accident sustained Misery's belief that harsh retribution always hung over the heads of those who indulged in drunkenness and sensuality.

'He's encased in plaster in the hospital. Be there for at least a month. We won't be taking the bugger back on board again,' he reported to the captain at breakfast, with an expression that came near to being joyful.

'How badly hurt is he?' demanded the master.

'Doctor says he has multiple fractures of the pelvis.'

'Broke his arse, in other words,' snapped the captain, closing the conversation.

Misery was further comforted by two matters that had for him a pleasing outcome. Both concerned Pete. The third mate had been threatening to buy a trombone for a fortnight. He had haunted several music shops, repeatedly examining their stock, haggling over prices until his appearance on the premises had drawn frowns from the attendants. Misery had expressed the hope that the dreaded instrument might never be bought at all. Then one afternoon Pete returned to the ship cradling a trombone. He displayed it proudly to me in his cabin.

'Well Sparks — what do you think, eh?'

'Quite a few dents in it here and there, aren't there?'

'That's the whole point. It's an antique. The fellow in the shop told me it had been played by some of the most famous musicians in New Orleans.'

'It's had a long life so.'

'Certainly. That's why it's tone is so mellow. Listen.' He blew a long blaring note. This brought Misery round. A look of pain descended on his bony face.

'What's that fucking thing, third mate?'

'Actually it's a new plumbing invention. You pour water in

one end and it disappears.'

'That thing will disappear completely if it's played in the accommodation after nine o'clock at night.'

'Don't worry, I can't play it yet. I have to learn.'

Misery turned on his heels and strode away. His anger turned to malevolent satisfaction a day later when an ugly rash broke out on Pete's mouth. Not only that, but it developed into painful sores. The cheap metal alloy of this bogus antique may have been the cause, or perhaps the mouthpiece had been caressed by diseased lips just before Pete had purchased it. He put the trombone away disconsolately, never to blow it again on board.

A few days later another object of Misery's detestation seized up. Pete's radio, its loudspeaker quivering under the strain of full volume, contracted a severe bout of electronic laryngitis. Pete, under the mistaken impression that the radio officer ought to be adept at repairing faulty radios, brought it to me. After some ineffectual poking about, pressing the valves in case one of them might have worked loose, I shook my head. Pete had to take it ashore to a repair shop; Misery was pleased to hear that it would not be restored to vibrant voice until we had returned from Houston.

'No wonder it packed up, at full blast night and day. We might get some sleep now.'

The event that afforded Misery most opportunity for gloating was the disappearance of the bosun. He made the announcement at breakfast with unconcealed satisfaction.

'Where's he gone?' Captain Thompson demanded.

Misery gave an unconcerned shrug. 'He was seen leaving the ship yesterday morning. Hasn't come back.'

'If he's not back by tomorrow, we'll have to call the police.'

'The bugger could have fallen into the river or been run over by one of them old trams,' said Misery hopefully. He was enjoying the captain's discomfort, knowing that the last thing Thompson wanted was to have the police and the agents involved. Already on bad terms with both, the master had no desire to provide them with more evidence of the

135

laxity on board.

After breakfast the captain called Pete and me to his cabin, and charged us with the task of finding Ben Jennings.

'Bloody rot,' burst out Pete as we came down the stairs, 'what can we do? Search every dosshouse and dive in the city? This is a job for the police.'

All we could do was make a few haphazard enquiries ashore and ask our shore-goers to do the same. Jennings's colleagues in the crew's quarters said that he had lately been given to dark moods of melancholy. The man who, at the start of the voyage, had voiced his unease about the crew's disposition to drink had himself drunk so much that his mental faculties were now showing evidence of damage. There was no sign of him after two days. His whereabouts was the subject of much speculation.

'He could be anywhere, that man,' said Pete irritably, returning tired after a search of some of the dockside bars. 'He could have got on a train to somewhere or be floating down the Mississippi with a buzzard standing on his belly.'

The following afternoon I went ashore, not with any express intention of looking for the bosun, but to read in the sun on a bench in a quiet part of the old residential area. Only the chiming of a clock within a nearby house and the hum of honey-seeking bees in the flowers could be heard in that peaceful bower. After a few hours I rose, stretched and wandered off on sandalled feet. I paused at the entrance to Pirate's Alley, a picturesque narrow laneway, once the haunt of the Barataria buccaneers. Here itinerant artists displayed their pictures, propped against the walls. Some undertook on-the-spot portraits of passersby in charcoal, chalk or pencil. At the far end an elderly artist with long white hair was thus engaged. He sat on a small stool, his clipboard on his knee, glancing at the sitter, making quick strokes, raising his head to study his subject, bending again to his work.

I was almost upon him when I was astonished to see that the sitter was none other than our missing bosun. His eyes were closed.

'Hey bosun!'

'Don't wake him up now, hear? Good thing I always start with the eyes — that's the hardest part.'

The bosun's usual woebegone appearance had been replaced by a weary tranquillity. The ravaged features of that square face were softened in repose. His mouth, into which such copious quantities of whisky had disappeared, hung open slightly. The artist achieved a remarkably perceptive representation of Ben Jennings. Granted he had an ideal sitter, who did not shift about, or purse his lips self-consciously; but he had captured something of the sadness and despair that shadowed the bosun's face during his waking hours.

'Best thing I've done for a long time. Guess I never done better,' said the artist wistfully, contemplating the work he had just completed. I wondered what ambitions and hopes that artist had as a young man, what kind of life he now led and what the future held for him.

Suddenly the silence was broken by a loud sneeze. The bosun sat bolt upright and wiped his mouth with the back of his hand. It took him a minute to regain his sense of time and place. Then he took the portrait in his big unwashed hands and gazed at it dully. Apparently satisfied, he hauled a fistful of notes from his trouser pocket and handed them over. The artist rolled up the portrait and inserted it into a cardboard cylinder.

'How are you, bos'?'

'Hello, Sparks.'

'Are you all right?'

'I suppose I am.'

'Where have you been these last three days?'

'Been? Just wandering about, I suppose.'

'Let's go back to the ship.'

'The ship? Oh yes. Okay.'

I left him at the door of his cabin. He hesitated about entering, the cylinder clutched in one paw, as if reluctant to once again confine himself to the scene of so much solitary drinking.

His return caused something of a stir on board. Even now,

so long afterwards, I still regret that I had not the compassionate wisdom to conceal the circumstances of his discovery.

'Getting his picture painted?' snorted Misery.

'Oh come now, Mr Muir, have you no feeling for art?' chided Mr Yardley.

'Painting the fucking ship is what he should be doing.'

Some of the less charitable knocked on his door, shouting 'Any chance of seeing your picture, bos'.' The door was never opened. All anybody heard was the occasional clink of bottle and glass. The extent of the harm he was doing himself became apparent only later when his supply of whisky ran out.

There were others on board whose zest for high living had diminished through overindulgence. The flickering flame was only rekindled in the evenings. There was less post-midnight shouting and yelling. Those who had established steady relationships with women had fallen into a more subdued pattern of visitation. Some men found themselves barred from various clubs where their nocturnal rumbustiousness had caused disruption. The frenetic pleasure-seeking was subsiding under the weight of satiation.

There was another cogent reason for the decline in exuberance. The cornucopia of pilfered whisky, which had paid for so many nights of celebration, was now beginning to echo emptily. Even the personal caches of the dedicated whisky-drinkers contained only a remnant.

It was out of the question that the Water of Life might be replenished from the cargo destined for Houston. The bright dockside lights lit up the decks at night. Moreover, a police car now occasionally toured along the dockside during the small hours; it was several times seen to stop opposite the *Allenwell*; one morning at 3 am two officers came on board and walked about the decks for ten minutes. Even the most desperate on board would not take any risk. Everybody realised that the eventual discovery of the gaping hole in the cargo would set off an almighty uproar. Anyone foolish enough to be caught red-handed broaching the hatch might have to carry the can for all the missing liquor. Only when the ship was under way to Texas would the whisky-bereft have a final chance to lay their hands on further treasure; with it could be funded a last uproarious fling when the ship returned to New Orleans.

Captain Thompson was restless to be back at sea. He had enjoyed himself immensely but, true seafarer that he was, he wanted to feel again the sea breeze on his ruddy face, sense the moving deck under his feet, hear the sound of the waves breaking against the prow. He would indeed have much preferred to be heading out into a cold windy sea rather than a two-day cruise over the placid waters of the Gulf of Mexico, followed by a sixty-mile journey up the canal to Houston.

At last, one sunny morning, the final sling of cargo was hoisted out of the hold, dangled in mid-air and then lowered to the dockside. The rattle of the winches ceased, the derricks were stowed, and our jaded crew pulled the hatch-covers into place. Our memorable stay in New Orleans had come to an end.

16

Moon Over the Mexican Gulf

Our departure from New Orleans had an after-taste of our revelrous sojourn there and an ominous portent of what awaited us on our return. On the quay were several women waving goodbye to their erstwhile lovers; there were also two police cars whose occupants had emerged to eye us as we cast off.

Some of the ebullient ladies shouted up intimacies to their men. Not all our fellows responded wholeheartedly. There were one or two coy ones who hunched their shoulders as they went about their work on deck.

'It's the first time those guys have seen their women in the sober light of day, and it's a bit of a shock to them,' Pete offered as explanation.

The policemen, slack-bellied and sun-glassed, chewed gum thoughtfully. They had the appearance of an overweight sheriff's posse watching a crowd of desperadoes leaving town. Also on hand to see us off was a delegation from the shipping agency; there were no friendly farewells from this group, as if they sought to distance themselves from visitors who had outstayed their welcome and had acquired a bad reputation. Their countenance might have been less grim were it not that we were due to return from Texas in ten days' time.

The broad river stretched ahead, rippling in the sunlight. The pilot called 'half ahead' and a gentle bow-wave glided out on either side and broke distantly behind us against the banks in a crumble of frothy water.

140

The most notable feature of our passage downriver was that the pilot bore a remarkable resemblance to the captain, both in figure and in temperament. Two soul companions, two fat old men, bonded by a mutual merriness, had providentially found one another. They stood together at the windows, and competed in telling jokes and stories, bellowing with laughter. Their jollity was infectious; Pete and I and the man at the wheel began to laugh, even when we overheard no more than a few words of the salty humour.

Down on deck the crew worked with some semblance of willingness. It was as if they were prompted to atone for the days of neglect. Many were glad to be back to the routine of sea-life, removed from the temptations to which they had so eagerly succumbed. They tidied the scraps of dunnage and litter into piles, ready for dumping over the side once we had reached the open sea. They hosed down the decks and swept the scuppers clear of grime. The bosun made an appearance; his attempt to make a show of authority was feeble, his performance largely went unnoticed.

It was late afternoon when the wide plain of the blue sea appeared ahead and the white sentinels on either bank of the South Pass came into view. After the fat pilot had jumped aboard his launch, exchanging shouted farewells with our beaming master, we made a slow turn to starboard, heading west for Galveston.

Captain Thompson went out to the wing of the bridge, breathing deeply of the sea air, scanning the waters all round. He shrugged his shoulders several times as if to slough off the smells of gasoline, cargo, perfume, riverbanks and magnolia blossom that had flavoured the air in New Orleans. Misery stayed out of his way, a spleenful presence on the opposite wing, and did not return to the wheelhouse until the captain had gone below.

The sun began to go down, laying a sparkling carpet of gold for us to follow. As it sank into the sea, it turned high streamers of feathery cloud a deep crimson. I enthused about this enchanting sight to Misery.

'Did you ever see such a marvellous red sunset, Mr Muir?'

'There will be some red faces in Houston when it's discovered just how much fucking whisky has been stolen.'

That night in the Gulf of Mexico was one of the most memorable I ever experienced at sea. After the sun went down, the whole western sky was charged with a luminous green light. Then the sky began to turn a dark blue, the stars appeared and seemed to lower themselves towards the earth, many twinkling brightly. Later on an enormous moon emerged out of the smooth sea, rested a little on the rim and then began to float slowly upwards. Its colour changed to cream, then to chalky white and finally, when it was high in the sky, to a bright porcelain blue.

When I had finished the last watch, I climbed up to the open deck by the monkey island to absorb the scene. It was almost as bright as day while our battered old ship murmured along over the sparkling ocean. This was a moment, rare in adulthood, when some of the wonder of childhood briefly returns; you gaze about, full of delight, stirred by vague longings and hopes. Then it is that you realise, sadly, how much you have lost the capacity to be exhilarated by natural beauty, to dream wondrous dreams. The enchantment of childhood and the ecstasy of early adolescence have been eroded and stifled by the obsessive concerns of the adult world. This was the kind of night which compensated for the dreary days of heaving decks and grey wind-tumbled skies. It induced a delighted tranquillity; you wanted to be nowhere else, to hold these moments for as long as you could, to try to let the scene become part of your being so that it remained somewhere in your memory for as long as you lived.

When at length I climbed down to the bridge-deck, Brad had come on watch. He was leaning over the parapet.

'You have to keep an eye out for shrimp boats in these parts, Sparks. It's hard to see their lights on a bright night like this,' he said, scanning the moon-glittered sea. I saw a man walking on the deck below, but thought nothing of it; anyone might stroll around on a warm night like this. On my way down I noticed the light off in the captain's cabin. But Pete's was still on and I knocked on his door to bid him goodnight. He was not there and I supposed he was down in the bathroom taking a shower. I read in my bunk for a while and had just put off the light when I heard voices outside. Then something heavy was dumped on the floor of Pete's cabin. My inquisitiveness was aroused. I leaned forward and put my ear to the iron bulkhead. I recognised Pete's voice, but I could not make out who the other person was, and indeed was never able to discover his identity. The big drawer beneath Pete's bunk was pulled out. It came as something of a shock to hear the clink of bottles being handled and stowed. It took a while to accept the fact that Pete had garnered a case of whisky from the raid that, I later heard, had taken place that night.

I was hurt that Pete had never confided in me; I would not have betrayed his trust. Perhaps he felt that I might have disapproved and tried to discourage him. He was a frugal, self-sufficient fellow, who never touched a drink, was without acquisitive instincts. But he had succumbed to the temptation to get in on the bonanza that so many were enjoying. When goodies are there for the taking — free drink, tobacco, samples of merchandise — it arouses a greed even in the most decent souls, especially when others are crowding round grabbing all they can; a loot-frenzy surges, touches honest breasts with a deprived feeling of being left out of the beanfeast. I too felt this tremor, but timidity and some in-bred scruples, which I found hard to discard, combined to keep it at bay.

Pete never made any mention of his barter-scheme during the following days, and it cast a small shadow over our friendship. Looking back on it, I regret that I had not the courage and concern for his welfare to broach the subject and to try to dissuade him from carrying out his enterprise. As it later transpired, he had made a deal with a black man in New Orleans to sell him a case of whisky on our return. He had no suspicion that this man was an agent of the federal authorities.

If memory serves me right, we reached Galveston the following evening and were directed by telegram to anchor in the roads until the next morning. There were other ships at the anchorage, all with their deck lights on, as were ours. Anyone who had neglected to stock up with hootch had now missed their last chance. One man who had failed to grasp this fact was the bosun. He had been in a deep drunken slumber the previous night. As it turned out, he had enough bottles to sustain him for another week, but when the well eventually ran dry, he would undergo a very hard time.

After taking the morning traffic list, I went out to the bridge to look at Galveston. It lay behind a long protective sea-wall, some ten miles in length, built after the hurricane disaster of 1900. We were opposite the older part of the town, near where we were to berth to discharge our small quantity of cargo of textiles. It looked like a sunlit eiderdown of red roofs, white gables and clumps of dark green trees. The flat sandy coastline, indented with shallow bays and lagoons, stretched in a long white line one either side, under the immense blue Texan sky. This was once the hideout of French pirates whose nautical skill and detailed knowledge of the shoals, shallows and currents gave them an advantage over pursuers.

We came alongside in mid-morning. Our cargo was discharged by mid-afternoon. We were the only ship in the old port area, and when work ceased that Saturday, the dock was deserted. We were to lie there in quietude until the pilot boarded on Monday morning to take us up the canal to Houston.

On Sunday afternoon I took a walk ashore, along pleasant streets lined with acacia trees and crusty shrubbery that sucked up whatever moisture there was in the sandy soil. There was not a soul about; one could almost hear the quiet breathing of siesta-takers behind the slatted shutters of the neat wooden houses. Tall sun-weathered telegraph and electricity poles splayed out wires to the red-tiled roofs and white clapboard walls. The yellow streets and sidewalks shimmered in the sun.

17

Texan Backwater

The *Allenwell*, with a lanky Texan pilot giving orders on the bridge, nosed her way into the canal for the sixty-mile journey inland to Houston. We passed through a metropolis of petrochemical plants, humming and hissing, their thin steel chimneys waving handkerchiefs of smoke. The intricate hives of buildings were interlaced with a mesh-work of piping which joined them to the acres of massive silvery storage tanks. When we left the tremor of industry behind us, our watery road ran straight into an immense flat plan. It seemed sandy and barren, though my Uncle Jim had told me that he had once worked on a peach-farm here-abouts. The sun glared harshly on land dotted with stunted trees and little dusty balls of tumbleweed.

On the bridge Captain Thompson was not at his best. For a start, the pilot was a laconic sort, as if years of peering along the canal had narrowed his vision of life, and he did not welcome our captain's flippant distractions. There was another reason for the master's touch of grumpiness. The presence of land so close on either side made him uneasy. Most of his life had been spent giving a wide berth to shorelines, headlands, reefs and sandbanks. He was the picture of the ruddy-faced British seafarer, weaned and nurtured on harsh North Sea and North Atlantic wind and wave, on rain and sleet. He was happiest on the wide ocean, no matter how stormy it might be. The Mississippi had been bad enough, but here we were confined between the narrow concrete banks of a canal leading us miles into the landscape, with the smell and feel of the sea left far behind. Perhaps he feared that some misguided hand might pull an enormous plug, draining the canal and leaving us high and dry. An engine breakdown or a steering malfunction might leave us in some lonely lay-by for days on end until repairs could be effected. Indeed, some distance on, we passed a deserted basin where an old Greek freighter lay rusting and lifeless. Captain Thompson frowned at it. To him this was akin to coming across the sun-bleached skeleton of a steer in the desert, whose eyeless skull warned wayfarers not to tarry long in this place.

The vast shelterless land under the endless blue sky made one feel vulnerable. You realised how lonely and overawed a family of settlers must have felt in their covered wagon, the cowpoke on his nag, the line of mounted soldiers, tiny dots moving along the sand-plain. Little wonder that the combative Americans set about countering the eeriness and solitude of the country's great spaces, laying down networks of railways and metalled highways, marking the map with hundreds of airports, big and small. The driver zipping along the roadway may see the buzzards wheeling aloft in the hot air currents, see long ranges of barren mountain on the horizon, but the radio is on full blast. From it comes a cacophony of comforting voices from dozens of stations, pouring out news, weather forecasts, pollen-counts, the time of day, the temperature, traffic information, details of barbecues, hoe-downs and the fantastic sale at Kaltenbrunner's emporium on the corner of Main and Jefferson. There is the reassuring sight of the line of telegraph poles beside the wide roadway, telephone kiosks in the most isolated places, television aerials over every solitary gas-station.

In the distance ahead a tall white obelisk glimmered in the sunlight.

'What's that thing, pilot, sticking up like a prick?' asked the master, focusing his binoculars.

'Why, captain, that there's the San Jacinto battlefield monument — where Sam Houston whipped the Mexicans. Eighteen thirty-six that was.'

'One thing you can't beat is a Mexican whore. Veracruz used to be a great place before the war. You could get your end away for a few pesos.'

The soaring obelisk was in an oasis of beautiful parkland. When we came abreast of it, a wide basin opened out to one side. Berthed there was an impressive battleship, festooned with flags and bunting; its light grey paintwork was spotless, its brasswork gleaming, menacing guns now stoppered.

'Why, captain, that there's the battleship *Texas*. Headquarters of General Dwight D. Eisenhower during, the invasion of France. He was a Texan, born in Denison, the pilot said with uninhibited American pride. 'Some man that. Some ship too.'

Misery and I went out to the port wing to view this famous warship. It was now a national monument and tourist attraction, its klaxon never again to sound 'action stations' nor its gums to belch fire. Misery refused to be impressed. A thin supercilious smile stretched his mouth as he focused his binoculars on the massive steel structure.

'They used have a dozen kinds of ice cream on them American ships during the war,' he sneered, implying that this kind of self-indulgence weakened the Americans' resolve to fight with the same gritty fortitude as did the British. 'Imagine going into battle with a ship full of niggers, dagos and wops.'

To him this explained the vital difference that made the British navy infinitely superior to that of the United States. The British ships were manned by sturdy, fresh-faced fellows, courageous lads with simple Anglo-Saxon names like Smith and Brown; these stalwarts were well able to endure hardships, to fight tenaciously when challenged. The American ships, on the other hand, were burdened by the presence of villainous and craven men of Greek, Armenian and African origin; Hispanics and Philippinos and Poles with unpronounceable names full of 'x's, 'y's, and 'z's like complicated algebraic formulae. This melange might be further vitiated by venal Jews and troublesome Irish. All right, the captain or admiral might be of British heritage, but there were an awful lot of people on board whose complexions and facial contours betrayed their base ancestry. These were the ice-cream eaters, the Coca-Cola sippers whose eyes flickered with fear when the alarm klaxon whooped and the 16-inch guns boomed.

British sealore is replete with wartime stories of British courage and composure, contrasted with Mediterranean hysteria and unreliability. Boom! The torpedo strikes the doughty British ship dead centre. A huge column of smoke billows upwards, black as the uniform of the U-boat captain. The stricken vessel is going down fast. But the men, with the sole exception of some Maltese galleyboys, set about launching the lifeboats without fuss, buoyed by wry humour and stiff upper lips. Comradeship comes to the fore. The lamp-trimmer had been knocked cold when the lavatory cistern fell on his head. A colleague finds him and carries him along the alleyway, now swirling with rapidly rising water. Even the bosun's foul-beaked parrot is rescued. Brave deeds are performed, but in an unobtrusive almost shamefaced way in case any act of heroism might be misinterpreted as showing off. There is no rush into the lifeboats.

What a different scene, what a contrast when a similar disaster befalls a ship manned by excitable Italians, Greeks, Spaniards, Egyptians and Lebanese! No need to shout 'Abandon ship'. While the explosion is still reverberating about the bulkheads, there is a headlong stampede to the boat deck. Too bad if you are unfortunate enough to fall on your face in a narrow alleyway. Nobody will stop to help you. On the contrary, you will be trampled on by dozens of panic-propelled feet. The boat deck is a confusion of gesticulating individuals, as men rush back and forth, bumping into one another. It's each man for himself. The captain and cook fight to be the first into the lifeboat. One man is seen carrying an enormous item of hand-tooled Indian brassware, intended for his mother in Piraeus. Chaos everywhere. Well no, not everywhere. Unseen by the struggling mob, the wily chief officer, a swarthy fellow with a head of greasy curls, has got away in the motor launch with a few accomplices.

These worthies have thoughtfully taken with them a goodly store of provisions, including a dozen bottles each of ouzo and retsina. They make off at great speed, heedless of the curses and pleas of their erstwhile shipmates. At the subsequent court of inquiry, held in Athens at war's end, the chief officer asserts that he left the scene 'in order to fetch help'. Fortunately for him, the presiding judge is a distant relative on his mother's side and he gets off with a verbal reprimand.

As we chugged further inland, many of our crew came out to loll about the deck, watching the featureless landscape slide slowly by. Some sat on the cover of the Number Two hatch which had been so efficiently broached two nights before. The raiders must have been uneasy at the imminent exposure of their depredations. Later, on the homeward voyage, when I was piecing together the whisky-saga, I heard that the final harvest had been dispersed about the ship, well away from the living quarters. I heard too that some had taken the precaution of carefully wiping all fingerprints from the bottles in case they might be discovered in a search by police.

Most of our fellows regarded our six-day sojourn in Houston as an opportunity for rest and recuperation. They intended to catch up on the nights of sleep lost in New Orleans, to erase dark pouches from beneath eyes, to write letters to neglected ones back home, to restore senses jaded and blunted by excessive revelry. After this period of refreshment, they could look forward to a final uproarious fling in New Orleans, provided that the whisky secreted aboard remained undiscovered.

If there were any on board who imagined they might have to fight off the temptation to make merry in Houston, they need not have worried. While that city was no more than an indistinct blur of skyscrapers in the haze of the horizon, the pilot called 'dead slow ahead'. We were coming abreast of a wide basin, lifeless as a stagnant black lake, with a few derelict buildings about it. A row of antiquated cranes stood on the cracked concrete of the dockside. Behind the dock were skeins of rusting railway tracks with tumbleweed and bushes growing amongst the sleepers; long lines of redundant freight wagons stretched out onto the plain. The only structure of any height was a row of disused grain silos, standing to attention like veterans in a commemoration parade. However, a modern metalled road was to be seen skirting the dock area; enormous trucks passed along it, dragging long cloaks of dust after them. Wooden telegraph poles, looking frail and lonesome, marked the road as it disappeared into the flat distance.

'Here we are, captain', said the pilot, instructing the man at the wheel to make a turn to starboard.

'Houston, pilot? This is like a ghost town'.

The pilot explained that this was one of the original basins constructed when the ship canal was first built. Houston, the hub of the American aeronautical, rocket and space industry, a hive of scientists, engineers and astronauts computer-planning to launch men onto the moon, seemed aeons away from this scene. This was America circa 1910.

Captain Thompson was annoyed. It was not so much that he wanted to wake up in the mornings in the shadow of skyscrapers, but he felt slighted that the agents had consigned his ship to this dusty backwater, like a hobo hustled round to the kitchen door. A grimy tug, perfectly in keeping with the environment, detached itself from the quayside and slid forward to nudge us alongside. We had the place to ourselves apart from a few senile vessels tied up on the other side. We were going to have to use our own derricks to discharge and load cargo.

'How do we get to Houston from here?' Pete asked the pilot.

'I guess there's a bus. But it don't go very often. Don't miss the last one back — it's a mighty long walk.'

When a representative of the agents came on board, the captain was uncharacteristically curt. He suspected that a bad report had preceded us and that the agents thought it prudent to dock us in this outstation.

The atmosphere on board was subdued. Nobody was in

151

any hurry to set foot on the hallowed ground of Texas. When the captain gave out a 'sub' on the evening of our second day there, men only drew enough to be able to go ashore for a few beers, buy souvenirs and post letters and cards home. When Misery set the crew to painting, under the direction of Tommy Carey, they wielded their brushes agreeably, seeing it as a form of leisurely therapy that would help renew their spirits.

The unloading of cargo went on steadily; work on the much-abused Number Two hold was not expected to begin until the third day. The level of drinking dropped off. For the first time in weeks, many men drew their daily six-can beer ration from Ted, signed for it and sipped it slowly as they lounged about the decks in the warmth of the evenings. Few ventured into Houston. Having become so used to strolling off the ship straight into the throbbing life of the French Quarter of New Orleans, everybody found it a tedious business to pick one's way across the railway tracks and tramp over the weedy ground to the bus stop. On my sole visit to Houston, I had to wait for over an hour for the bus. Despite the time of the year, the heart was intense and the glare from the flat scrubland brought on a headache. All I can recall of Houston is the intimidating traffic, the hot pavements, soaring skyscrapers, men wearing ten-gallon hats and ornate cowboy boots, and the amount of Spanish heard in the streets.

Captain Thompson also made only one visit to the city. He was stung that the agents had not seen fit to invite him ashore in the customary manner. The likelihood was that the agents in New Orleans had forewarned their colleagues in Houston of the risks involved in offering hospitality to our lively master. But he had a small measure of revenge. When one of the agents' men came on board one morning to collect some documents, Thompson told him that they had been mislaid. He would probably lay hands on them by the afternoon and would deliver them himself, provided a car was sent for him. The man left the ship annoyed. What arrived on the dockside that afternoon was a shabby taxi.

Thompson made it clear to the Mexican driver that the cab was at his disposal for the rest of the day, to be charged up to the agency. According to his later report, he had chucked the bundle of documents across the counter in the agency office and then had taken off on a conducted tour of the city, with the cabman as guide. The Mexican began to extol the delights of his native cuisine and they ended the evening in a restaurant, with the taxi-driver as the captain's guest. They parted company, late that night, the best of friends; Thompson was chuckling to himself as he climbed the gangway.

'I've a good mind to charge the bill for the meal to the agents and all', he beamed at breakfast the next morning.

'You dined well, I take it?' Mr Yardley asked.

'Tortillas, tabasco sauce, chillies, garlic — hotter than any bloody Indian curry', said the captain with remembered relish. 'I was blowing fire from both ends all night. I thought my ring would take alight.'

Mr Yardley nodded. 'That's precisely the kind of colourful comment they ought to include in the *American Good Food Guide.*'

On the third day in the 'Ghost Dock', as the crew had christened our strange berthage, the moment of revelation at last arrived. In the early afternoon the slingloads of whisky-crates started to come out of the Number Two hold, to be loaded straight into big trucks on the dockside. This was one day that Misery did not take a siesta; he stood, arms folded, at the edge of the hatch. Two of the agents' men were there also, armed with clipboards and tally sheets. It was quite clear that they were aware that much was amiss with our cargo; one man held a little metal computator, which he clicked every time a slingload came out; a third man counted the crates on the dockside before they were loaded onto the trucks. The deck crew on cargo duty acted with a show of indifference, but they watched the scene from the corners of their eyes.

On my way up to the bridge deck for a grandstand view, I noticed Little Alex peering out of one of the saloon's for'ard portholes. From the bridge one could see a number of off-duty men lounging about, watching the expressive hand-signals of the head longshoreman as each slingload came up, was swung slowly out from the ship and lowered gently onto the quayside.

There must have been a certain sadness amongst the onlookers. The source of solace, joy and not a little profit would soon be no more. There might still be a secret hoard on board, but when it had been spent in New Orleans, the final curtain would come down. These cases of the best Scottish whisky being so purposefully stowed on the trucks were destined for greedy American guzzlers, people whose taste-buds had long been blunted by rye, bourbon, mash and other inferior distillations and who could never properly appreciate the exquisite tang of Scotch.

When the last sling went over the side, Misery and the two agents drew together. The tally sheets were consulted. Heads were shaken. Misery held up his hand to the head longshoreman to order a temporary cessation of work. He and one of the men climbed down into the hold to look about before the rest of the cargo was unloaded. When they climbed up, they all went straight to his cabin to inspect the cargo plan and manifest. After a short interval they came up the stairs to the captain's cabin and knocked urgently. From the door of the radio room I could hear voices raised in argument and, as I tiptoed past on my way down, I heard Captain Thompson shouting, 'How do I know, eh? How do I know?'

Finally the agents came down, faces dark with frowns, clutching their briefcases. They hurried down the gangway, jumped into their cars and sped away. When Misery appeared in the foyer, there was a look of vindictive triumph on his face. Soon the news was out and spread like wildfire round the ship.

'Eighty fucking cases missing, Sparks,' whistled Pete innocently. 'That's 960 bottles. An awful lot of whisky.'

It certainly was, considering that our total crew was around forty-five persons. By my reckoning, at least fifteen had in no way participated in the theft.

Two hours later one of the senior men from the shipping agency boarded. A big red-faced man, he stomped his way aggressively up to the captain's quarters. While he was closeted there, a police car drew up on the quayside; a tall captain and two officers came on board. They also went straight to the master's cabin. Misery was summoned, carrying the cargo plan.

There was now some disquiet amongst the raiders of the *Allenwell*. Men spoke in whispers, conferred in corners. Some pessimists predicted a stem-to-stern combing of the vessel. A search might reveal at least some of the caches. If that happened, then individuals might be selected for questioning.

Beams of rage and vilification were directed at a few uncivic-minded persons, the bosun amongst them, who had rejected all persuasion to part temporarily with their life-sustaining bottles in the interests of collective caution. Ben Jennings continued to drink away in his cabin, as did one of the engine-room greasers, Reilly by name.

'If there's trouble, these piss-artists will get us all hung,' the men said indignantly.

In the saloon that evening Misery preened himself vengefully. 'A lot of questions are being asked up there,' he said, nodding to the deckhead above. 'And questions will be asked when we get home.'

'Our esteemed master won't talk his way out of this one so easily,' chimed Mr Yardley. 'Cunard will think twice about chartering this benighted ship again.'

There was a pallid glow of spleen about Misery. He knew that reports would be made out, sent clicking on the teleprinter to New York, London and to the owners in Sunderland. Cunard would lodge a claim against the *Allenwell*. The insurers would be involved. There might even be a court case. The reverberations would last for months. The red face of Mr Hall, our marine superintendent, would be waiting on the quayside in London as we drew alongside.

'That's what happens when there's no discipline on board a ship. When I was master, nothing like this would have happened,' said Misery.

'Yes — but what a dull ship it would be, Mr Muir,' returned the chief engineer.

We heard footsteps coming down and glimpsed the figures of the agent and the police as they passed through the foyer. Presently Captain Thompson trundled into the saloon. He was still ruffled from the angry exchanges that had taken place. He became aware of the malicious exultation being exuded by his two senior colleagues.

'Thought I'd never get rid of that big bugger of an agent,' he said, mustering a grin, 'and that police captain — long miserable streak of piss.'

'Very tiresome people, I'm sure,' noted Mr Yardley flatly.

'How do I know where the whisky is gone? We've been in four ports — stevedores and sods and bods from ashore coming and going, all over the ship, night and day.'

This dishonest attempt to exonerate the ship and its crew at the expense of outsiders was received in silence.

'I don't give a fuck about them all — Hall or the owners or anyone. Don't talk to me about shipowners. Sitting in swivel chairs in big offices. Most of them would spew their rings up at the first sign of a heavy sea.'

The unease on board was heightened when, later that evening, some of our men walking over to the sleazy bar and eatery near the road were pounced upon and frisked by police who had been lying in wait. It was felt that this might be a preliminary to determined police action. Yet the next day came and nothing happened, apart from men being searched at random when they went ashore to the road-house.

Misery was disappointed. He expected the police to search cabins, to ask men how they had been able to afford the suits, shoes and expensive souvenirs packed in wardrobes and drawers. He railed against the forces of law and order. 'Lazy buggers. Corrupt too. What can you expect when it's full of Mexicans and half-castes?'

Our own genial half-caste, Brad, had a more realistic explanation. 'Look, this is Houston, Texas. Every bugger carries a gun and they let fly at one another as the fancy takes them. There's a murder a day in that city. Buggers get plugged all the time. The police haven't the time to bother with small fry like us.'

I believe that neither Captain Thompson nor Misery had any inkling of the loot hidden about the vessel. I sensed that Pete was worried, even though he most likely had removed his treasure from his cabin and had hidden it elsewhere. The trepidation engendered by the caches began to subside when it seemed that the police in Texas had little interest in the matter. Indeed its presence helped to keep morale up at a time when working routines, normal on any other ship, were now the daily lot of our lively crew. As they painted, cleaned and refurbished the vessel, they were buoyed up by the thought of a renewed debauch on our return to New Orleans.

Some men did not bother to go ashore. Most who did merely strolled over to the roadhouse for a few beers. This was a squat clapboard place, patronised by passing truckers and the small gang of stevedores working on our ship. It was dim and dreary during daylight hours. Whenever some sweaty docker or burly trucker came through the fly-screen door, they seemed to be overcome by the torpor there, spoke in low tones, gazed at their glasses of beer, listening to the sizzling of hotdogs on the greasy ranges.

In the evenings, however, the roadhouse took on a squalid semblance of life. The garish neon sign began to flash outside and the massive jukebox inside glowed and rumbled. A strange assortment of people came in to shake off the dust of long days: hobos, drifters, elderly men who had once worked in the dock and had been left stranded hereabouts when the river of commerce had changed course. There was one lanky man, whose leathery face seemed to denote Texan toughness and manliness. Our men learned to avoid his company for he turned out to be a rapacious homosexual, looking about restlessly from cold blue eyes for any likely pick-up.

About ten each evening, when men had had a good deal

to drink, hard-faced prostitutes came in to ply their trade. Couples got onto the middle of the board floor and slouched about to the boom of the jukebox in a fog of tobacco smoke and the blue fumes from the hot plates. One night Pete and I sat at the counter watching a remarkably handsome woman roving amongst the drinkers, chatting and bantering, raising a pencilled eyebrow seductively. Every so often she would take a man outside. They returned after twenty minutes or so and she would continue her way amongst the crowd.

'This is real American time-and-motion stuff, production line,' Pete observed. We speculated about where she took her customers. There did not seem to be any dwelling house nearby; we could not imagine her taking them into some deserted warehouse. Nor was the good earth of Texas hereabouts the place to fornicate; it was adorned with small cacti and thorn bushes. Moreover, bodies writhing on the ground were liable to disturb some reptilian creature which might take its revenge by sinking forked tongue or steely pincers into the private parts of the lovemakers.

One of the barmen heard our musings. 'She's got a station-wagon out back, with a big spring mattress. Yessir, a big spring mattress,' he said, with a certain amount of pride, as if this was the kind of adaptability, ingenuity and efficiency that had made the United States a great nation.

Mistress of the hot-plates was a fat girl in a loose grey dress. She moved about cumbersomely, slapping down the hamburgers and steaks, juggling the skillet full of French fries, sawing at the bread rolls. She had a round colourless face, hair pulled back into a coil; she fingered back from her face a long wisp which perpetually escaped. From behind small round spectacles she peered out at the world of masticating jaws, beer-gulping gullets, hunched shoulders and shadowy dancers. Now and then she would take coins from the till, waddle across to the jukebox, clink them in and press the bright yellow buttons with podgy fingers.

I imagined this forlorn girl had never known romance in any shape or form, succumbing to over-eating and languor. This assessment proved incorrect. The sandy-haired Alasdair told me that he had a brief love-session with her.

'I got pissed last night and started making eyes at her. She was very friendly. I was only half-joking when I asked her could I leave her home. I nearly fell off the stool when she said, "Fine, but we got to wait until I close up." It was two in the morning when the joint was emptied. The barmen shagged off and left her to do the cleaning up. We were alone. Just as we were going out the door, she jumped back in and dragged me with her. "There's two Mexican hookers out there in a car, waiting to get me. They tried to run me down the other night." We were there in the dark, peeping out at the car parked over to one side. These Mexican whores had kicked up a racket in the place one night and she had phoned the police. They were fined and now they're out to get her.

'We had to wait until nearly three before the car moved off. The booze had worn off too. I didn't fancy a bit with her at all, but I couldn't back out. We walked along the road in the pitch dark. We cleared off the road any time we saw the lights of a car coming. My trousers were torn by wee spiky bushes.

'She lives in a flat over a little store. I got the shock of my life when I saw a wee babbie asleep in the bedroom. I don't know who was minding it, but it was hers. She told me she had been married at nineteen and divorced at twenty. We screwed on the settee. I didn't like the idea of making my way back to the ship at five in the morning. I thought those women might still be driving around. I'm supposed to be seeing her again tonight, but I'm not going near that road-house again. I don't want to get my arse in a sling — run down by Mexican whores.'

Morale on board got a further boost when crates stencilled 'London' were deposited on the dockside and began to be hoisted aboard. This is the watermark in any voyage. The tide begins to turn, however slowly, and starts to carry the voyagers towards hearth and home. Men come out on deck just to watch. It evokes a flurry of calculation; calendars are consulted, distances reckoned, likely weather conditions assessed.

'Okay — two days to New Orleans. A week loading there. A day's sailing to Mobile. One day there. Two days to Tampa. Three days loading there. Then we're away. Two weeks across the Atlantic with a following wind and sea. By my reckoning we should get to London . . . . If we sign off next morning, we might be in time to catch the afternoon train to Newcastle-upon-Tyne. Get in before the pubs close. How about a few pints of Newcastle Brown Ale, Geordie lad, before going home to goose the missus?'

This is the powerful cycle of expectation that dominates the sailor's life. He looks ahead to the day of return to his homeland. As he meets neighbours outside his house, they all say, 'How long are you home for?' A few days there and people ask, 'When are you going back?' Even before his ship sets off again, he is asking, 'When do we get to Recife?' When that port appears on the horizon, he is saying, 'Four days here and we are off to Santos.' The sailor's today is overshadowed by the tomorrow. His eyes look towards some point below the curve of the globe, anticipating events a week or a month ahead. It is very hard to avoid stepping onto a conveyor time-belt where the reality of the here and now is blurred and diminished by the future. Moreover, the constant physical movement about the oceans, the varying vistas of sea and land can act as a soporific to the sea-trapped, lend a comforting illusion of change to those whose lives are in stasis.

'I won't be sorry when we leave this place,' I heard Ted say, as if our leaving would somehow wrest some significant change in his lifestyle. He made one rather typical journey into Houston. Once arrived, he had sat in a cantina drinking tequila for several hours. On the bus back he fell asleep. By the time he woke up, it had gone two miles past our stop. He had jumped off in a fluster; only when the bus was a receding cloud of dust did he remember that he had left on board several souvenirs, including an ornate silvered sombrero and a ten-gallon hat. It was late afternoon when his bedraggled figure appeared on the dockside.

The one successful shore-goer was the Lambton Worm. On our first full day there, he had set off, neat as a new pin, and gone directly to a big hotel of some renown, called, I think, 'The Shamrock'. Thereafter a purring saloon, driven by a good-looking woman, would arrive to pick him up and leave him back. Ever reticent about his affairs, he put it about that this woman was a distant cousin of his and that he spent his evenings and nights in the company of boring relatives.

Even though the prospect of a police investigation receded with each day, there was still a surge of collective relief when the last of our cargo was loaded and we prepared to sail. The luck of the *Allenwell* had held out. The caches of whisky were intact, ready to be unearthed for a whopping six-day rout in New Orleans. With a bit of luck there might even be enough left over to help anaesthetise the rigours of the North Atlantic crossing.

18

Time of Calamity

The flat coastline of Texas ebbed away over the edge of the ocean behind us and we ploughed steadily across the smooth waters of the Gulf. The sun went down, disappearing into the yellow mirror of the sea astern.

After midnight the alleyways were full of the sound of careful footsteps and murmured words. From the depths of the pounding, oily engine room, from the shadowy recesses along the propeller shaft, from beneath the deck-boards of the lifeboats, from paint lockers and musty cubbyholes, the bottles of whisky were retrieved.

There were, I understand, a few cautious souls who advocated that the whisky be left in hiding until a day or two had passed in New Orleans. Their argument was that the authorities at the scene of the great whisky-mart might show a much greater interest in the vessel, would know that a search had not been conducted in Houston.

All objections were swept aside in a tide of euphoria. The danger had passed. If the police had not bothered to investigate the theft in Texas, had not struck when the iron was hot, their colleagues in New Orleans would hardly expect to uncover any evidence almost a week later. There was another reason that impelled men to lay claim to what was 'theirs' and to take personal possession of it. This was the last hoard mined from the seam; men were reluctant to leave precious nuggets lying in neutral areas. There were always the few unscrupulous ones about, greedy fellows who might act dishonourably at the expense of their companions. So all

162

the bottles were secreted in men's cabins, under bunks, behind wardrobes and drawers, under settees.

It was at this juncture that Ben Jennings drained the final drop from his last bottle. Stumbling out into the alleyway, he became aware that the last of the harvest was in transit. He was downcast, and began to beg of his alleymates a small share, even a single bottle. His pleas were brusquely rebuffed. Even the generous ones felt it would be unwise to give him any; he presented a wretched picture of one whose balance of mind had become unsettled by constant drinking. This was demonstrated sometime in the small hours when he went out on deck and began to uncover the Number Two hatch. Brad spotted him from the bridge and sent one of the men on watch to take the demented bosun back to his cabin.

Ben Jennings declined to be confined there. He emerged into the alleyway, hammering on doors, craving whisky. There was a brief scuffle when several men pushed and dragged him to his cabin. He put up little resistance; the strength in that bear-like body had been sapped by weeks without proper food. He lay down, fully clothed, on his bunk. Then an aggrieved colleague, soured at being woken up by the toper whose drinking had endangered all in Houston, came rushing in and punched him in the face. Next morning Jennings appeared with a spectacular black eye, like a huge oyster; the white was covered by a film of blood.

'Yes — that's the best time to hit a man – when he's lying down,' said Mr Yardley scathingly.

'That man has been allowed to drink himself into a cabbage,' Misery said, without sympathy.

Sometime in mid-morning the bosun was seen wandering all over the ship, searching for whisky in every nook and corner. He made his way onto the bridge, stumbled into the chart room and fell in a heap at Captain Thompson's feet.

That was the end of Ben Jennings's ill-starred reign as bosun of the *Allenwell.* The captain sent for Tommy Carey and appointed him boss of the deck crew. The fact that Thompson did not consult Misery was a deliberate snub that rankled deeply with the mate. The lamptrimmer, though partial to a drop of whisky, had taken no active part in the pilferage. He had the respect of the men. Even so, he might have had a difficult time establishing and enforcing his authority if the anticipated carnival was to get under way on our arrival in New Orleans. One of the first acts of this kindly and humane man was to appoint a reliable young fellow as guardian to his deposed predecessor. The captain decided that Ben should be taken to hospital for examination and treatment as soon as we arrived in New Orleans.

We picked up the Mississippi pilot in the early morning of the following day and had an uneventful passage upriver. As the hazy vista of New Orleans began to come into view on the great curve of the water ahead, men appeared on deck to watch. They smiled and joked. They punched one another playfully, and made the upthrust forearm sign of sexual penetration. Many had women waiting for them, supposedly with a ten-day accumulation of passion ready to be discharged in the piercing embrace of their returned lovers. A trio, standing on Number Two hatch, sang 'There'll be a hot time in the Old Town tonight.'

'Who's for the "Bootlegger"?'

'I won't leave this city without climbing up alongside Andrew Jackson on his fucking horse.'

This was the great returning to a city that had provided our men with an unforgettable fiesta, unequalled in the sea-experience of most. They knew every street and alleyway in the French Quarter, knew where the best value lay in wine, women and entertainment. The only apprehensive person on board was Toni.

'I hope I'll be taken on again at "The Riverboat", Sparks. You never know with showbusiness — one minute you're up and the next you're down.'

By chance, we found ourselves in exactly the same berth we had previously occupied. First up the gangway was the silvery-haired senior man from the agency. He went straight to the captain's quarters; a noisy argument took place.

Brad took the bosun to hospital. They did not return until evening. Ben's appearance was startling. His face was the colour of boiled lobster. A pink patch covered his dis-coloured eye; his shoulders were slumped. He bore the expression of somebody who had undergone a fearful ordeal. Brad told us that Ben's stomach had been pumped out, that he had been given an anal emetic of volcanic effect, been almost parboiled in a steamy bath and finished up having a huge draught of nauseous medicine poured down his throat.

'That doctor turned him inside out like a rubber doll and scrubbed his insides,' said Brad. This reported mediaeval treatment, at variance with modern medical practice, had at least had a deterrent effect.

'I wouldn't wish that on my worst enemy,' said Ben as Brad gave him two of the prescribed tablets, and saw that he swallowed them.

Tommy Carey detailed the same young fellow to stand guard over Ben. There was always a chance that someone, moved by misguided pity, might present him with a bottle from a well-stocked larder. Indeed Pete and I were very doubtful that he would be able to survive the six-day baccha-nalia that was in prospect in the alleyway. As it transpired, events were to remove all temptation from his environment. Under the effects of the tranquillising tablets he went off into a deep sleep.

That afternoon there had been a small but disquieting inci-dent. A police car had drawn up on the quay opposite the ship. Toni, hurrying ashore to discuss his future in showbusi-ness with the proprietor of 'The Riverboat', had been subjected to a frisking. One or two of our men, nipping ashore to the nearest post-office, had also been briskly searched. After half-an-hour the car drove away. This hardly curbed the rising hum of gaiety and chatter coursing through the ship as the sun dipped towards the west and the lights of the French Quarter began to flicker and flash. But it induced a note of caution. A gentlemen's agreement was made that no whisky be taken ashore that first night. Consequently, when the captain doled out the 'subs' in the saloon after the evening meal, there was an unusually long queue; many drew only enough to tide them over the night until the barter system had been re-established.

To Misery's gratification, loading of cargo began within an hour of our coming alongside and would continue until ten o'clock; he was able to put a gang of disgruntled men on cargo duty, with Pete as duty officer. When I was returning aboard after a long stroll about the Vieux Carré, I was nearly swept back down the gangway by the rush of impatient deck-crew men. In their haste they had again beaten some of the longshoremen to the gangway. I noticed Pete in conversation with a coal-black man who had a markedly sloping forehead topped by a parapet of thick fuzz. I assumed this man to be one of the stevedoring gang.

It must have been about two hours later, sometime after midnight, when, reading in my cabin, I heard a rumbling negroid voice talking to Pete next door. When I heard the heavy creak of the bottom drawer being pulled out, I put my ear to the bulkhead; the bottles were being unearthed. The whisky transaction was under way.

Suddenly Pete shouted. His cry was followed by a loud babble of other voices. Fearing that he was being robbed, I rushed out into the alleyway, just in time to see the black man scampering away. A man in a light tropical suit and wide-brimmed hat was standing inside the door of Pete's cabin.

'What's up, Pete? Are you alright?'

Pete was standing in a state of shock and hurt, with bottles of whisky all about the floor, like someone who has been shamefully disqualified in a game of skittles. The man turned to me. He had a revolver in his hand.

'Get back from that door.'

'Who are you?'

'FBI — that's who. This man is under arrest. Stand back.'

'Is that right, Pete?'

Pete nodded, crestfallen.

'Get back I told you.' The FBI man pointed the revolver at me. I retreated and stood by the door of my cabin, still doubtful about what was going on. Then other men came hurrying down the alleyway and went into Pete's cabin. I heard the bottles being gathered up. Pete asked permission to go out to the lavatory.

'Okay. You go with him. Make sure he don't do anything funny,' a voice said. Pete's face was full of pained dejection as they passed by. When they returned from the toilet, Pete was allowed to collect a few clothes into a handgrip. Then the FBI men and Pete emerged and went up the alleyway. As they reached the foyer, Pete turned and waved back to me with his free hand; the other was handcuffed to one of the men's wrists.

I followed at a distance. In the foyer, dumbstruck, stood Brad, Rat, Little Alex and Ted, just returned from a subdued, self-financed night ashore. We all crowded to the railings to watch Pete being bundled into a big black car. The door slammed and the car purred away, trailing twirling red feathers of exhaust round its circular tail lights.

Ted, smiling amiably, said, 'Third mate's gone ashore for a night's drift.'

'Shut up, you dumb cluck,' rasped Little Alex. 'He's being taken to police headquarters, that's what.'

Ted blinked, puzzled and offended.

Rat's little rubbery mouth twisted with vehemence. 'It's that fucking nigger. He approached me too, but I didn't trust the bugger. If I'd known that the third mate was doing business with him, I'd have warned him off.'

Little Alex flexed his shoulders threateningly. 'If that black bastard ever sets foot on board again, I'll split him with the meat cleaver.'

'Don't worry — you won't see him again. But we'll see plenty of police and customs. Sooner rather than later,' Brad predicted ominously.

Captain Thompson, who had been informed of the arrest by one of the FBI men, came down in dressing-gown and slippers. He was angry and upset, thrusting forward his lower lip, blowing out his cheeks. This was one time he could find no witticism to lighten the occasion. After telling us that Pete was going to be questioned at police headquarters, he stomped back up to his cabin.

Mr Yardley, disturbed by the commotion, came wheezing out of his cabin.

'I'm sorry for that young fellow,' he said when he had been given the news. He looked darkly at Rat, Little Alex and Brad. 'He hadn't the cunning of the old thieving hands. They'll save their own mean skins alright,' he said, turning away.

The old thieving hands were in a state of fear and panic.

'The third mate will be grilled just as soon as they arrive.' Little Alex's eyes twitched, pointed nose sniffing about, smelling danger. There arose an alarming image of Pete sitting on an upright chair, blinking under a harsh spotlight while beefy men, chomping cigars, rasped questions at him.

'How much does he know?' Brad wondered, his habitual tranquillity ruffled.

'Well, he's not fucking blind or deaf,' snapped Rat, 'God knows what they'll drag out of him.'

'This ship will be searched from stem to stern.' Little Alex's face was shiny with perspiration. 'They could be on their way down here right now.'

This dire expectation caused dismay and consternation in the alleyways. Men came out of their cabins to whisper urgently in huddles. Celebrants returning back on board, flushed of face and loud with cheer, were lassooed at the top of the gangway by hoarse warnings. Songs ceased in midnote, bouts of hiccuping and burping were instantly cured. They hurried to their quarters, mumbling and muttering.

An immediate search of the *Allenwell* would reveal enough incriminating bottled evidence to send men to jail along with Pete. The spectre of toiling under a broiling sun, in striped convict's garb, constructing by hand-labour a roadway over the unhealthy Louisiana swamplands, loomed in many imaginations. When a big limousine drew up on the dockside, it almost led to a frightened stampede.

'This could be the first of them now,' someone shouted.

A false alarm. Out stepped the Lambton Worm, waving a brief goodbye to the lady driver. But it was enough to shock men into a desperate escape scheme.

'We'll have to get rid of every fucking bottle. If anyone is caught we're all done for,' Rat said.

'Hang on. Let's do this thing right,' cautioned Brad. 'If we panic, something will go wrong.'

Thus began one of the great dramatic incidents of the *Allenwell's* visit to the USA. Lookouts were stationed on the starboard side to watch for the approach of police or FBI cars. A man was posted at the port railings in case one of the launches of the port police might come cruising by, sweeping its searchlight along the river. The alleyways resounded with scurrying feet, with cabin drawers and presses being pulled open. Those whose cabins were on the starboard side carried their store of bottles through the cross alleyway, clutching them nervously in case one might fall and break, leaving a smell that might be picked up by the quivering nostrils of some police sleuth.

I heard later that someone had suggested that at least some of the loot, with fingerprints wiped off, might be hidden once again, well away from the living quarters. Wide-eyed alarm put paid to such a risky idea. Whisky found aboard might have led to some of the crew being questioned, one at a time. A nervous man, under prospect of arrest, might crack, incriminating himself and his fellows.

When the lookouts had given the 'all clear', the great jettisoning began. Portholes were opened, like a wooden man-of-war about to loose a cannonade. The bottles came flying out, flung well away from the ship, tumbling in arcs and plopping into the Mississippi. There was great dismay at having to resort to such a heart-rending solution. The shiny new bottles, sealed red tops intact, were now being carried downriver by the current. But it was seen as a vital, if agonising, act of self-preservation, like precious food stores being heaved out of a hot-air balloon to try to prevent its descent onto some jagged, impenetrable mountain range.

Even so, for some men the pain of parting was greater than the fear of being caught. Little Alex, in a frenzy of fright and perhaps some guilt, was one of the leaders of the great disgorgement. After the main cannonade had been fired, he and several others went from cabin to cabin to ensure that no foolish fellow had decided to retain a few comforting bottles. A row broke out when they came upon Reilly, the greaser, clinging doggedly to his store. This gaunt, skeletal man, with a shock of wiry grey hair, could not bring himself to throw the very elixir of life into the dark river outside his porthole.

'You silly prick,' yelled Little Alex, 'you'll get us all in the shit!'

The other men backed up the cook. Reilly gave in, big brown eyes looking sadly about. For him this was to be a prelude to a prolonged period of distress.

'Do whisky bottles float, Sparks?' asked Alasdair anxiously. I could not tell him and still do not know. It was expected that the bottles would be carried well downriver by the powerful current. Many of them probably ended up bobbling about at sea or bumping along the silted bottom. I can only hazard a guess at the number of bottles flung overboard; somewhere between a hundred and fifty and two hundred is my reckoning.

There was a great sense of relief on board that enough time had been given to ditch the evidence. But there was foreboding about what the morning would bring. If there were any on board who were beginning to have regretful second thoughts about the draconian sacrifice, made in such haste, their doubts were sharply dispelled at 7.30 am. A formation of cars roared onto the dockside. From them poured a task-force of FBI men, led by the man who had arrested Pete. They rattled up the gangway and went to see the captain. When the others had come on board, a contingent of port police stood guard at the bottom of the gangway, barring the way of longshoremen trying to board for cargo working.

Captain Thompson appeared, scowling, in the foyer. 'The ship is going to be searched,' he announced in a croaky, bad-tempered voice. The hunt was, apparently, to be carried out under the supervision of the FBI, since Pete's crime, the

170

illegal importation of contraband, was a federal offence. The searchers dispersed purposefully about the vessel. On a more orthodox ship, the officers might have been exempted, on the assumption that they would not risk their careers by indulging in unlawful activity. The *Allenwell* was a ship of a different kind, with its third mate caught red-handed and now under lock and key. The FBI men were to undertake the search of our alleyway; they insisted on the captain accompanying them as witness.

They began with my cabin. 'You the guy I saw last night?' asked the man who had nabbed Pete. 'Alright — let's go.' While Thompson and I stood in the doorway, they set about pulling the cabin apart. The drawers of the writing-desk were wrenched out and dumped on the floor; those beneath the settee and under the bunk were piled on top of them. Torches were shone into the gaping spaces. My greasy rain-coat, mottled uniform and single suit were yanked out of the wardrobe and thrown on the settee. The search was carried out in a vindictive way, which added to the sense of outrage at seeing one's personal possessions, clothes, letters, books and private papers being subjected to a rough handling. One man even riffled through the pages of the dog-eared note-books from which these reminiscences are compiled and then chucked them aside; he would have found nothing of a compromising nature in them, anyway, since it was only on the homeward voyage that I was able to piece together the whisky saga.

It was when the cabin was in a shambles and yet the men still continued to probe and hammer away at every possible hiding place that it struck me that they regarded me as a prime suspect, a possible next-door accomplice of a man in the same age-group. For some unaccountable reason, a sense of guilt began to take hold of me. But Thompson, his humour returning, lightened the tension. He grinned when the prying hands of the FBI man uncovered two magazines of doubtful literary merit — *A Manual of Sexual Massage* and a publication bearing the title *Bum-Biters Illustrated.*

'You won't find anything in Sparks's cabin except his

collection of French Letters of the World.'

'Now let's try the radio shack,' the head man retorted.

They stomped into the radio room, pulled out the drawers and heaped them on the floor. It was hard to restrain a rising hostility when they roughly swept out all the neatly stored items in the spares lockers.

'Hey – some of those valves are fragile.'

'Yeah? We're feeling kinda fragile ourselves right now,' rasped the leader.

Captain Thompson caught my eye and winked. I am not sure if he was ever aware of the cascade of whisky which had gone over the side the previous night, but he certainly realised that in arresting Pete and then allowing five or six hours to elapse before conducting a search, the FBI had bungled badly. The searchers did not ask me to take the covers off the equipment, as I had expected. I could have told them that it was possible to stow bottles in the direction finder and on the valve-tops of both transmitters.

While the FBI men were searching the radar hut up top and the battery locker abaft the bridge, I caught sight of the boiler-suited brigade rummaging about the lifeboats.

It took a full hour to restore the radio room to order after the uncouth searchers had departed, in the company of the captain, to continue the quest below. Brad told me later that Misery had been seething as his privacy was violated, while the captain stood at the door grinning. The mate was embarrassed when a store of washing-powder was unearthed; he was meant to distribute the packets to Pete, Brad and I at intervals during the voyage but, like a greedy squirrel, had kept them all in his possession.

There was great anxiety in the crew's quarters during the treasure hunt. Each occupant stood by uneasily, watching his personal effects being scattered about. Some quaked, fearing that during the scrambling panic of the previous night, a bottle had been overlooked in some dim recess.

There was a jarring scene when the searchers hammered on the bosun's cabin door, waking him from a dark nightmare world. Imagining that they had come to take him back

172

to the hospital for a further ordeal of treatment, he began to wail. The men, disturbed by his frightful appearance and alarming behaviour, did no more than glance about the cabin before moving on. It later transpired that up to a dozen empty bottles were lying about in the drawers.

The search went on for several hours. Every hole and corner about the decks was probed; down in the engine room the boiler-suited squad tapped bulkheads, squeezed into oily lockers, crawled along the length of the propeller shaft.

At last the operation came to an end. The rummaging parties, sweaty and grimy, gathered in the foyer, wiping dust and oil from hands and face. The FBI men were sour with frustration and failure. They must have realised that the sound of the trap snapping on Pete's naive head had alerted the resourceful whisky-scavengers. There was relief when the empty-handed task-force filed down the gangway, got into their cars and sped away. The longshoremen were allowed on board to begin cargo work, and a semblance of normality returned. But there were worries about the possibility of further investigation. Before leaving, the chief FBI man had shaken his finger in the captain's face, saying, 'We ain't finished with this ship, not by a long whiles.' From that time onward there seemed to be a police car lurking somewhere about; men going ashore were regularly frisked and those returning were often compelled to produce means of identification.

There was a good deal of worry that Pete, with a jail sentence hanging over him, might be under pressure to disclose whatever he knew about the gaping hole in the whisky cargo. I do not believe he could more than make a surmise of who the principal predators were: his own code of honour would not have allowed him to be an informer. Just the same, there was no knowing that other members of the ship's company might be taken ashore for questioning, especially those whose cabin contents denoted an opulent lifestyle, as well as those for whom bloodshot eyes were a permanent facial feature.

'Could you imagine them grilling the bosun? That man might say anything — his brain-box is pickled with alcohol.'

At the evening meal, the first proper repast served up on that day of disruption, Mr Yardley and Misery were still fuming at the humiliation they had had to endure during the search. Their chagrin was exacerbated by the knowledge that the rummagers had made a sole exception of the captain's quarters.

'Shame and dishonour are no strangers to this ship,' Mr Yardley said.

Misery's indignation was somewhat salved by the fact that the captain had been brusquely summoned ashore by the British consul. 'Well, that's the end of all the boozing and whoring on this ship,' he said with malignant satisfaction.

Before the meal was over, Captain Thompson appeared. He was irked by having been stopped at the foot of the gangway and compelled to identify himself before being allowed to board his own vessel.

'Where's our third mate?' asked Mr Yardley, with an ironic stress on the 'our'.

'In the federal penitentiary in Baton Rouge, that's where. Federal law and state law and all the rest — I got a pain in the arse listening to that consul going on. Toffee-nosed bollocks.'

The Old Man had learned that an approach for leniency might be made to the Governor of Louisiana before Pete was put on trial. He had been heartened to hear that the Governor was one Jimmy Davis, better known as a guitar-playing entertainer who years before had written a song of worldwide popularity called 'You are my Sunshine'.

'I might go and see the bugger myself. He can't be too bad if he can sing a song,' the captain said, beginning to regain his humour.

'Why not?' chimed Mr Yardley. 'If there's a piano in the Governor's drawing-room, the two of you might perform a duet.'

'When will we know what's going to happen?' asked Misery, indirectly.

'How do I know? It could be weeks,' snapped the master, sensing Misery's lack of concern for Pete's predicament.

'We'll be a watch-keeper short for the homeward voyage, then,' Misery said vengefully, indicating that from now on the master would have to stand full sea-watches. The Old Man grunted, shot a glance at the mate's prim face. It was not the watch-keeping that bothered him as much as the prospect of unavoidable contact with the mate in the chart room and on the bridge.

19

The Voyage Turns Sour

That memorable day marked a watershed in the fortunes of the *Allenwell* and her pleasure-bent roisterers. The atmosphere on board was transformed. The halcyon days were over. There was an almost unnatural quiet in the evenings. No more the sounds of exuberant huzzahs on the dockside at night, of unsteady feet stumbling up the gangway, of singing in the alleyways, of retching in the toilets. The drunken dart games were at an end, much to Misery's pleasure.

On the first post-search evening, only a handful of guilt-free men went ashore. The once ebullient revellers huddled in their cabins, fidgeted about the decks, held furtive conversations, sometimes peeped at the police car stationed by the cargo sheds. During the search it had been learned that the federal authorities and police had reacted to complaints from the owners of well-run nightclubs that the seedy dockside haunts were awash with bootleg Vat 69, selling at well below the normal price. Apparently, some of these shady places had been visited by the federal agents and their proprietors had been questioned. Our whisky-princes considered themselves lucky that they had not been fingered on the previous night when they had returned to their familiar territory. Now that the whole business was under open investigation, they feared to set foot in these places again; a harassed receiver of stolen goods might betray them to some agent sitting unobtrusively at the far end of the bar-counter. Some men, with an exaggerated estimation of the FBI's determination, were loathe to go ashore at all, imagining a voice calling out 'That's the guy' as they turned a corner of the cargo sheds, while lawmen closed in from the shadows. Anyone on board who had traded in whisky envisaged the possibility of ending up, like Pete, with menacing criminals for company.

The high livers on board had spent their 'subs' on the first night ashore. Now Captain Thompson declared that there would be no more. It was not a punitive action on his part; the agents were unwilling to advance any more money, realising the likelihood of a prolonged wrangle between agency, Cunard, shipping company and insurers.

Several passionate liaisons, renewed the previous night, now had to endure a collective coitus interruptus. The women hung about the seedy clubs and drinking dens where their shipboard swains now feared to venture. Some of the more enthralled took chances and sought out their women; almost all found that ladies who had previously welcomed them with open arms and thighs now had turned markedly cool when their nautical lovers were unable to provide them with 'presents' of money, to wine and dine them. Those who had boasted that their love affairs were solely dependent on their own persuasive personalities and amorous prowess now sullenly referred to their former love-partners in execrable terms. Even the few who had established relationships with respectable suburbanites faltered; they had hardly enough money to make telephone calls or for bus fares, let alone appear on the doorstep with some small token of endearment. These genuine affairs wilted in the atmosphere of anxiety and despondency that enveloped the ship. Only the Lambton Worm, game to the end, persisted in his pursuits.

After a few days lying low, some men did go ashore, sneaking circuitously around the French Quarter to find quiet places off Canal Street where they nursed a beer all evening. The love affair between tramp ship and city of wine, women and wassail was ending in disillusion. The disenchanted could no longer bear to revisit scenes redolent of departed gaiety. They sat on board sullenly, wanting nothing more than to let go the ropes and head downriver without a backward glance.

The Old Man reached into his repertoire of obscene anecdotes, telling them with gusto. Misery picked at his food, as if sour satisfaction was sufficient to keep skeletal body and mean soul together. Mr Yardley chuckled, not at the captain's stories but at his blustering performance. On one occasion Captain Thompson, with an aggressive grin, announced that he had received a telegram of censure from the owners over the missing whisky.

'You can expect another one soon if, as seems likely, the third mate ends up sewing mailbags,' said Mr Yardley.

One positive outcome of the glum sobriety on board was an improvement in the food served up. Little Alex and Old Charlie still bickered in the galley but the brio had gone out of their arguments. No longer handicapped by blurred vision and shaky hands, their culinary efforts became more palatable. A less welcome aspect of this improvement was that Little Alex once again began to concoct that dessert known as plum duff. As I hesitantly surveyed this glutinous mass of boiled dough, dotted with raisins and sultanas, Mr Yardley chided me: 'Come on Sparks — eat it up. We English appreciate this delectable dish entirely on the basis of its density and weight. This is the kind of food which made England a great nation. It engenders a hardy stoicism. It enabled us to build the British empire when you Irish were subsisting on potatoes and shooting at landlords from behind hedges.'

One unappreciative Englishman was Misery. He prodded his portion vindictively with his fork. But a smile of mitigation curved downwards on his thin lips. 'The third mate won't get any plum duff in the federal penitentiary.'

'That will be one of the greatest hardships he'll have to endure there,' responded the chief engineer.

Misery was quick to take advantage of the strangely docile attitude of the deck-crew. He declared to Tommy Carey that the rust-bubbles, which had been wilfully overlooked during our first stay in New Orleans, must now be scraped, red-leaded and painted. Misery picked his way over decks resounding to the sound of chipping hammers and scrapers, a look of sour satisfaction on his face. There were no dissenters. No one felt it wise to shirk the punitive regime. Men were afraid that the mate might well be able to point a finger at the former high livers if there were further police enquiries. In the engine room Rat made a great show of carrying out Mr Yardley's instructions to clean the place up and to overhaul the generator. He reported regularly to the chief engineer with an unaccustomed show of subservience. The deck and engine room crews worked with a will; perhaps some felt that to do so was an act of supplication from further attention from the FBI. Others may have been glad that the source of so much temptation had been flung from the ship.

Drinking was now confined to the six daily cans of beer from the ship's stores. This ration did not sit well with men whose palates had become used to copious amounts of whisky. They found beer an insipid substitute. It was difficult to achieve a satisfactory level of insobriety.

'The way I am now I'd need a whole case of beer to get pissed,' I overheard one worthy say as he emerged from Ted's cabin cradling his cans. It was also irksome that drink now had to be actually paid for.

The sudden change in drinking habits seemed to have no appreciable effect on Ted. It was assumed that he was one of the few on board who had sufficient money left to be able to buy bottles of spirits ashore. With glazed eyes and distant smile, he doled out the beer ration. Sometimes he forgot to ask men to sign for their allotment; some unscrupulous fellows managed to draw double rations.

'His accounts are in such a mess he's giving half of it away free,' said Brad, with a kindly sigh. 'The poor devil doesn't know his arse from his elbow.'

It never seemed to have occurred to anyone that in his sodden state Ted might be keeping no proper tally of the beer-store, ensuring that there was enough on board to see our alcohol-loving ship safely home. An unpleasant shock, followed by painful deprivation, awaited those for whom alcohol was an important as food and sleep.

In the gloom over the *Allenwell* one star shone brightly. Not alone had Toni resumed his twice nightly performances at 'The Riverboat' to great acclaim, but he had also been given an increase in salary. He now embellished his act with his sleight of tongue. He would hold up his hand before beginning the next item and, in the brief silence, cast a burbling whistle towards one of the tables near the stage.

'Please – no interruptions,' he would wag an admonitory finger towards the group of drinkers. They would invariably look at one another in puzzlement. Just as he seemed about to get on with his act, he would repeat the trick.

'If I find out who's whistling, I'll go down there and kiss him — if he's handsome enough.'

This gambit almost caused a row one night when a heavy-faced Swede accused one of his companions of being the source of the whistle. They began to push one another. Blows were not far off when Toni defused the situation by launching into a whistling version of 'If I were a Blackbird'.

One of the rewards of Toni's rise to stardom was that he was sought after by several suitors. One day I saw him mincing along the street, accompanied by a retinue of unhealthy-looking individuals.

The proprietor was again pressing him to jump ship. 'I'm all a dither, Sparks. It's the chance of a lifetime for me. Only trouble is, I'd be putting myself completely in his clutches. Proper crook, he is. But you've got to take chances if you're going to make it big in showbusiness, Sparks. Get your name up in lights. Just the same, I'm worried about the police watching the ship like hawks. Trouble is, I'm too well known now just to fade away. I really don't know what to do, I really don't.'

His dilemma was solved in a rather dramatic manner two nights later. Brad witnessed the event and related what had occurred. A noisy argument had broken out between sailors and longshoremen just as Toni had started one of his seductive songs. Punches were thrown, chairs raised and about twenty men got to grips in a thunderous set-to. In the best tradition of showbusiness, Toni carried on; but his small voice was drowned in the din. He had, apparently, become piqued that he was being ignored . He stopped abruptly and began to abuse the battling mob, shouting obscenities at them. The demented proprietor roared at him to continue singing. Like an enraged prima donna, Toni waved him aside dismissively.

'Stop it! Wops and wogs, Huns and Frogs!' he screamed. This provoked a muscular German to leap onto the stage and deal the entertainer a resounding blow, knocking him into a heap on the stage.

By the time the police arrived, the place was a shambles. Some arrests were made. Ambulances were called. The proprietor stalked about in a white-hot fury. Toni, smarting from the blow and from wounded pride, unwisely chose this moment to accost him with complaints. Toni was sacked on the spot. He began to protest. The proprietor responded by booting him out the door, flinging his wages after him.

When Toni appeared in the saloon next morning to serve breakfast, we were taken aback by his appearance. He had attempted to hide a huge purple bruise on his face by a heavy daubing of rouge. It made him look like a circus clown who had fallen off the tight rope and landed on the magician's equipment. The silk shirt and bow tie had been discarded in favour of his drab steward's uniform. He was downcast as he served the meal, all flourishes and theatrical mannerisms disappeared. Captain Thompson, who had heard what had happened, made no attempt to hide the happy twinkle in his fat-enveloped eyes. For several days Toni was inconsolable, moping amongst the shreds of his shattered dreams. In time his Londoner's humour and resilience reasserted itself. Long before the end of the voyage he was able to talk with wry amusement of his meteoric rise and fall in US showbusiness.

Men came out on deck to savour the loading of cargo for home. 'It's going too bloody slowly for my liking. Them fat

American dockers are swinging the lead.'

'It won't worry me if we never see this place again. Good job we'll only be a day or two in Mobile and Tampa. I want to get back to the wife.'

Right up to the day before we sailed, there had been a faint hope that Pete might escape with a hefty fine and be able to rejoin us. Then the British consul sent word to the captain that such a process would take several weeks. Pete's belongings were to be removed from his cabin. A station wagon was sent down to the ship for them.

'Will you give us a hand packing his gear, Sparks?' Misery was reluctant to undertake this task himself. Yet, once inside Pete's cabin, his narrow face gleamed with a satisfaction that bordered on delight.

'He won't cheek the guards in the federal penitentiary, you can be sure.' Then he held up Pete's sextant in its polished mahogany case. 'He'll hardly be needing this again,' he said, implying that Pete's nautical career, at least as a deck officer, had most likely come to an end. In the top drawer of the writing desk there was a collection of group photographs, taken at the many navigational colleges that Pete had unsuccessfully attended. There he was, among men with fresh faces full of life and hope, with his crew-cut, big ears and lopsided grin. On the desk was a framed photograph of his parents, a solid couple who would be dismayed to learn of his misfortune.

Just as Misery pulled out Pete's trombone from the drawer beneath his bunk, the gasping presence of Mr Yardley appeared in the doorway.

'We won't be hearing this thing any more,' said Misery, holding up the instrument triumphantly.

'Well, he might distinguish himself as a member of the prison orchestra,' said the chief engineer. 'Many famous musicians spent time in jail for one misdemeanour or another. He would be following in a hallowed tradition.'

It was sad to watch Pete's trunks and bundled possessions being heaved into the back of the station wagon and driven away. It is sad also to reflect that, in my own introversion and impoverished sense of human relations, it never crossed my mind to write him a note of encouragement and consolation.

Unlike Misery, Mr Yardley did not gloat over Pete's fate, but he took a keen pleasure that the focus of events had largely shifted to the ship itself, where he was front-seat spectator, instead of being the lone figure at the railings at night, looking out at the city where most of the action was taking place. On one of our last days in New Orleans, browsing about the bookshops, I came on a second-hand copy of a book about the Roman poet Ovid. When I presented it to Mr Yardley, his watery eyes flickered with delight.

'Ovid got on the wrong side of the emperor and was banished to a barren outpost on the Black Sea, right at the far edge of Roman civilisation,' he said. Long afterwards it occurred to me that nobody understood the poverty of the poet's isolation better than Mr Yardley; on the *Allenwell* he was in an environment totally inimical to his classical enthusiasms.

On our last afternoon in New Orleans I revisited the favourite seat in the blossomed corner of the old residential quarter, once more savoured the bee-droning quietude, the aroma and the benign sun. Afterwards I repaired to the fountained patio of the restaurant where I had spent so many tranquil hours, drank so many cups of coffee. I had a wistful feeling that I would not be seeing these places again.

We sailed from New Orleans on a bright, calm morning. There were no fond farewells, no tearful girlfriends on the quayside; only glowering groups of police, shipping agency men and FBI officers watched our departure. There was no rush to the railings to take a last look at the city where the wildest seafaring fantasies of port life had once been a reality. The telegraph rang 'half ahead', marking the end of another episode in the *Allenwell*'s story.

'Forget New Orleans,' said Little Alex as he hatefully heaved a bucket of slops over the side.

20

In Mobile and Tampa

We had hardly tied up in Mobile, Alabama, when the longshoremen came clambering aboard. The loading of cargo began straight away. A man from the agents hastened on board and informed Captain Thompson that every effort was being made to have us on our way the following evening.

'The sooner the better,' rasped the master, who had the impression that his ship was regarded as a troublesome visitor whom everyone was anxious to hustle off without delay. As if to confirm this, a police car appeared and a fat officer hauled himself on board. He accosted Captain Thompson in the foyer.

'We don't want any trouble from this ship now, hear?'

'We're here to load cargo and shift our arse out of this place as fast as we can.'

Their big bellies confronted one another and the two jowly faces puffed combatively.

'Nobody better get out of line, hear? Otherwise they'll end up in the cooler pretty smart, hear?'

'I hear. I'm not fucking deaf.'

Word of this threat got about quickly. It put paid to plans by the inveterate spirit-drinkers to buy bottles to supplement the beer ration and help tide them over the voyage ahead. They had no money, but the intention had been to carry ashore the suits, shoes and souvenirs which had materialised from bottles of Vat 69 and to convert them back into bottle-form once more by barter. Now nobody ventured ashore.

If memory serves me right, it took us a day and a half to reach the beautiful port of Tampa, halfway down the western side of the Florida peninsula.

We glided into the sparkling bay, with palm trees shading the avenues of St Petersburg on the port side and Tampa itself gleaming immaculately under the afternoon sun. Many of our men came out on deck to enjoy the panoramic view, gazing up at the graceful steel bridge that spanned the bay, pointing at the rows of pleasure-craft moored in the marinas. Their spirits were rising, not so much at the verdant prosperity of this haven, but because it was our last port of call. When we had taken on board our cargo of citrus fruit from the groves of Florida, we would be on our way. Once this final hurdle had been cleared, any lingering fears of retribution by the FBI would be laid to rest.

Captain Thompson had a noisy argument with a tall, sallow man from the shipping agency who came on board when we docked. The captain's strategy to handle the row when the ship got to London was already clear. He would counter all accusations with a broadside against the incompetence and negligence of the agents. He revelled in this kind of fracas with shipowners and agents, observing no rules of honesty, bending the truth to suit his case.

'He'll blame the agents for the disappearance of the whisky, just you wait,' said Mr Yardley, who well understood the master's character.

Our captain was a performer. He could play the buffoon, simulate anger, astonishment, concern and puzzlement at will. He could be cunningly devious; but he was never less than his own man, was without pretence, never put on airs and graces. He never curbed his robust vulgarity, no matter in what company he found himself. Some were repelled by it, but many found it refreshingly honest.

One person who took to him in a matter of minutes was a lady of some distinction who was escorted on board next day by the sallow agent. She was middle-aged but, like many American women, was carefully preserved, elegantly groomed in a way that lent attraction to her plumpness. It was from her vast citrus estates that our cargo had come. With businesslike vigour and vivacity, she toured the decks, watching crate after crate of oranges, lemons and grapefruit being loaded into the holds.

I was lounging about the bridge in the sunshine when she climbed up the outside companionway, accompanied solicitously by the agent. She introduced herself with a firm handshake, exuding warm American conviviality from bright blue eyes. Then Captain Thompson appeared from the chart room. He was clad in a pair of old khaki shorts, sandals and a string vest through which his wiry body hair protruded. He reminded me of a brown gooseberry which clings to the bush far past the end of the season. The agent, frowning, introduced them with some reluctance.

'Like citrus fruit, captain? she said.

'Never touch 'em. They give me the runs.'

She laughed. 'Why captain, I thought you English people had good digestive systems.'

The master thrust out his beer-belly and patted it patriotically. 'An English stomach can hold nearly everything.' He eyed her own ample figure with unhidden speculation. 'All them citrus fruits haven't done you any harm, that's plain to see'.

She rocked with laughter at this unusual compliment. Thompson, sensing that he might be on to something, asked her if she would like a beer.

'Now that would be just fine, captain', she said. He took her below to his cabin, ignoring the agent, who went sourly away.

Some time later, on my way down the stairway, I peeked into the captain's quarters. There was nothing to be seen, for the curtains had been pulled across and the door shut, but hearty laughter and giggling were to be heard.

Two hours afterwards Captain Thompson left the lady down to her big saloon parked on the dockside. Her coiffed hair was somewhat dishevelled, her facial make-up less evident, the expensive dress puckered. But she had an air of zesty satisfaction as she joked and bantered with our redoubtable captain.

His amorous exploit was soon being admiringly related all over the ship. Even Mr Yardley conceded a rare compliment. 'Not bad for a man touching sixty-four — and with only one ball at that.'

Next afternoon there was a perceptible surge of exhilaration as the last sling of cargo was swung on board. The deck crew whistled and shouted cheerfully as they hauled the heavy hatch planking into place and let it drop into the grooves with conclusive thuds. The rasping canvas covers were dragged over the boards with unusual vigour, as if to hasten the hour of departure. When the gangway was levered up, the last link between our boisterous vessel and the United States, with its hostile forces of law and order, was severed.

'Next time a ladder goes down, it will be for the Thames pilot off Dover', announced Little Alex with some relief and triumph.

We sailed out of Tampa Bay into a calm, sun-bright sea. Toni brought a cup of tea into the radio room, where I was tapping away to the short-wave station at Halifax, Nova Scotia: 'MV *Allenwell* leaving Tampa bound London'. From the portside porthole we could see a long line of white beach, fringed by a palisade of tall palm trees.

'I can't wait to see the town hall in East Ham,' Toni chirped. No matter that, in murky smog, it was often hard to see any more of the grimy tower than the orange moonface of its clock. Home for him were the little rows of red-bricked houses, the pinched shops pressed together along the main street, the public houses heavy with the smell of beer and damp clothing.

I looked forward to seeing the dark, craggy outline of Slieve Foy brooding over the stony shores of Carlingford Lough, smell the tang of the brown seaweed and hear the brief piping call of curlews over the mountains.

In the chart room Brad laid off our course. It would take us around the tip of Florida, out into the North Atlantic by the

Bahamas and across to the Azores, two-thirds of the way across; from there we would plough our way up towards the Bay of Biscay and Europe. We were likely to encounter the usual rough weather as we moved into the northern latitudes, but at least the wind and sea would be following us, pushing us forward.

There were some fourteen days sailing ahead of us. For most it meant climbing back onto the dull treadmill of watch-keeping, life inexorably governed by the hours on the clockface. On any normal ship an uneventful passage could be expected: drab days of voyaging, with discomfort to be endured when the region of storms was reached.

21

Dismaying Discovery

Our last view of the United States was the broken yellow line of the Keys before we turned out into the Florida Straits towards the Atlantic. The sea was dark blue, choppy under a fresh breeze. Captain Thompson stood on the wing, breathing deeply through hairy nostrils. For the first time in many weeks the deck swayed a little beneath his bandy legs. The prow rose and fell with a refreshing splash. Our master mariner had a look of contentment on his round face.

During the first few days, the crew, clad in shorts and singlets, gave the finishing touches to the painting programme. This was the time to get deck work done, before we ran into heavy weather in the northern latitudes. There was some surprise when Ben Jennings came out on deck and quietly began to take a share in the work. He spoke little. With his humble mien and shaven head, he had the air of a penitential monk atoning for having guzzled sinfully of the monastery's famed elderberry wine. None of his fellows cast any mocking remarks in his direction. He had endured with fortitude the jolting journey of withdrawal from the dim alcoholic underworld in which he had for so long existed. Tommy Carey had visited him regularly, plying him with words of encouragement and bottles of mineral water. Tommy had warned everybody to keep beer out of Ben's sight, but the bosun had made no attempt to cadge. He had regained some of his self-respect and had earned regard from his alleymates as well.

The sight of Ben going about, even in recuperation, was

disturbing for some. He was a walking example of the ill-effects of overindulgence and of the acute discomfort awaiting anyone who might be deprived of their daily supply of alcohol. The heavy drinkers were having to make do with the ship's beer. Several of them prevailed upon the occasional or moderate drinkers to hand over their daily ration, on promise of payment at the end of the voyage. Ted doled out the sustaining cans at five o'clock each evening. There was always a queue of impatient men waiting in the alleyway as the hour of deliverance approached. Lips moistened as the chief steward fumbled in the beer cases on the floor of his cabin; signatures were quickly scribbled on the chits and the cans were carried away hurriedly.

It must have been about five or six days into the homeward voyage, when cloud-cover was beginning to encroach on the blue sky, that people started to notice a change in Ted. He no longer smiled hazily during the beer-dispensing ceremony. He seemed unnaturally preoccupied with some weighty problem. On one occasion he mumbled about 'having to go easy on the beer.' This was interpreted as a reference to some physical discomfort caused by his own intemperance. Even when he was seen several times in the storeroom looking about in a puzzled manner, it only caused some amusement. 'I seen him standing there like a goat looking at lightning.'

Nobody suspected that anything was amiss. Then one afternoon Reilly went to Ted's cabin to collect the allotment which his engine-room workmate, Joe Coughlan, had compassionately assigned to him. Reilly's bloodshot eyes bulged when he saw Ted reach down into the single beer carton and heard him say, 'I can only give you two. We're running short.'

'Running short? How do you mean, running short?'

Ted, utterly deflated, handed him two more cans. The carton was now empty. 'That's all there is. There's not another can on the ship. Sorry, mate.'

'Sorry mate! Are you fucking joking?'

Ted made no reply, hanging his head. Reilly, dumb-

190

founded, disappeared at speed.

In no time word was round the ship. If plague had broken out, it would not have caused greater consternation. A crowd of men converged on Ted's cabin.

'What's all this about the beer running out?' they shouted. Ted sat on his settee, in despair, smoking deeply.

'Come on – give us those keys. We'll look for ourselves.'

The mob surged down to the storeroom, flung open the door, rampaged about angrily. Men began to take boxes of provisions from the shelves, to heave about cartons of foodstuffs piled on the floor. The hope that a case of beer might be uncovered beneath cartons of tinned beans or bully beef subsided sourly. The ransacking brought it home to them that the beer-cupboard was indeed bare. They turned on Ted, who was standing dolefully at the door.

'You silly twat! Why didn't you order more in the States?'

'I did, but it never arrived,' whispered Ted, without conviction.

'Why didn't you check your stores? That's what you're paid to do.'

'I thought we had enough.'

Someone said accusingly, 'A pound to a pinch of shit that bugger has enough for himself.'

Several infuriated men ran back up to Ted's cabin and began to rummage through it roughly.

'I haven't a drop, I tell you, not a drop,' said Ted sadly. One man, bitter and sulphurous, gave him a shove. Ted flopped onto his settee like a sodden sack.

'Piss-artist! Some chief steward you are.'

Many of the mob stalked away to their cabins in rage and dismay. But a group assembled noisily in the foyer.

'The captain is going to hear about this.'

'What can he do?'

'He can do something, so he can.'

'Like what?'

'Like putting into the Azores for a few hours. This ship is supposed to have beer on board.'

'You must be fucking joking.'

The argument became heated and was only quelled when Captain Thompson, hearing the hubbub, came down the stairs. He frowned with annoyance when he was told the news, but he offered little sympathy and no solution to the dilemma.

'If there's nowt beer left, there's nowt I can do about it,' he barked authoritatively and went back up.

'All very well for him,' someone said. It was well known that Captain Thompson, like many masters, customarily maintained a store of beer in his quarters for his own use and to entertain visitors.

'Leave the Old Man out of this.' One of the deck crew pointed a warning finger at the speaker. Others nodded loyally. They would not brook criticism of the benign master, who had been so tolerant of their own excesses and misdemeanours. The crown dispersed, grumbling.

A bad-tempered mood rumbled through the alleyways. The heavy drinkers, who had imbibed so zestfully during the prolonged whisky-fest, had been finding it something of a trial to adapt to the paltry beer ration. The meagre supply had come to be regarded as a precious commodity. These men would be disgruntled by the enforced abstinence. But the prospect of days without a drop of alcohol was going to discomfit the dozen or more who were addicted. Deprivation would try nerves and metabolisms.

In the saloon that evening, Misery was aglow with spiteful satisfaction. He would not miss the single beer, which he sipped each day like a mean sparrow. It gave him immense pleasure to contemplate the drink-lovers who had roistered so noisily for so long now going about with shrivelled tongues hanging out.

'It's all caught up with this ship at long last — as it was bound to do,' he pronounced with a rare smile.

Mr Yardley was amused by the irony of this extreme turn of events, of a ship on which heavy drinking had been part of the weft and weave of daily life now sailing across the wide ocean like a puritanical pilgrim ship.

'Well — we've had the feast. Now for the famine,' he

chuckled. 'The captain's boozing pal has fallen down on the job.'

'When I was master, the chief steward had to present a stores check every week,' said Misery righteously. He glanced towards the galley. 'We might get some better food from now on.'

The following morning, after breakfast, Captain Thompson went to see Ted. He kept the door of the chief steward's cabin open and, knowing that several pairs of interested ears were cocked, went through a performance of rebuke. He concluded with, 'Alright then – let's have a look at all the bloody stores.' He led the way below, with the guilt-stricken Ted following behind, bearing a jumbled sheaf of stores lists.

They were there for over two hours, compiling a rough inventory of the food stores on board. Not surprisingly, the ship's provisioning proved to be in a dreadful mess. Some of the stores lists proffered by Ted actually related to the previous voyage. While the stock-taking was in progress, several men peeped in.

'Sparks — that place is like Al's Great Oklahoma Emporium after the tornado has swept past', said Alasdair. A hopeful rumour went about; so low were we in essential foodstuffs that we would be forced to put in to the Azores to reprovision. 'There's plenty of cheap Portuguese plonk there.'

When the captain eventually emerged, he scotched all such fantasies. He declared that we had just enough food to see us home. But we had run out of cornflakes and coffee, butter was in short supply and the bread would have to be carefully rationed.

Misery, who only nibbled on a few cornflakes each morning, now professed a great liking for this unobtainable commodity. 'Imagine sailing without cornflakes,' he whined.

'Abstinence is good for the character and for the development of spirituality,' responded Mr Yardley, 'Why do you think those hermits fasted in the desert for years on end?'

'And bread rationing! I've never been on a ship like it.' Misery shook his head in disgust.

'Never discount man's ingenuity, Mr Muir. Why, in Russia during the last war, they made a reasonably palatable substitute out of sawdust and onions. The ship's carpenter may have some extra work to keep him busy.'

At table, Captain Thompson weathered with gruff bluster Mr Yardley's scarcely veiled implications of execrable ship management. 'If Hall can't find a better chief steward, there's nowt I can do about it,' Thompson said, as if he himself had been making some efforts to have Ted replaced. Mr Yardley shook his head disdainfully at such blatant dishonesty.

In the dark of the wheelhouse during the evening watch, the captain pronounced his sea-spun philosophy towards the discomfort on board. 'You have to take the bad with the good at sea, Sparks. If you go ashore for a night's drift and two weeks later find you have a dose, it's no use blaming the whore.'

He was not greatly concerned about whatever anguish the alcohol-deprived might have to endure. If a man drank himself silly for weeks on end, then he ought to be willing to endure the consequences — delirium tremens, depression, pink elephants stomping about the cabin. Had he not had his private supply of beer, he would certainly have missed it, but he would have borne the loss with amused stoicism. All his life he had grinned in the face of hardship. He had no time for anyone who complained when things got rough.

No cheerful forbearance was in evidence amongst the drink-desperate. Ted was the scapegoat. But suspicions were now voiced that some on board had played leading roles in the depletion and rapid disappearance of the beer stocks. I noted a venomous exchange between Reilly and Little Alex at the door of the galley.

'You've had more than your fair share. Don't try to tell me, mate,' accused Reilly, hands shaking with agitation.

'Look who's talking, will you.'

'If it wasn't for you, we wouldn't have ditched all the whisky.'

'You're blaming me now, is that it? I had no fucking intention of ending up breaking stones, mate.'

'I'd like to see the stone you'd be able to break.

To make matters worse, the weather unexpectedly deteriorated. Wind-hustled clouds fled across the sky. A strong wind blew from the northeast. The waves began to increase in size and power. This was Thompson's kind of weather. He made no complaint about having to keep a watch and took over from Misery with the air of a man about to enjoy himself for the next few hours. He spent long periods standing stolidly on the open wing in his dirty duffle-coat, enormous black beret clamped on his round skull. Whenever he looked in the door of the radio room, where I sat cursing the North Atlantic, his russet face glowed a healthy, wind-beaten red.

'Nothing like a good blow to get rid of the cobwebs, Sparks', he would say. He laughed at the weather forecast, which told of a storm beginning to blow in our wake.

Down below, men were undergoing the nerve-wracking ordeal of drying out. On the gloomy, heaving ship, they wandered about fitfully, fidgeting in their cabins, trying to sleep when they could, hauling themselves on watchkeeping duties.

'There's a lot of people gasping like stranded fishes on this ship,' said Toni.

One man made another assault on Ted's cabin. He was convinced that the chief steward had a hidden cache, because even three days into the alcohol-drought Ted still appeared to be pleasantly drunk. Brad reckoned that Ted had drunk so much during the previous year that he was now saturated with it, could live off the residue, the way corpulent men can live off their own fat in conditions of starvation.

195

22

Mid-Ocean
Turbulence and Medication

Big black waves began relentlessly to pursue the cheerless *Allenwell*. The massive slopes, tops shredded by the gale, lifted our stern out of the water, plunging the bow deep into the sea. Sometimes they smashed over the poop and a tumbling white deluge swept forward along the decks. Doors and portholes were shut tight. Nobody ventured onto the cargo decks.

Brad marked the storm centre on the chart. A huge depression was churning powerfully five-hundred miles to the northwest, gaining on us by the hour.

'The bugger will cross our course just off the Azores,' he said. His face was shiny with perspiration, as if we were sailing in torrid equatorial waters. I could never be sure if Brad was an alcoholic. He was one of those heavy drinkers whose flabby frame could absorb vast quantities of liquor without visible effect. He bore any strains with oriental serenity. Only once did I hear him mention the subject. 'I'd give anything right now for a pint of ale, Sparks,' he said with a wan smile.

He told me that he had been knocked up one morning at 4.30, just as he was turning in. Two men had implored him for any kind of medicine that might allay their distress. Brad was meant to be in charge of the medical locker and to act as a sort of medical orderly. He had to search about for the key. Perhaps the supplicants had been hoping that the locker would contain the traditional medicinal bottle of brandy.

However, when Brad unlocked the dusty cupboard, all that could be found was a bottle of congealed cough mixture, a well-matured bottle of syrup-of-figs and a flagon of black draught, a notoriously violent bowel-scourer. The men had had to settle for a glassful of this powerful emetic, hoping it would clean out their writhing systems. They hurried away to clamp themselves over the toilet seats.

The *Allenwell*, stout-hearted ship though she was, began to roll and plunge alarmingly. The storm howled round us in a rushing torrent of sea, wind, spray and rain. For alarming seconds, with our stern out of the water, the ship shuddered as the propeller flailed helplessly in the air. The ship was becoming difficult to control. When Captain Thompson took over at eight one morning, he decided that there was no alternative but to turn her about into wind and wave.

This was not an easy manoeuvre in mountainous following seas. With the wheel full over, it took a long time before the ship's head began to swing round. Then, for at least two minutes, we were broadside-on to the waves. The ship began to roll awesomely, hidden under a flying screen of spray and foam. I lost my footing in the radio room and fell onto the threadbare strip of matting; it began to slide back and forth over the linoleum-covered deck, carrying me along with it. Each time it fetched up against the bulkhead, I had to swing my legs around and brace them. Several times I tried to rise, but the deck was canting so steeply that I kept toppling over. In the end I decided to enjoy the ride and laughed like a child on a magic carpet at a fun fair. But I kept a wary eye on the brackets that clamped the emergency transmitter to the port bulkhead; this heavy piece of equipment was at times almost overhead during the tremendous rolling. Eventually the *Allenwell* turned her stubby nose into the storm and began to ride it out. We were heading westward, now at half-speed. Captain Thompson grinned with exhilaration. 'I thought she'd never come round.'

Not everyone on board found amusement in the master's mid-ocean turnabout. Cuts and bruises were sustained. Everything that had not been securely tied down had been thrown about. The drawers under my bunk and settee lay on the floor; even the books on the shelf had jumped the wooden lath and lay scattered about.

'Half the fucking crockery is broken,' Little Alex declared, standing at the door of the galley with sweeping-brush in hand. Mr Yardley was furious, fingering a sizeable red bump on his forehead as he sat down for breakfast. 'He should have given proper warning. That's how people get maimed in the engineroom.'

'I thought we were going to turn turtle, I did,' said Toni familiarly to the chief engineer. Mr Yardley sulkily ignored him.

Misery, with Tommy Carey and the carpenter in tow, carried out a painstaking tour of inspection. The cargo had not shifted, as had been feared, but one of the lifeboats had been stove in and would need extensive repairs. Railings and bulkheads were dented and woodwork splintered.

There were a number on board who were visibly shaken by the experience. Everyone knew that ships founder in storms. Lloyds' register of shipping lists the vessels that disappear each year, many with not even a scarred lifebelt washed up on some shore to tell their fate. Over the years I had heard Morse-cries for help from ships listing perilously, fighting fires, drifting towards rocks with engines broken down, heard the urgent exchanges as rescuing ships tried to grasp survivors from lifeboats. Despite this, I could never bring myself to imagine that any ship I sailed on was ever in danger. There were others like me, trusting or unimaginative, who sailed blithely on in the face of reality and never had a moment's fear.

There were many wretched hours for fearful and fear-free alike. For two days we pitched and plunged westward, while the gale howled, spray and rain thundering against the windows of the wheelhouse. Only once did I don oilskins and ride the roller-coaster on the wing. For the most part I sought to cocoon myself in the radio room relapsing into a state of dumb hibernation, twirling the knob of the receiver across the broadcast bands to assure myself that somewhere were solid lands and cities round the curve of the globe, places where fields of winter wheat were sprouting and cawing crows were building nests in tall trees.

The tiresome struggle with the North Atlantic was renewed: holding the railings and doorposts grimly, staggering below to one's cabin, lying on the settee with arms and legs braced against wardrobe and writing desk, trying to get some rest.

'If we keep going like this, we'll be back in Florida soon,' said Toni, his chirpy Cockney humour under strain.

This was the nadir of the entire voyage. Those who were undergoing the turmoil of drying out had been in part sustained by the thought that each turn of the propeller was taking them home, where they might recuperate or slake overwhelming thirsts in the dockside pubs of London. Now we had turned about on the road to succour and shelter, with our backs on the distant pinpoints of light at the end of the long bumpy night-road. Morale was low.

'Chief steward's in his cabin, shaking like a leaf,' said Toni. In a fog of cigarette smoke, portholes bolted against wind, sea and the outside world, Ted lay on his settee. A musty smell of whisky, gin and beer hung about the cabin. He ate nothing. He told me later that he felt as if an endless steel thread was being drawn from his bowels like a tapeworm. Ted rarely put his nose out into the hostile environment his negligence had engendered.

Some men, emerging from the dark regions of alcoholism, began to find their appetites, despite the rolling decks which made for queasy seasickness. For weeks they had been uncaring about food; it had merely served as an appetiser, a stomach-liner before the main course of whisky. Now, with taste-buds no longer anaesthetised, they began to eat ravenously. They became quickly aware of the poor quality of the food. Their chagrin was directed not alone at Ted, but at Little Alex as well.

I saw two men standing at the door of the galley, firing hostile jibes at the chief cook. Little Alex shouted angrily at them: 'Look here, I'm the cook. The chief steward's in charge of stores. That's his business.' He had been careful to distance himself from the unpopular Ted. It occurred to me later that he might also have a disquieting premonition that when Ted came to his sober senses, he might assert his authority over the catering department. Ted's transformation in character and behaviour was going to be one of the talking points of the latter part of the homeward voyage.

One person who had no complaints about the nauseous food was our rotund master. He wolfed the ghastly stews with relish, burping with satisfaction, while Mr Yardley, Misery and I reluctantly chewed small morsels of fatty meat. I learned to avert my eyes from the brown mess swashing about the plate.

'I hope we're not going to be like *The Flying Dutchman*, destined to wander the seven seas to the end of time,' wondered Mr Yardley.

'Storm's passing over. I'll turn her about tomorrow when the sea slackens off.'

'Kindly let us know when you're going to do it,' the chief engineer said sharply.

The master grinned, a mischievous old practical joker. On the bridge he was never less than cheerful. He was at his best in rough seas. Each evening, after I had taken the traffic lists, I went out to join him in the wheelhouse.

'My father was shipwrecked on the Azores. They were there for six weeks before they could get a ship home. He didn't mind — pissed every day on Portuguese plonk and humping some lassie there as well.'

Standing beside the Old Man in the chart room or wheelhouse at night, one caught a distinct smell of ingested beer. Sometimes he came into the saloon for the evening meal with a merry glow on his weathered face. His belching presence aroused the resentment of his two senior colleagues. They felt that Thompson, the man ultimately responsible for so much of the poor conditions on board, ought somehow to be penalised, be made to feel as deprived as Mr Yardley without his coffee and Misery without his cornflakes. Yet here he was, aglow with ruddy health, fat face beaming beerily, devouring the atrocious food, spinning yarns everybody had heard before, chuckling at his own witticisms with out-thrust lower lip, bushy eyebrows bristling with joie de vivre.

The Old Man did not invite anyone to his cabin to share a beer. I thought this at odds with his generous nature, but Brad pointed out that, even during the great drinking era, the master had never asked any of his drink-mates to his quarters; he had preferred to meet them in Ted's cabin.

'Look, Sparks, the captain has to keep some small distance between himself and everybody else. After all, you have to have some kind of order and authority on board ship,' Brad said.

This subtle barrier was fully accepted and understood by the Old Man's former quaffing-companions. He was entitled to his own supply without any obligation to share it. Not even the impudent Little Alex would have had the gall to ask the captain for a single can. But, in an odd and secretive way, our hearty master was to expend some of his precious store on the most distressed member of the ship's company.

After the weather had abated, Captain Thompson turned the ship about and once again we began to head homewards. By the time we had come abreast of the Azores and had altered course to take us up to Biscay, it seemed that all the alcohol-addicted had got over the pain of enforced sobriety. Even Ted began to come out of his cabin. He took to endlessly walking back and forward across the foyer. The acute physical turmoil was now replaced by a slow mental awakening. When I looked in on him one afternoon, he was sitting on his settee, staring into the middle distance with some concentration. He spoke slowly and hesitantly. He was like a man who had woken from a sleep so deep and lengthy that it was taking him time and effort to come to terms with the waking reality about him. Perhaps Ted was trying to cast his eyes back along the dim, sodden road he had been hazily plodding for so long, wondering where he had been and what he had done. 'Rip Van Winkle of the high seas' was how Mr Yardley described him.

The tempers of the one-time topers improved markedly.

There was a certain sense of pride that they had endured the very worst that could have happened and had survived, however shakily.

'I'll remember this part of the voyage as long as I fucking live,' Little Alex said swaggeringly to Brad in the foyer. The second mate smiled sturdily.

Then Rat reported to Mr Yardley that Reilly had fallen ill, was unable to rise from his bunk, seemed unable to eat anything. The chief engineer was scathing. 'If a man can't get on with his job because of drink, then he shouldn't drink at all. He's brought it on himself and now the burden is thrown on his workmates.'

Mr Yardley felt obliged to make a personal assessment of the lying-low of one of his staff. Wheezing and coughing, he struggled down to the crew's quarters.

'That man has almost drunk himself out of this world,' he reported at lunchtime. 'He's lying there like Tutankhamen waiting to be embalmed. The prince of topers has reduced himself to skin and bones. But you have to hand it to him, his feats of drinking have brought him fame and renown – not an easy thing to achieve on this ship.' Mr Yardley then looked challengingly at Misery. 'He has upheld the proud tradition of the engine room. We engine-room men have always been the champion drinkers of the British merchant fleet. Your bosun couldn't match him – look at the way he dropped out of the race at the halfway stage.'

Captain Thompson, accompanied by Brad, visited the sick man. Our shambling medical orderly carried with him the bottle of syrup-of-figs as a symbol of office rather than as a healing potion. The master, after a cursory examination of the patient, prescribed a course of meat broths. He ordered Little Alex to prepare them daily. Alasdair was appointed medical attendant, reporting to Brad twice a day.

'This is the cook's big chance to redeem himself,' said Misery, who was enjoying this mid-ocean crisis.

'Hah! If he sets about making those broths the same way as the meals, it will put a full stop to Reilly's illustrious drinking career,' said the chief engineer.

'The third mate broke out the only decent funeral flag we had on board,' said Misery thoughtfully.

Reilly was unable to stomach the cook's concoctions. 'Make him drink the bloody thing!' the captain said emphatically to Brad. 'Otherwise he won't last until we get to London.' Brad did his best, visiting the sick man before and after each of his watches, coaxing him to swallow a little of the broth. But two days later Brad reported that Reilly was showing little sign of improvement. That night I stayed on with Brad for the first few minutes of his watch. I was about to make my way below when the door of the captain's cabin opened. The master emerged, carrying one of those small canvas satchels intended to hold important documents in the event of any hasty departure from the vessel. He staggered when the ship rolled; I heard the muffled but unmistakable tinny clang of full beer cans. From the door of the radio room I watched him go down the stairwell.

From then on, each night after he had finished his watch, Captain Thompson carried the canvas sack below to Reilly's cabin. Once, when he heard me at the top of the stairs, he thrust it inside his windcheater. Between beer and broth, or despite both, Reilly held up until we reached London. The master's ministration was one of the best-kept secrets on the gossipy *Allenwell*, where the alcohol-dearth was a constant topic of conversation. I do not believe that even Brad knew. Only long afterwards, when Reilly was no more than a legendary memory on the ship, would the Old Man begin to boast that he had once saved a man's life by beer. A colourful, exaggerated version would be part of his repertoire, an addition to the corpus of sealore which laid much illness at the door of alcohol while also extolling its virtues as a cure-all.

23

Recovery and Rejuvenation

As we left the Azores behind and moved slowly towards Biscay, the first sounds of Europe began to be heard at night on 500 kilocycles. The rustle and crackle of static diminished in the earphones as our vessel chugged further and further away from the region of electric storms. On the far edge of the late-night hush came a faint chirping. Each night it grew a little louder. It was like approaching a wood where dozens of different birds called and whistled.

The trained ear of the radio man focuses easily onto one single course of twitter, locks onto it, follows it amongst the curling streamers of Morse-sound. He comes to recognise each station's distinctive timbre and tweet. He can identify the varying national Morse-styles and, often, the characteristic 'fist' of individual signallers. The practised ear can build up an aural map of the night world, know what are normal and what are freak conditions and made a good estimate of how far distant is each transmitter.

The Spanish and Portuguese stations, on the Iberian peninsula itself and on the Canary Islands and Maderia, were first to be clearly heard cheeping away at intervals. Two nights later the French and British coastal stations began to emerge distinctly from the night-chorus.

The weather was still rough and the ship swayed and groaned, but the end of the voyage was not far below the horizon.

'Only five days more, Sparks,' Toni said lightly as he went about dusting and cleaning my cabin. 'One voyage on the

Allenwell is enough for me, thank you very much. I'll look for a Union Castle ship when we get to London. Fun and games all the way down to Cape Town.'

An immediate advantage to sticking with one ship was that at the end of each voyage the radio officer, with the captain's compliance, could take off on unofficial leave until the ship was ready to sail again, all the while accumulating a store of Marconi-leave, which could provide him with nine months or a year's holiday when he felt like it. I knew that if I remained on the *Allenwell* and Thompson retained his command, I could head off home for at least three weeks' 'captain's leave'.

However, Mr Yardley now began to speak of the uncertain future of the ship. 'God only knows where we'll end up if we lose the Cunard charter.' He did not relish a return to the sweltering, vapoury tropics. During the previous voyage, when the vessel had wallowed in the steamy equatorial fog of West Africa, his emphysema had been exacerbated in the damp heat; he had fought exhausting battles for breath every hour of every day until the ship moved towards drier or cooler climates. 'Hall might have to get on his bicycle and look for another charter,' he said, evoking a picture of our flabby red-faced marine superintendent pedalling in perspiration down Leadenhall Street from one shipping office to another. Mr Yardley's real fear was that the ship might be laid up for a few months, swinging at anchor in the river Tyne with only a skeleton crew on board. He was afraid that if he had to leave the ship on which he had sailed for eighteen years, he might never be allowed to return. For the past two years, he had not set foot ashore, let alone in the engine room. In Liverpool he had made light of his infirmity in the presence of Mr Hall, belittling any notion that he was unfit for duty. He might rail and fulminate about the shabbiness and shoddiness of the *Allenwell*, but he was aware that in any well-run company the medical officer would never allow him to sail. He would be packed off home to his little terraced house in Hull, a semi-invalid awaiting the end.

'The sea has been my life, Sparks. It's been good to me —

a lot of the time anyway — and it's only fair that I should provide some nourishment for fishes and crustaceans when my time comes. Going over the side, wrapped in canvas and weighted with lead, is a dignified way to go; none of the hysterics and histrionics which characterise shore-side burials.'

It was a source of some satisfaction for the chief engineer that Rat was departing the vessel in London, even though he was well aware that the second engineer's replacement was unlikely to be a man of unblemished record whose exemplary character would inspire diligence in the engine room.

Rat now appeared every afternoon in the doorway of my cabin. He would never come in and sit down. Leaning against the door-jamb, bracing his boiler-suited body against the roll and sway of the ship, seemed to reflect his uneasy state of mind. He had recovered from any discomforts suffered when the beer-well ran dry. What was preying on his mind was the wrenching transition upon which he was about to embark.

'Well — this is my last voyage,' he always began, in an indeterminate tone of voice, as if it was a matter of doubt. 'It won't be easy after twelve years. I've nearly forgotten what living ashore is like — and I don't like what I remember of it.'

He had come from the Tyneside shipyards, working in drab machine-shops and draughty slipways, where the clang of riveting reverberated against iron plate and concrete wall and the intense blue sparkle of acetylene torches lit up dim hangars.

'I don't fancy going back to it. I hated when the alarm clock went off in the mornings — couldn't wait for the hooter at the end of the day.'

Rat talked circuitously, endlessly, about the coils of his quandary, pink lips writhing under his big white nose.

'At least I'll have a steady bed to sleep in at night, with her ladyship beside me, not rolling about the sea like a bitch. I've had enough of this life.'

He would look across the cabin to the porthole, where he

could see the murky grey horizon rising and falling, tilting and sliding, see the dreary black waves.

As the *Allenwell* moved into the outer reaches of the Bay of Biscay and, against normal expectation, the seas moderated further, morale on board began to rise. With the exception of Reilly, all those afflicted by the alcohol-drought had got over the trauma and depression of readjustment. Men began to come out on deck, breathing deeply of the cold wind, letting it buffet their upturned faces. A few even indulged in a tentative form of callisthenics, waving arms about, doing partial knee-bends, flexing their shoulders. Some opened cabin portholes to let the blustery wind disperse the musty smells of confinement.

The most remarkable restoration was manifested in the person of Ted. He had been the slowest of all to recover from his private purgatory. He continued walking endlessly back and forth across the foyer with a look of unusual concentration on his face. 'He's like Demosthenes preparing an important speech for delivery to the assembly at Athens,' commented Mr Yardley. Once, as I entered the saloon, I caught sight of Little Alex peering out the door of the galley at his former drinking companion. When Ted's back was turned, the cook nodded towards me in faint amusement, tempered, I thought, by a certain wariness.

Then, one morning, Ted's ceaseless journeying ended. He emerged from his cabin, not in the familiar navy cardigan and crumpled grey trousers, but in a neat dark suit that I had never seen him wear before. It had the authority of a uniform. At breakfast he stood at the door of the saloon like a commanding maître d'hôtel. He greeted me affably, but with some formality. The puffiness had gone from his face; his eyes were clear and alert, the pupils a bright blue. He reminded me of my father when he had pulled himself together after a long drinking bout.

'Clean shirt and all, by golly,' said Mr Yardley, unimpressed by Ted's metamorphosis.

After breakfast Ted went below to the storeroom with

sharpened pencil and new notebook. He attacked with vigour the jumbled disarray of cartons, boxes and crates, sorting, selecting, tidying. He began to make a brisk inventory. News of his transformation got about. Several men gathered at the doorway, eyeing him curiously. They had never before seen Ted sober.

He rounded on them. 'Yes? Can I do anything for you?' They were taken aback by his interrogative tone, but one man spoke up. 'You can give us better food, chiefy.'

'That's exactly what I'm about right now. Okay?' He turned his back on them dismissively. The sightseers dispersed, nodding to one another and marvelling.

When he had concluded his stocktaking, Ted then concentrated his new-found force on the galley. It was mid-morning. Little Alex and Old Charlie, in their soiled aprons and checkered pants, were lumbering about preparing lunch. The ranges were grimy with a hundred overspills of stew; the walls and floor were mottled with grease-spots. There was rubbish and dirt in every corner.

'This galley is to be cleaned up,' the chief steward ordered. Leading by example, he took off his jacket, neatly folded back the cuffs of his spotless white shirt, seized a brush and began to sweep the litter into a pile in one corner. The two cooks stood about uncertainly, mouths agape, while Alasdair and I loitered watchfully in the foyer.

'Empty the gash bucket', he ordered the chief cook.

'It's only half-full.'

'I said empty it.'

The little ferrity cook, his long fine hair falling over one eye, did not take this approach very well. 'Talk about Dr Jekyll and Mr Hyde — this is the best I've seen yet.' He made a loud, false laugh.

The chief steward advanced towards him, jaw squared, and raised one finger. 'I won't tell you again.'

With great bad grace, aware that there was an audience, Little Alex succumbed. He lugged the big galvanised bucket over to the leeside and dumped the contents overboard.

'Now scour out that can with Jeyes fluid and boiling water.

Right away.'

It was in the afternoon, when the cooks normally took a few hours' rest, that the real purging of the slovenly galley began. First the scrubbing brushes, mops and squeegees, which had been regarded by Little Alex as unnecessary frills, had to be retrieved from the dark closets to which they had been consigned. These had to be cleansed in hot water, soap and disinfectant. The scouring of the galley took two full days. It became a kind of running show, with random spectators appearing at various times to grin at the harassed faces of the cooks wielding mops and brushes in a mist of steam and cleaning fluid, while the renaissant Ted stood by in stern supervision.

'Herakles cleaning the Augean Stables had nothing on this,' said Mr Yardley, who delighted in the humiliation of the cooks, particularly Little Alex, whom he especially disliked.

With the rejuvenated Ted in full control, the quality of the food, rationed as some commodities were, took on a marked improvement. A matter for some astonishment in the saloon was that the menus were now neatly typed.

'My God — what's this? Vol-au-vent no less. And spinach! What have we done to deserve this?' asked Mr Yardley.

'It's a bit late in the day for the vol-au-vent and spinach,' said Misery, dourly resisting any show of appreciation. It transpired that Ted was a qualified master baker. He had uncovered a quantity of corn meal in the storeroom and, to compensate for the shortage of white bread, himself baked some delicious brown bread. Like a fastidious restaurateur, he closely directed the culinary efforts of Little Alex, prodding him into producing a variety of soups, main meals and deserts which seemed exquisite compared to the squalor of the former regime.

'Bakewell tart, by God,' exulted Mr Yardley. 'Sparks — in later years, when the news is published in the quality newspapers that our chef had been awarded the gold medal of the Société Internationale de Gastronomique, you'll be able to turn round to all your pals in Ireland and say, "I once ate a Bakewell tart baked by that famous chef".'

Ted undertook a tour of inspection of the accommodation. He found no fault with Toni's territory, but he severely ticked off Alasdair for the dust and grime of the portside cabins.

'A new person he is', remarked Toni. 'Cold showers every morning, out on deck doing exercises at the crack of dawn. He's even stopped sucking his teeth.'

Ted's rebirth was one of the talking points on board. He gained some respect; he could no longer be condescendingly dismissed as a hopeless toper. Gone were the days when the smell of burning and stewy vapours wafted about the galley. It was no longer the scene of bad-tempered brandishing of skillets and cleavers, of the angry clanging of pots and pans, of oaths, abuse and obscenities. The cooks were like slapstick comedians upon whom vows of silence had been imposed.

'I'm really worried about those hash-slingers', said Mr Yardley. 'There must be something seriously amiss when you see them doing their work properly.'

I bumped into Little Alex in the alleyway. His face was twisted with resentment. 'I like that chief steward a lot better when he's drunk than when he's sober.'

Misery would not have been satisfied with cordon bleu cooking, but it was a little saddening to note the way Mr Yardley's implacable dislike of shipboard caterers was unrelenting. The criticism of the food had been a daily ritual which both men were unwilling to discard.

'The chief pisspot jerker need not think that this eleventh-hour conversion is going to get him anywhere,' said Mr Yardley. 'He's going on the theory that sailors have short memories and that we'll imagine we've been feeding like lords the whole voyage.'

'A few cornflakes is what I'd like instead of all that fancy stuff,' said Misery, who clearly had no intention of allowing his memory to be manipulated.

One afternoon, on the bridge, Brad volunteered some information about Ted's troubled life. His wife had left him because of his drinking, taking with her their two children. Shortly afterwards an appalling tragedy had occurred. All three had lost their lives in a fire which had engulfed the house in which they were staying. Ted was shattered. He had sought refuge from grief and remorse in a state of steady drunkenness.

The first seagulls appeared when we were a day's sailing from Île d'Ouessant, our first landfall, on the tip of Brittany. They began to accompany us, gliding and sliding along the air currents over and about the ship, like well-wishers encouraging a weary marathon runner towards the finishing line.

'Won't be long now,' men repeated. For the first time in many days laughter and banter began to resound. Those with radios were picking up the BBC on long and medium wave.

'Never mind all that about some government minister accused of buggery – just tell me that there is no rail strike, that the trains to Newcastle are running.'

'As long as the pubs aren't on strike, I won't worry.'

Some of the good humour of the old hands, however, was to be disturbed a little. That night in the radio room, when I was listening intently to Radio Eireann, trying to burnish my rusty knowledge of the Irish language, I became aware of our callsign beeping from the loudspeaker of the second receiver. Land's End radio was calling 'QTC — telegram for you'. It was addressed to Captain Thompson. 'Cunard charter discontinued. Please prepare report of voyage. Hall.'

The master was out on the bridge, warily watching several pinpoints of light scattered about the black horizon; we were now approaching an area of heavy marine traffic. He came into the chart room.

'Don't tell me the missus has fucked off with the milkman, Sparks', he said, leaning over the chart table, holding the telegram under the funnel of light from the desk lamp. His bushy eyebrows seemed to unroll, protruding to focus on the message like supplementary eyes. The big flat lower lip pouted aggressively.

'Prepare report, my arse,' he exploded. 'I'll prepare fuck all. I'll wipe my arse with this.' As if to signify this intention,

211

he roughly thrust the telegram into the back pocket of his wide, baggy trousers.

Many another captain would have been circumspect in the way he made known such an uncomplimentary item of news. Not so our modern-day buccaneer. At breakfast next morning he had a roguish twinkle in his eye as he produced the telegram, like a fat, mischievous schoolboy who has shattered a prize pumpkin with a well-aimed stone. Ignoring Misery, he read its contents out to Mr Yardley.

The chief engineer was not amused. 'Charter discontinued — that's a subtle way of putting it, I must say. Well, it's uncertainty that lends life its fascination. A year carrying phosphates from Morocco to Burma would be just dandy. There's a mosquito-infested creek amongst mangrove swamps just waiting for this noble vessel,' he spat savagely.

'Hall better get his lazy arse into gear and find something,' said the Old Man, with a tone that implied that the marine superintendent was the one responsible for the loss of the charter.

Misery's eyes were on his plate. He smiled faintly, moving his dentures in a show of disinterest in the ship's uncertain future. It was now known that before we left Tampa, he had received a letter confirming his appointment to another company.

'Well — anything is better than going back across the Atlantic to the USA,' said Little Alex. 'We've had our bellyful of that country.'

'It might be better than an eighteen-month trip plugging between the Persian Gulf and Borneo,' said Old Charlie.

'Anything is better than the ship being laid up, with everyone paid off,' said Brad. This was the prospect that worried all the old limpets who had made the *Allenwell* their seahome. They, along with Captain Thompson, had created a happy-go-lucky environment that would be hard to find elsewhere. On the other hand, there were the dozen men, who for one reason or another, intended to quit. Many were quiet, sober types, unwitting newcomers who had signed on for the first time in Liverpool; they had failed to appreciate the hilarity of being kept awake half the night in port by singing, bawling and brawling in the alleyways; they were men of good appetite who had grown lithe and sinewy under the unpalatable food. For the waverers like myself, the news added another element of doubt.

On a cool, misty morning, with a moderate sea running and a fresh breeze out of the northwest, we made the first land-fall. Captain Thompson asked me to stand by the radar. I put it on the 40-mile range. The trace line sweeping around the circular display tube soon began to daub a small yellow blob on the outer rim and to solidify and extend it.

'That's it, captain.'

'We'll wait till we see the bugger.' Thompson regarded the radar and other electronic devices of navigational equipment as mere aids to his own sea-honed sight, sense of smell and hearing instincts; he was reluctant to accord the radar any more than marginal importance. He went out onto the star-board wing and gazed towards the indistinct horizon. It was a long time before he put his binoculars to his eyes. 'That's it alright,' he said. One could make out a dull grey patch of land, see faintly the tall lighthouse of Ouessant. Misery, who had come up to the bridge to take over the watch, kept out of the master's way. Only when the Old Man went into the chart room did he move to the starboard side to view the smudge of land. On the wings, in the wheelhouse, in the chart room, at the radar viewer, the two kept their distance silently. It was like a seemingly natural but carefully con-trived ballet whose smooth movements had been meticulously spaced and timed.

That night Captain Thompson played a jolly, bibulous role on the bridge. When I came up for the evening watch, he stuck his head into the radio room.

'Sparks, that bloody radar's all gone to cock again,' he said, as if delighted with this evidence of electronic unreliability.

When I stood in the dark at the viewer, restoring the pic-ture he had managed to erase by his thick-fingered fumbling, I could get the whiff of beer.

'That radar has never got over the way the third mate used to fuck about with it,' he said. He began to wrench the range control backwards and forwards. I winced.

'I'll stand by the radar, captain.'

The screen was dotted with the yellow blobs of other ships in this highly congested seaway. 'Good, good,' he said. I knew that what he really wanted was an audience, someone in addition to the man on the wheel, to listen to his chatter and witticisms. He trundled from wing to wing, watching the navigational lights of the score of other ships, near and far, passing up and down and across this narrow strait. This dangerous stretch of water, where collisions and near-misses were common, induced a tension and anxiety in many navigators. It did not bother the intrepid Thompson. Slightly merry he might be, but he was not careless. He had a jaunty insouciance that inspired confidence. He was like a happy driver of a battered old jalopy scudding skilfully down a busy street while owners of sleek limousines frowned lest their expensive vehicles might get a rear light broken or a fender stove in.

A big cross-channel ferry, looking like a floating palace with its rows of lighted windows, crossed ahead of us. In the manner of a street urchin rasping at a toff, Captain Thompson blew the *Allenwell's* blabbery siren. The steersman chuckled.

Every now and then the master went out to either wing to survey those ships nearest us. 'There's a bugger astern creeping up on us. You have to watch for Greek arse-bandits in these waters.'

I was still on the bridge at midnight when Brad appeared.

'She's all yours, second mate, to do with her as you will,' said the Old Man. 'I'll just go below to see how Reilly's getting on before I turn in.' With that our cheerful captain went heavily down the stairway.

'I hope he won't be sacked or anything like that, Brad,' I said.

Brad shook his brown face with slow emphasis. 'Naaw. He might act the comedian, but he's no fool. He can look after himself. Bloody good navigator. Hall knows it too. All the captains I ever heard of who put ships aground or collided were worriers, cautious blokes.'

I waited on for a while to share some of the last graveyard watch with Brad as our old tramp trudged the homeward pathway. Before I went below, I watched the sweep of the trace on the 40-mile range begin to brush in the headlands of the English coast on the edge of the screen.

24

A Floating Theatre

Next morning the south coast of England was in near sight, clearly visible in the first shafts of broken sunlight we had seen for many days. Men came out on deck and lined the railings, looking at the chalk cliffs and the rolling green downs behind them. They squinted at the tiny buildings and hamlets clustered here and there along the shoreline. They laughed and joked, enveloped in a homecoming euphoria.

'Hey — I think I see a boozer up there over those cliffs.'

'What I want to see is the first boozer outside the dock gates.'

There was whistling and humming in the alleyways as men packed. Souvenirs and presents were being made up in bulky parcels that would live a precarious existence in buses, pubs, station buffets and trains until finally they were carried across the threshold of some expectant home. The hard core of revellers and eccentrics who had made the ship their sea-home and hoped to remain on, were looking forward to leave. The dullards, the sober ones who were quitting, were clearing out their cabins.

As I passed down the alleyway on the way to breakfast, I peeped in the open door of Misery's cabin. He was bending over an open suitcase on his settee, carefully lining it with his meagre store of shirts and underwear. On the shelf above the wash-basin was a small silver-backed hairbrush that might have been a present from a maiden aunt on his first voyage. Beside it was a shaving brush, its bristles so worn down that they formed a small yellow cone. You could easily imagine his winning it in a raffle at the Mission to Seamen in Grimsby when he was third mate; not until the last bristle had fallen out would he think of replacing it. I mentioned Misery's preparation for departure to Mr Yardley.

'The trouble with that man is that he has no appreciation of melodrama or spectacle. Here we are on a floating theatre where comedy, slapstick, tragedy, music-hall turns and generous dollops of low farce are performed regularly, and he's sitting in the front row like someone inflicted with piles. The only things which would make him smile was if one of the performers tripped and broke his leg or the tightwire artist was electrocuted when his balancing pole touched a live wire.'

After breakfast we were abreast of the chalk cliffs of Dover. A big pilot cutter came sweeping out to us, curved alongside and the Thames pilot jumped on board. He was spruce and businesslike, looking curiously about our seedy vessel as he made his way to the bridge. Captain Thompson greeted him heartily.

'She's all yours, pilot. Take the bugger to London,' the Old Man said and went below for the first of many end-of-voyage beers.

Misery, conscientious to the end, had Tommy Carey set the deck crew to tidying up the sea-blotched ship. They worked happily in the mild air, under a bright sky, hosing down the decks, brushing off the salt-streaks, wielding mops and squeegees, shouting to one another.

'Can't wait to get my arse off this fucking ship.'

'You won't know how good she is until you join another bastard.'

'I nearly died of thirst this last fortnight.'

'You nearly died of whisky before that.'

'Well, I'll have some stories to tell about this voyage.'

'You can oil your vocal chords in the pub tonight.'

'We've had good times on this ship. We'll drink to that.'

Already the memory of our disagreeable voyage home was beginning to soften. We were starting to recall fondly the uproarious times, to mellow and dramatise the tensions and discomforts that had begun on the calamitous night when the whisky was jettisoned.

Our last lunch was light-hearted. Even Misery had a less spleenful air about him. Mr Yardley was looking forward to having only a skeleton crew on board after the pay-off the next day. Captain Thompson came in, beaming and burping, not in the least troubled by the prospect of Mr Hall's bloated face waiting on the dockside.

Our excellent lunch was enlivened by a little incident which typified the bizarre character of the *Allenwell*. When Toni brought in the teapot, it was accompanied by a platter of crackers and a small glass bowl containing a viscous black substance. Mr Yardley peered at it with watery eyes, picked up the bowl and poked his spongy nose towards it.

'My God! Caviar, no less. We're being fed like Roman emperors.'

Captain Thompson chuckled. He took the bowl and concentrated his bushy eyebrows on it. 'Caviar. Well I'll be a pox-doctor's clerk.'

A sarcastic smile stretched Misery's thin lips. 'The chief steward is excelling himself — but I don't think I'll chance it.'

Mr Yardley examined the bowl again. 'It must have been put on board the day the ship was launched — for the delectation of the owners, of course. He's unearthed it in some dark corner of the storeroom. Hah! We've been fed like swine for most of the voyage and now we're getting caviar. The *dîner d'adieu* on the *Queen Elizabeth* wouldn't beat this.' He pushed the bowl towards the master. 'Well, captain, this is where you exercise your *droit de seigneur.*'

The Old Man accepted the challenge. Like a heroic food-taster in some melodramatic intrigue, he took a teaspoonful and brought it towards his mouth. He hesitated theatrically for a moment and then plunged it in. His fat jowly cheeks ballooned and contracted. He swallowed it with a gurgling gulp. Then he pronounced his verdict.

'Tastes as if some bugger pissed in it,' he said, pushing away the bowl. It was one occasion when his indiscriminate appetite failed him.

'Come on, Sparks,' said Mr Yardley. 'Show a bit of courage. When you go back to Ireland, you'll be able to tell your pals that you sailed on a ship where caviar was served.'

With the amused eyes of the three upon me, I was overcome with shyness. 'I don't like caviar,' I lied. I had never tasted any.

Then Captain Thompson hit on an idea that appealed to his impish humour. He summoned Toni. 'Steward – take that caviar up to the pilot.' Toni took the bowl and the crackers away on a tray.

'Maybe we ought to wait until the ship is safely berthed first,' Mr Yardley suggested. He shook his big fuzzy head in a philosophic gesture. 'Stew, burnt toast and plum duff has roughened our palates. We'll never be able to savour the finer delicacies.'

The pilot consumed the entire bowl and later declared to the master that the caviar was first-rate.

Mr Yardley asked me to call to his cabin. I waited outside while he underwent a horrendous, rasping cough-bout. With shaking hands he handed me a message he wanted sent to his wife, asking her to come down from Hull the next day. 'I'm sure she can't wait to be back in the arms of her vigorous spouse,' he gasped, dabbing his streaming eyes with a handkerchief.

That was the last telegram of the voyage. I cleared it while the ship was throbbing evenly along the wide estuary of the Thames, with the grey-brown mudflats slowly closing in on either side. Up ahead the edges of the immense, grey-tufted carpet of buildings that was London came in sight.

The voyage records had to be gathered together. It did not take long to tot up the figures on the telegram account sheets; hardly thirty telegrams had been sent and received during the trip. The telegram copies and the weather reports, curling at the edges, were rolled into small bundles and secured by elastic bands. The clerks at the depot riffling through them would have no idea of the kind of voyage they represented. The radio log would have to go into the big manilla envelope as well. This record of communication, like the mundane telegrams and battery log, only marginally reflected the reality of the past three months on the *Allenwell*. It was meant to be signed daily by the master, but, when I had presented it to him on our first day at sea, he had waved it aside. 'Never mind all them regulations, Sparks. I'll sign the bugger once, at the end of the voyage and that's it.' I would have to choose an opportune moment to get him to sign, before he got really tanked up.

If I stayed with the *Allenwell*, it would simply be a matter of handing in the records at the Marconi depot the next day and disappearing out the door to go on 'captain's leave'. But until I knew what the future held in store for our wayward tramp, I was reluctant to take a decision. However, the vehemence with which I had vowed it would be a one-trip, once-in-a-lifetime experience was weakening; I was having to suppress a rising hope that I could remain on board.

'MV *Allenwell* entering Port of London from Tampa and US ports' I tapped out to the coast station as the curve of the river took us towards the great dockland, and two tugs stood by up ahead to nudge and pull us in. 'Station closed' was the final entry in the log.

When I climbed up to the radar hut to throw the mains' switch, we had just entered a long rectangular dock, with rows of cargo ships lined on either side and at the far end. They were large vessels, some gleamingly new, and all looking shipshape and elegantly seaworthy. We looked very much the down-at-heel tramp in such company. Yet, when I stood alongside Captain Thompson and saw the contented look on his weathered face, I knew that he was proud of our crusty ship and of himself too. We had caught some of the worst storms and had come through. We had fulfilled our mission, more or less. If we had not delivered intact part of our tempting cargo, it was because you could not expect to muster a virtuous crew on such a dilapidated vessel. Thompson never actually said so, but I believe he took the view that on a ship of scant comforts, the crew were deserving of any windfalls that might come their way, provided they did not commit murder to lay hands on them.

As the ship was pushed broadside towards the dock, between two impressively neat cargo liners, there by a bollard stood the plump figure of Mr Hall. His beltless grey raincoat, crumpled and creased, was like a collapsed tent. His scuffed black briefcase was that of a shabby salesman who plodded about on flat feet, offering cut-price rates in the competitive world of shipping. He turned his red face towards the bridge and waved to Captain Thompson with a wan smile.

Hall came up the gangway along with the customs and immigration officials. In the foyer he assumed a paternalistic air. 'Had a good voyage, then?' he asked. We were standing about, not to greet him, but for our mail. We knew that he already had a Cunard version of some of the more colourful events of our voyage. From his briefcase he wrenched a bulky bundle of mail, 'Here we are. You'll all be waiting for your letters, eh?' With that the bundle burst apart, scattering the letters about the deck.

I took mine up to the radio room to read them there, leaving the door ajar to eavesdrop on the captain's cabin below. I was able to note some of the exchanges.

'Harry, I'll need a report.' Mr Hall's voice was pleading rather than authoritative.

'I'm reporting to you now.'

'Old Gunther wants a written report. He went up the wall.'

'Fuck him. I'm a seaman, not a fucking scrivener. I've brought his ship through ten days of storm and I didn't have time to write things down.'

'We'll have to make up some kind of report, Harry.' Mr Hall's tone was conciliatory, conspiratorial.

'I'll dictate it to you then.'

'I'm not a fucking scrivener either.'

'We'll think about it. Come on, man – let's have a bloody beer.'

In a penny-pinching outfit like the one-ship family concern which owned the *Allenwell*, it would be as difficult to engage a dynamic marine superintendent as it would be to acquire the services of a captain of impeccable record and behaviour. But there was another reason why their brief confrontation was not more heated. Lazy and bumbling as Mr Hall might be, he had managed to secure another charter.

When I went to the captain's quarters to get him to sign the radio log, I heard the news. The new charter was with the Ghanaian national shipping line. It would be another three-month voyage. The ship would first go to Hamburg and Antwerp to load cargo and then down to West Africa — Dakar, Conakry, Freetown, Abidjan, Takoradi, Lagos and the river-ports of eastern Nigeria.

Mr Hall's face was flushed a deeper red when he stumbled into the saloon along with Captain Thompson for the evening meal. His eyes were glazed and his speech slurred. The Old Man burped bibulously, grinning.

'Well, Sparks, you can look forward to plenty of black ham next trip. Off to bloody Africa again.'

'We're working for the blacks now, is that it?' said Mr Yardley acidly.

'I don't mind working for the niggers as long as we get paid.' Mr Hall raised his head with some effort, 'It's as good as we can get.'

'It's the river-ports of Nigeria that I'm looking forward to,' said Mr Yardley with a savage smile. 'Two weeks loading mahogany logs in Sapele should be just dandy. I've always liked those vapoury, pestilential places amongst tropical swamps, strange as it might seem. It's the Englishman's addiction to barren deserts and inhospitable jungles, I suppose.'

The master was smiling, watching Mr Hall fumbling with knife and fork, clumsily trying to co-ordinate the movement of fingers, hands and mouth. The captain took him back to his cabin when the meal was over.

Mr Yardley shook his head sagely. 'You'll be staying on, of course, Sparks, eh?' I sensed the hope behind the offhand tone.

'I'm not sure.'

'Not sure! This ship has been good to you. If you haven't

filled your stomach with food, you have filled several of those little notebooks of yours. If you stay on – why, you'll collect enough to write several books – all about one single ship. The only trouble is, people won't believe it. They'll say you made it all up. Baron Münchhausen with an Irish brogue.'

Mr Hall had brought good news about Pete. He had been released from prison after three weeks, been fined and deported. He was now on board a Liverpool-bound boat as a Distressed British Seaman. I heard this with great relief and gladness. If this blot on his record put paid to his seafaring career or stunted it, I felt sure it would not affect his bubbling good humour or resilience.

The expectation of arriving in a home port engenders elation. Yet as soon as the ship ties up fore and aft and the gangway goes down, there is a perceptible change of mood. The sense of sea-borne comradeship begins to weaken and fragment as men receive letters from home, and telephone loved ones. Family concerns now overshadow shipboard matters. Men were preparing to go their own ways. There was, among the old regulars, a great sense of relief that they could return after home leave. There was joy that their easy-going captain had not got the boot. A three-month voyage suited everybody. All this put them in good form for a night in the pub.

The ship's company was to be paid off the following afternoon; the small number remaining on board for port duties would sign temporary articles. Captain Thompson, well aware of the overwhelming urge that many felt to slake long-endured thirst in a great celebratory gathering, had arranged for a 'sub' to be paid out after tea. Even many of those quitting the ship for good wanted to mark the end of the voyage in a drinking session, to recall its memorable moments, to say goodbye to shipmates.

The big pub outside the dock gates was designated as the oasis. As soon as men collected their money, they began to hurry the last few steps at the end of the parched journey. But not all were going to the pub. I saw Toni make off in a surprisingly muted suit, with carefully wrapped presents under his arm. I wondered if he was going to visit his estranged wife and two teenage children. His cheeky, fluttering presence would be missed on the ship; as a cabin steward, he would be hard to equal.

In the mild evening air, I wandered about the ship, trying to make up my mind what to do. I came across the gaunt figure of Reilly standing outside the lower port alleyway. A heavy black overcoat hung loosely on his emaciated frame; his face was thin and shadowed, pouched eyes deep in his head, bush of wiry hair dishevelled.

'Doctor's putting me into hospital. That's it. It's goodbye to this ship. Five years I've been on her. Well – I never liked West Africa anyway.'

I had never been near the West African coast nor indeed in the bustling ports of Hamburg and Antwerp. A chimera of glamour hovers over places one has heard stories about but has never seen — even the muggy, feverish mangrove swamps of the Nigerian river-ports so detested by Mr Yardley.

At the railings, watching the groups of men clatter down the gangway, was Ben Jennings. He was neatly dressed and had regained some weight. He had let his hair grow, so that his round skull resembled a grey coconut.

'Going ashore, bosun?'

'Don't know. I don't think it would be good for me. I've been through a lot.'

'You'll be signing off?'

'I can't stay on this ship after all that's happened, Sparks.'

'Will you go home for a while?'

'Don't have any home now. I know people in Devon. I'll go there for a few days. Some of them might be around, if they're not at sea.'

While we were chatting, Misery passed, in overcoat and dark suit. 'Ah'll go ashore, phone the wife', he said, 'tell her we've arrived. Might go to the pictures afterwards.' He ignored the bosun. As I watched him make his pigeon-toed way along the quayside, it struck me that the *Allenwell* would never be quite the same without him. His unfailing spleen and mean spirit had contrasted with the cheery vulgarity of the captain and had evoked some of the best witticisms from Mr Yardley. The meal-time entertainment would not have the same pungent flavour when he was gone.

Brad leaned against the door of the galley, rolling a cigarette. He was duty officer that night, and would be staying on board at least a fortnight while the cargo was being discharged. 'Aw — I'll get up to South Shields for a few days before we sail. See the old aunt.'

I decided to go ashore for a meal in a Chinese restaurant in East Ham that I knew well. On my way to the gangway, I knocked on Mr Yardley's door to see if he wanted anything. He was sitting with book in hand, breathing laboriously.

'Yes – a bottle of Gordon's gin. Seeing that everyone else is going on the piss, I don't want to be regarded as an oddity by remaining sober. Anyway, when her ladyship arrives tomorrow, that will be the end of all drinking for me.'

At the top of the gangway I fell in with Rat. We walked towards the dock gates together.

'This will be my last booze-up with shipmates. Last night aboard ship too – unless she calls it off.'

'She'll hardly do that.'

'You never know with women.' His tone seemed to hold a faint perverse hope that the unwanted might occur. 'It would be too bad if she did. But it's bad leaving the sea now that the time has finally come.' I promised to call into the pub on my way back to join him in a farewell drink. 'This is one night I'm really going to get pissed, Sparks.'

It was foggy and damp on the streets of nearby East Ham. There were plenty of people about; the little cafés and pubs were alive with light and life. To a sailor after a long voyage, every girl seems immensely attractive and desirable. The clicking of high heels on the pavements acquires an erotic rhythm. Even a shopping bag slung over a girl's arm has a sensuous significance as it brushes against her thigh. In the restaurant, eating prawn curry among the dragon murals and the tasselled lanterns hanging from the dark red ceiling, I envied the confident boyfriends of the girls at the tables about.

Afterwards, on my way to the bus stop, I passed the corner of Wakefield Street. Some distance down it was the flat-topped brick building that housed the Marconi depot. On the bus I indulged in a reverie which was becoming established as part of the turbulent thoughts of the dissatisfied radio officer. When the staff clerk appears and opens the conversation blandly with, 'Well now — what can I do for you?' I reply curtly, 'You can make up my pay and have it sent on to me, please. I'm resigning.' And I turn on my heel.

The bus stopped beside the pub by the dock gates. The pub had a massive, grimy exterior, but its windows were aglow with welcoming yellow light. Even on the pavement one could hear the rumble of voices from within. I hesitated outside from shyness; but I had promised Rat and had also to buy Mr Yardley's gin. When I pushed in the inner door, a barrage of loud conversation assailed my ears. The place was jam-packed with sailors, struggling at the counter, shouting for service, yelling at the aproned waiters who shoved their way amongst the crowded tables. I squinted through the mist of tobacco smoke, looking for our fellows. The clamour seemed loudest of all in one area and sure enough there were our jolly mariners spread about six or seven tables.

Hands and arms, when not engaged in conducting glasses to mouths, were waving about graphically. Faces assumed and discarded simulated expressions of ecstasy, anxiety, hilarity, distaste. The high and the low points of the voyage were being recreated. Already the experiences had been sifted and selected, dramatised, shaped into yarn form. Even the most painful incidents were now softened by humour.

'If anyone told me I'd fling twenty full bottles of whisky over the side, I'd have said they were mad.'

'Never mind that. I thought I'd fling myself over the side in mid-ocean, I felt so bad.'

'I've been on some binges, but not one that lasted six fuck-ing weeks.'

'I screwed so much that I thought I'd have to grow a new one.'

I squeezed in beside Rat, who was ordering another round of farewell drinks. 'Here's to the good old *Allenwell*,' he yelled. Little Alex and Old Charlie were shouting at the tops of their voices, competing in vivid description of the memorable moments of the voyage. Duty officer Brad was there, glass in one hand, looking about with a dentured smile. Ted, sadly, had reverted to his old sozzled self. The eyes, which for seven days had been so bright, were now reglazed. It was impossible to hear very much in the din, but from the regular twitching of his mouth, one could tell that the tooth-sucking habit had been re-established. The fractured friendship between him and Little Alex had been alcoholically restored.

The adventures of the *Allenwell* were being told, with no small amount of exaggeration, colour and boasting, for the benefit of interested listeners from other ships at nearby tables. The entry of our bedraggled ship into the dock had aroused some curiosity. Seafarers have an insatiable appetite for sea yarns and gossip. There were many eager hearers, heads shaking and nodding as the stories were being told. The fame, or infamy, of the *Allenwell* already was being propagated by word of mouth, spreading quickly amongst the story-loving seafaring fraternity. When I took my leave and pushed towards the counter to buy Mr Yardley's gin, I found myself wedged between men from the ship astern of us.

'That scruffy-looking crowd over there — from the old hulk that docked this evening — broached the cargo of whisky, they did. Drank like fishes. Ran riot in New Orleans. Ship placed under arrest. Third mate put in jail and all.'

'Lucky bastards. How come we never sail on a ship like that?'

'Oh, I don't know. Fighting and boozing to beat the band. A real rough-house she is.'

Within a few days inflated versions of the happenings on board would be all round the dock. Sailors passing by would nod towards the rust-bumpy hull and say, 'That's her. That's the one.'

As I made my way along the quayside, I surveyed the other ships tied up there. They were clean and well-maintained. Rows of portholes gleamed. One could imagine the spacious cabins, the pleasantly furnished recreation rooms where films were shown regularly, the white linen tablecloths and glistening cutlery in the saloons.

The *Allenwell* looked as tatty and run-down as when I had first seen her, a tramp sleeping it off after a long and eventful wandering. Yet Mr Yardley's description of her as a floating theatre was apt. If one was looking for entertainment and some racy, comic and sad insights into the human condition, she was hard to beat. On the stage were performers whose distinctive personalities made them particularly memorable.

I waited outside Mr Yardley's door until a long series of painful raspings and heavings had subsided. When he opened the door, his bony, boxlike chest was jerking spasmodically. Tears of struggle filled his eyes. He took the bottle gratefully, hands quivering.

'If only I had the energy, I'd wait up until 4 am and then go round the accommodation kicking up a row, waking up everyone else for a change. And how indignant some of them would be! They'd say "That old bollocks Yardley has finally gone mad."'

When I crossed the foyer and was turning down the alleyway towards my cabin, I heard sounds from the recreation room. Captain Thompson and the boiler-suited Lambton Worm were playing darts. I had wondered why the master had not been ashore in the pub; he gave me the reason when he saw me peering in the door.

'That boozy bugger Hall flaked out on the floor of my cabin. Pissed in his pants and all over the carpet too. He's up there snoring like a hog.'

He paused, darts in hand. 'Well, Sparks, Africa next trip, eh?' Drunk as he might be, the cunning little eyes took in the hesitancy on my face.

'We'll need one reliable, sober bugger on board. Able to

send messages without his hand shaking from the DTs and keep the bloody radar going off the West coast.'

This honest praise struck a warm chord deep in my insecure soul. I nodded gratefully. 'Well, I haven't been to West Africa before, captain.'

'You won't regret it, Sparks; not when you're holding a black cheek in each hand.' By way of illustration, he formed his fat hands into two rounded claws and held them before him at crotch level.

The decision to make another voyage on the *Allenwell* lifted a weight from my mind. I went to my cabin with a light step. There were to be times in the months ahead when, badly bitten by mosquitoes and suffering from a virulent form of diarrhoea contracted from the contaminated shipboard food, I would regret it. But that's another voyage and another story.

I climbed into my bunk contented, looking forward to three weeks' captain's leave by the shores of Carlingford Lough. Before I fell asleep, I heard the crowd returning to the ship, shouting and singing. Just as I fell into unconsciousness, I heard from below the sound of Taffy's mandolin and his high tenor voice rising and falling, as it had on that first night aboard the trampship *Allenwell*.

Afterword

You turn to these words, I would hope, with regret, sorry to be done with *Seaspray and Whisky*. I know I certainly didn't want the crazy, incredible voyage of the grubby old *Allenwell* to end; from the moment I joined "Sparks" Freeman as he stood in "stunned dismay" in his dingy cabin that first night on the disgraceful old tub, I was an avid (if unobserved) member of the shambling crew, aghast at the goings-on but eager to watch and always thoroughly entertained by it all. The roguish big-bellied captain; Yardley, the physical wreck with the sarcastic tongue; peevish Misery Muir, world-class sourpuss; mincing Toni, cabin steward and (all too briefly) celebrated New Orleans cabaret *artiste*; the battling cooks with their nightmarish cuisine; the hardcore sots, pickled in Vat 69; unlucky Pete, the only one the Feds managed to nab: they were a gang I was loath to take leave of, personalities realized with such unassuming artistry that I suspect they'll live in memory more vividly than if I'd known them in the flesh. Indeed, when Sparks revealed he was signing on for another tour aboard the *Allenwell* I was all set to join him, unwilling to lose touch with such unforgettable hooligans, and had there been a further installment of their adventures I'd have turned to it immediately.

Which reminds me – it was only by chance that I got to turn to *Seaspray and Whisky* in the first place.

I've described in the pages of A COMMON READER how I happened to learn about this quirky seafaring classic, and since this COMMON READER EDITION of the book is only available through our catalogue, chances are that most of you will already know the story. The anything-but-festive book fair. My downcast progress round the claustrophobic hall. The overheard snatch of enthusiastic, Irish-accented commentary.

My excited reaction to the opening pages. A reader's discoveries are often serendipitous, but this one seemed more so than most: at a truly miserable trade show, I had stumbled upon a little masterpiece.

Of course at the time all I really knew about the book was what could be gleaned from a handful of paragraphs read hurriedly in uninspiring surroundings. But I had a hunch: my hasty sampling seemed to indicate that here was a writer who could tell his unique and outlandish story memorably. Perhaps what initially intrigued me most was the sharp contrast between the reserve of the narrator and the wild-and-woolly shenanigans he was apparently going to be describing. There was even, I thought, a hint of schoolmarmishness about the storyteller (and what quality could possibly be more out of place?). For example, when he noted that the missing booze "most certainly accounted for a prolonged whisky-fest, which engendered riotous living afloat and ashore," something about the turn of phrase and choice of words made clear he'd no part in any of *that*. But if he hadn't, how could his account of those who metaphorically went overboard be anything other than sniffy and censorious? Had I discovered an ocean-going variation on *The Odd Couple*?

As it turned out, the painfully shy and unwordly Sparks does keep his distance from the mayhem on board. From first day to last he remains the outsider, the onlooker taking everything in. And it's here, I believe, that Norman Freeman shows himself to be a genuinely gifted writer. His portraits of the crew and his descriptions of their activities are built up out of a wealth of finely observed details, the fruits of concentrated watching, noting, assessing, and remembering. But it isn't only Sparks's eyes which are trained on the *Allenwell*'s bizarre cast and their egregious antics: he observes them with his heart as well. It's Freeman's ability to convey his affection for, and empathetic understanding of, a group of men so utterly different from himself, which makes *Seaspray* the lively, warmhearted, distinctive, and memorable chronicle it is.

A final word or two about old Sparks. In my opinion, Norman Freeman's depiction of his shipboard self is a masterly bit of self-portraiture. It's aptly and judiciously self-scrutinizing, a subtle and intelligent portrayal of an insecure and bookish soul who finds himself caught up in a bacchanalian whirlwind. In short, there's neither too much nor too little of Sparks, and, as I've said, I was left with a desire to put to sea with him again. That's in fact what prompted me to ask Norman Freeman, during a recent exchange of faxes as we prepared for publication of this COMMON READER EDITION, whether he'd written anything more about the *Allenwell* or other voyages he might have made. In reply, the author, who now works for a public relations consultancy in Dublin, acknowledged that he had served a second tour on the decrepit vessel during the trip to Africa mentioned at the end of *Seaspray*, but afterwards left the ship and heard no more about her. And while he has two other books to his credit, and a fourth in the works, none of them involve further nautical adventures. I'd like to think I speak for every reader of this wonderful book when I say how much I hope Norman Freeman does eventually revisit his days at sea. I'd sign on for another volume any time, just so long as I don't have to weather another of those fairs to discover it.

Thomas Meagher
Editorial Director, A COMMON READER